THE IMAGE OF JAPAN:

From Feudal Isolation to
World Power, 1850–1905

THE IMAGE
OF JAPAN:
From Feudal
Isolation to World
Power, 1850-1905

JEAN-PIERRE LEHMANN
Lecturer in History, University of Stirling

London
GEORGE ALLEN & UNWIN
Boston   Sydney

Printed in Great Britain
in 11 on 12 point Baskerville
by W & J Mackay Limited, Chatham

To My Father

ACKNOWLEDGEMENTS

I am very grateful to Mr Peter Leek of George Allen & Unwin. The idea of this book was his; he discussed it with me, provided many useful comments, and then showed extraordinary patience in having to wait so long for its completion. I wish to record my thanks to Professor Victor Kiernan of Edinburgh University, who, though he may not know it, was influential in the organisation of the material for this book. Mr Richard Storry, Director of the Far East Centre at St Antony's College, Oxford, and my former supervisor, read the first draft of the manuscript and suggested extensive pruning and some tightening up of the style. For this, and for many other things, I shall always be deeply grateful. I should like to express my thanks to Miss Betty Neech who typed the final draft of the manuscript quickly, cheerfully and with great care.

CONTENTS

Introduction   *page* 13
1 The New Japan – Far East or Far West?   20
2 Western Encounters with Japan – Enchantments
    and Disenchantments   42
3 The Women of Japan – In Reality and Fantasy   68
4 Politics – Oriental Obscurantism to Occidental
    Enlightenment   97
5 Industriousness, Industry and Industrialisation   123
6 Yellow Hope – Yellow Peril   143
Appendix   181
Notes   187
Bibliographical note   194
Index   199

LIST OF ILLUSTRATIONS

Between pages 64–65 and 80–81 :

Samurai and servant. (*The Mansell Collection*)
The Japanese. (*The Mansell Collection*)
New Year's Day – old and new. (*Mary Evans Picture Library*)
Caged prostitutes. (*The Mansell Collection*)
The interior of a Tokyo brothel. (*Mary Evans Picture Library*)
A high-class geisha. (*The Mansell Collection*)

Between pages 128–129 and 144–145:

The opening, by the Mikado, of Japan's first railway. (*The Mansell Collection*)
The Emperor inaugurating the Parliament of 1890. (*Mary Evans Picture Library*)
Yokohama, the Mikado in procession. (*Mary Evans Picture Library*)
The Yellow Peril
Figaro cartoon of the Russo–Japanese War. (*The Mansell Collection*)
Baron Kuroki, Commander-in-Chief of the First Japanese Army. (*The Mansell Collection*)

INTRODUCTION

The name of a country conveys an image. This image is not constant; it varies with the times and with the different minds on to which it is projected. Images, perhaps by definition, are caricatures, or at best impressions. They relate to an aspect of reality, but often exclude other aspects, other realities. They also tell us something about the perceiver of the image. Western images of Japan have varied, reflecting not only the changes taking place in that country, but also the changing attitudes of people in the West towards themselves.

In this book we are concerned with the attitudes towards Japan held by people in the West in the second half of the nineteenth century and the first five years of this century, from the country's 'opening' to the Western world in 1854 to its victory over Russia in 1905. The sources are primarily British and French, to a slightly lesser extent American and to a small extent German; Russian material, although undoubtedly of very considerable importance and interest, has not been used because I cannot read Russian. Tolstoy is the exception. American attitudes towards Japan have received considerable attention in a number of works and especially in two recent books by Akira Iriye.[1] The general problem of Russo–Japanese relations has been dealt with in great detail and with great erudition in the numerous works of George Alexander Lensen.[2]

The half-century that we shall be dealing with was one in which Japan conducted an intensive programme of modernisation, industrialisation and, to a certain extent, Westernisation; the country also became involved in international politics (following more than two centuries of peace and isolation from the outside world) with the inevitable treaties, trade, alliances, and wars. Generally speaking, in the West this period was marked by a considerable degree of self-confidence, perhaps arrogance, coupled with reassuring pseudo-scientific theories of white racial superiority. This permitted Westerners to treat Japan and her efforts at

13

modernisation with a certain amount of condescension, paternalism, and indeed at times a combination of contempt and alarm. Certainly Japan did not lack advice, usually gratuitous, on what to do, what not to do, where to go, where not to go.

Needless to say this advice was often contradictory. There were those who felt it was simply impossible for Japan to modernise, to reach levels of economic, military and political power comparable with those in the West. There were those who felt that the Western powers should unite in ensuring that Japan never reached those levels. Others believed Japan could succeed in becoming a modern and 'civilised' state, but only if she were prepared to Westernise completely not only her institutions, but also her culture, in particular to abandon her ancient form of writing in favour of the alphabet and her religions in favour of Christianity. Finally there were those, significant both in number and influence, who felt very strongly that under no circumstances should Japan be allowed to modernise; they saw Japan as a pre-industrial earthly paradise which should be preserved from the evils of modernity.

Another point perhaps needs to be made. With the benefit of hindsight, we now know that tremendous changes were taking place within Japan – at many levels – during this period of half a century. And indeed most Western observers of Japan were keenly aware of this. Others, however, were not. Images do not necessarily change at the same pace as reality. One must be conscious of the Western prejudices of the day – many of which are still alive and well in the 1970s. Certainly in the Victorian period it was believed that there was a clear distinction between West and non-West, White and non-white, Christian and heathen. It was firmly held – though obviously there were numerous exceptions – that Western civilisation, race and religion were possessed of certain properties, denied to members of non-Western civilisations, races and religions. These properties were presumed to emanate either from the grace of God or from the very nature of the evolution of man – 'scientific' theories comfortably embedded in that loose set of doctrines called social Darwinism. This was certainly racialism, but was not necessarily always expressed as such. The theories were often expressed in an eminently humane way. Furthermore, on the face of it, in the period we are dealing with there was every reason to subscribe to such views. Western civilisation, the white race and the Christian religion stood paramount in the world. Perhaps more misleading, however, was the tendency to think that the non-Western world was more or less homogeneous, albeit with slight variations in degree; much the same sort of attitude is evinced today in using that rag-bag euphemism, the 'Third World'.

All this is to say that, although Japan was changing fairly dramatically, decade by decade, during the period we are dealing with, realisation in the West of these changes, if it existed at all, tended to come in fits and starts, although obviously there were exceptions. Also, one sees and believes largely what one wants to, giving far more credence to what seems to confirm one's prejudices. Those who believed that a non-Western, non-white, non-Christian country such as Japan could not possibly, by the sheer force of things, develop into an industrial society or towards more progressive politics refused to accept evidence to the contrary. The excessively pro-Japanese side, on the other hand, tended to exaggerate changes out of all proportion.

Thus it seemed to me that chronology was not necessarily a trustworthy guide for the writing of this book. I have therefore preferred to make a thematic approach. Within the various themes, which correspond generally to chapters, chronology is taken account of. A word about which themes have been included and which excluded may be helpful. The emphasis I wished to give to this book was on attitudes to *changing* Japan. Thus the reader may discover with some dismay that such vital and magnificent facets of Japanese culture as art, literature and architecture receive scant treatment and are, perhaps unfortunately, lumped together in one chapter (Chapter 2) with a number of other topics. Of course art, architecture and literature did change during this period, in the sense that new expressions were found, many of them fascinating, but Western awareness of them was minimal. And I am not giving an account of the attitudes of the specialist in Japanese studies or of the erudite connoisseur of artistic or literary matters, but of those of the educated, albeit non-specialist, general public. I think it safe to assume that at the time in question the educated general public was more interested in Japan than would be the case today. The educated classes had more time, more money and were more outward-looking. The periodicals and newspapers which catered for this public contained numerous articles on Japan, dealing with a very wide variety of topics.

The many travelogues about Japan contained vivid descriptions of the Japanese countryside – landscape, gardens, temples, houses, villages, and so on. Again, however, these are not aspects of *changing* Japan and so have been set aside. There are, however, aspects of Japan's modernisation which I have also left out. Two areas of change which will no doubt spring to the reader's mind are law and education. Some aspects of law are covered in the first chapter, where I look at the problem of treaty revision. There are a few comments on education interspersed here and there in the text when relevant to one of the themes under study. I have preferred to treat in some detail those themes which I consider to be more important. Finally, the question of religion, as is pointed out in Chapter 2, is a *leitmotiv* throughout the book, as is the question of race.

The themes which I have concentrated on are: the attitudes toward Japanese modernisation in general (Chapter 1), women (Chapter 3), politics (Chapter 4), industry (Chapter 5) and, finally, the West's reaction to the Russo–Japanese war (Chapter 6). Chapter 2 contains a number of different themes which I felt should be included, but to which I could not devote entire chapters. The selection of these themes requires no explanation, with the possible exception of the chapter on women. It can hardly be argued that the position of women was one of the more striking aspects of changing Japan. On the other hand, as should be made clear in Chapter 3, probably no aspect of Japan was of as much interest as her women. Western attitudes toward Japanese women, whether based in reality or fantasy, deeply influenced Western attitudes toward Japan in general. No doubt readers may take exception to the attitude toward Japanese women in particular, and the female sex in general, which is depicted in a number of passages quoted. I think their inclusion is important. I have refrained from passing any judgement in the course of the text. Victorian attitudes (though not necessarily mores) toward women and sex were, needless to say, different from those of today; and it is no use attempting to judge these attitudes with our present values.

Material for this book has been collected from the writings of Occidentals whether or not they visited Japan. By and large, however, and for obvious reasons, those most important in creating and developing images of Japan in the West were people who visited the country either for short periods of travel or for longer periods of residence. Japan had her share of fascinating and, in some cases, eccentric, visitors.[3] Kipling toured the country in 1889, and the French novelist, Pierre Loti, made a number of seafaring tours. Of the longer-term residents, the best known was undoubtedly Lafcadio Hearn. Hearn wrote numerous books about Japan, became a Japanese citizen (taking the name Koizumi Yakumo), married a Japanese, and died in the country. There were scholars, early pioneers of Japanese studies, such as Basil Hall Chamberlain and W. G. Aston, and experts in diverse fields employed by the Japanese government to help in the programme of modernisation. There were painters such as the American John LaFarge, the Englishman Charles Wirgman, the Italian Antonio Fontanesi. One of the most interesting and influential Western residents was Ernest Fenollosa. Fenollosa was an American of Italian descent, invited to Japan to teach Western art. Soon, however, he became convinced of the aesthetic superiority of Japanese art. He emerged as one of the leading exponents of the revival of traditional art and an ardent critic of the new school of Western painting. There were also the ubiquitous diplomats, traders, visiting politicians and statesmen (Nicholas II, then Tsarevich, just escaped assassination in Japan in 1891), journalists, teachers, missionaries, sailors, and adventurers or 'globe-trotters' (a term dating from that period).

Many of these visitors and residents wrote books or articles about Japan – not only the distinguished scholars, the politicians or diplomats, the accomplished writers and journalists, but also ordinary tourists recording their impressions and experiences. The variety of background and interests was naturally reflected in the writings. What preoccupied George Curzon or Valentine Chirol in Japan was different from what interested or amused Rudyard Kipling or Pierre Loti. It is obvious that there cannot emerge one single image of Japan; rather, the image is a mosaic. The aim of this book is to illustrate the more striking aspects of this mosaic, those which caused the greatest impression.

As I said earlier, what I am concerned with here is the educated general public of the period. Therefore I have excluded from the selection of material anything which would not normally have been available to the public, such as diplomatic or consular correspondence. I have made extensive use of *The Times* (of London) on the reasonable grounds that this was the most influential and prestigious newspaper of the Western world during the period we are dealing with. To get another point of view, a non-establishment one, I have also referred (in Chapter 5 and especially in Chapter 6) to *Justice*, a weekly edited by the social democrat Henry Hyndman. The *Edinburgh Review, Blackwood's Magazine* and *MacMillan's* contain numerous articles on Japan and it seems reasonable to assume that my ideal educated man or woman would either receive or read regularly one or more of these periodicals. In France the *Revue des Deux Mondes* was considered a 'must' for the person wishing to be in touch with world affairs, art, history and so on.

In the bibliography at the end of this book I have given a fairly wide selection of books on Japan and of course the notes contain references to all material used. The important thing seemed to me to be to obtain a cross-section of various interests, careers and backgrounds; thus material was selected from the writings of politicians, journalists, missionaries, artists and writers, academics, and the ordinary tourist. Obviously there were bound to be different impressions of the country depending not only on profession and perhaps sex (though the number of women writing on Japan were few, no doubt for the simple reason that during this period there were relatively few Western women in Japan), but also on the date and the length of residence. Kipling's visit was short (part of a world tour); Hearn spent fourteen years in Japan. Also, there were varying degrees of knowledge of Japan's culture, history, social mores and language. Basil Hall Chamberlain, a professor at the University of Tokyo for many years, was a man of great erudition so far as Japan was concerned. So was W. G. Aston, the pioneer of Western study and appreciation of Japanese literature. This knowledge could hardly be claimed by the globe-trotter.

My ideal educated person with an interest in Japan would have read fairly widely from a variety of different sources: the press and periodicals already mentioned, as well as books he would find in bookshops, libraries, borrow from friends or be given as Christmas presents. In the appendix I have given very brief notes on some of the authors more frequently quoted than others; some, such as Kipling, needless to say need no introduction. I must make it clear, however, that the main emphasis of this book is not on the conveyors of the image, but on the image itself. Hence this is an impressionistic work.

Japanese names have been written following the Japanese order, i.e. family name precedes given name.

THE NEW JAPAN –
FAR EAST OR FAR WEST?

> *If Lemuel Gulliver had recently returned from a fourth voyage to 'Laputha, Balnibari, Luggnagg, Glubbdurb and Japan', his narrative would not have been more full of strange incidents and novel observations. . . . Indeed, it was by a happy conjecture that Dean Swift ranked Japan with those creations of his own misanthropic genius, where all the conditions of European society were at once reflected, distorted, and inverted.* (1863)[1]

> *Japan is no longer the hermit of the East, but the most Western of the nations of the West.* (1903)[2]

Japan consists of a cluster of islands off the mainland of East Asia. The similarity between Japan's geographic position in Asia and Britain's in Europe did not go unnoticed, and as Japan became industrialised (and especially at the time of the Anglo–Japanese Alliance of 1902–22) it was not uncommon to refer to the country as the 'Britain of Asia'. (The alliance, as a Japanese government minister proclaimed, joined the Empire of the Rising Sun with the Empire over which the sun never sets.) Although both Britain and Japan are island nations, their histories are very different. Japan, unlike Britain, was never conquered by a foreign power, until the American victory of 1945. There was no equivalent to Roman or Danish invasions, no 1066 in Japan. Britain participated in European affairs and wars; Japan's involvement in continental Asian affairs remained minimal. When Japan came closest to being invaded, in the thirteenth century by the fleet of Kublai Khan, she was saved by a typhoon which destroyed the bulk of the enemy fleet; the typhoon was baptised the *Kamikaze* (Divine Wind). In the nineteenth century, while the Western powers carved up most of Asia as colonies, Japan remained a sovereign state.

Yet, if it is true to say that Japan never experienced military invasions until 1945, she was subjected, as a modern historian has pointed out, to a number of cultural invasions.[3] The first and most important of these took place from the fifth to the eighth centuries of our era when Japan adopted practically all the cultural features of neighbouring China (architecture, writing, religion, etc.). China remained Japan's fountain of civilisation until the nineteenth century, though to varying degrees. Thus, although from the seventeenth to the nineteenth centuries Japan entertained no official relations with her neighbour (apart from limited trade centring around the port of Nagasaki), the achievement of scholarship, for example, depended on one's knowledge of and erudition in the Chinese classics. The cultural imports from China were 'japanised' over the ages, that is adapted to indigenous customs and needs. The second though far less significant cultural invasion took place in the sixteenth century and marked the first contact of Japan with the West, mainly in the form of Portuguese Jesuits.

Following this second cultural invasion, and partly as a result of it, from the early seventeenth century Japan's policy towards the outside world was one of almost total isolation. The only exception was a small artificial islet in the bay of Nagasaki, Dejima, where Dutch traders were allowed to reside. This small 'window to the West', as it has been called, in fact proved invaluable: Japanese authorities were able to keep in touch, albeit remotely, with political events in the European world, while the availability of Dutch books and the presence in Dejima of doctors enabled a handful of Japanese scholars (the *Rangakusha*, or scholars of Dutch learning) to study Europe's scientific discoveries and developments.

In many respects, however, this isolation was fruitful. Japanese political history prior to the seventeenth century was not unlike the history of all other feudal countries in that to a great extent it consisted of bloody battles, intrigues and assassinations between rival fiefs. Indeed the century preceding the policy of isolation is called the *Sengoku jidai*, or era of the country at war with itself. Following the last great battle of feudal Japan, the battle of Sekigahara in 1600, peace was achieved, both internally and externally.

The following two and a half centuries witnessed a great flourishing of the arts, a phenomenal expansion of literacy, a very considerable increase in economic activity. There can be no doubt that this period sowed the seeds for Japan's later modernisation. By the end of the eighteenth century and increasingly in the beginning of the nineteenth century, however, a number of factors developed which seriously weakened the viability of the government and its policy of isolation. Serious economic difficulties were reflected in the increasing number of famines experienced during this period which caused numerous peasant uprisings. Political and intellectual dissatisfaction found expression in a variety of schools which tended towards a greater emphasis on national learning, as opposed to Chinese learning, and to a questioning of the government's legitimacy, favouring a return to both the temporal and the spiritual power of the Emperor. Although the imperial dynasty remained unbroken, since the twelfth century the Emperor had been little more than a figurehead. The rulers of Japan came from successive dynasties of *shōguns* (generalissimos); the ruling shogunal dynasty from 1603 to 1867 was the Tokugawa family. During this period the shogun ruled in Edo, while the Emperor in theory reigned in Kyoto, though under strict shogunal surveillance. Furthermore, Japan's political institutions were full of contradictions. Whereas political power theoretically remained in the hands of a high-ranking, landowning nobility (*daimyō*), economic strength was increasingly acquired by a rising merchant class (the bottom of the feudal social hierarchy) and administrative ability was to be found in the ranks of the middle and lower gentry (*samurai*). Japan, therefore, in the early nineteenth century was facing grave problems and tensions with the government finding it more and more difficult to cope.

It was under these circumstances that Japan also had to face a menacing situation from abroad, in the form of Russian, British, French and American ships in Japanese waters demanding an end to the country's policy of isolation. In 1853 the American Commodore Perry invited Japan to sign a treaty of friendship and commerce with the United States, leaving the Japanese a year to make up their minds. The shogunal authorities were in a state of panic and the country in general in considerable confusion. Although the mood of the ruling class was definitely not in favour of treating with the 'barbarians' (as Westerners were called), wiser counsels prevailed and, no doubt partly with the example of China before them (the Opium War), the shogunal government complied with the American demand. Japan, therefore, was not opened by force – as was China – but certainly with the threat of the use of force. The Japanese government had had to recognise that in material terms at least Western civilisation was superior.

The reaction of the people, however, was initially xenophobic. For the thirteen years following the first treaty with the United States (which was quickly followed up by the British, French, Russians and a host of other Western and some Latin American countries), the shogunal government found itself caught between two forces: on the one side the Western powers insisting that the doors to the Empire, only slightly ajar, be opened far wider; on the other, consistent and powerful pressure from within the country for the doors to be shut and bolted again. The first cry to capture the popular imagination was that of *jōi*, or 'expel the barbarians'. The imperial court in Kyoto, under Emperor Komei, became a centre of intrigue against the shogunal government. To the slogan *jōi* eventually was added that of *sonnō*, 'revere the Emperor'.

In 1867 Emperor Komei died and in the following year a major political revolution took place: the shogunate was overthrown and the restoration of the Emperor (the Meiji Restoration as it is called) was proclaimed. The original xenophobic character of the restoration movement was completely abandoned. One of the first proclamations emanating from the new government, the Charter Oath, boldly announced as its fifth principle that 'Knowledge shall be sought throughout the world in order to strengthen the foundations of imperial rule'. Almost at once the government began to institute far-reaching and radical reforms: feudalism was abolished, education made universal and compulsory, military conscription established, religious toleration accepted, fully fledged embassies set up in Western countries, civil and criminal codes promulgated along Western lines, and so on. Just as the political structure of Japan was apparently undergoing a process of Westernisation, so was the economy: railways, lighthouses, factories, brick buildings, foundries, and all forms of armament industries were established.

The government's intention, as the Charter Oath made clear, was to strengthen the country (and itself) by importing what was useful from the West. To the people, however, it meant more. From xenophobia in the 1850s and 60s, by the 1870s and 80s they had reached the other extreme – uncritical adulation of all things Western. The people in this context means mainly the upper middle-class urban dwellers. The life of the Japanese peasants, the vast majority of the population, was not significantly Westernised – except for a minimum amount of schooling, military service for boys, and textile factory work for girls. To the better off, however, experimentation in Western habits seemed limitless. Their diet was affected they began drinking beer and wines and eating meat, for example – the latter responsible for the culinary innovation of *sukiyaki*. So was their attire: Western hats, jackets, trousers and shoes were donned with enthusiasm, separately or together (the gentleman in Japanese dress with bowler hat was not uncommon). More important, Western literature, philosophy, politics, religion, architecture, painting, sculpture, and music all had their impact on Japan. Thus in the latter part of the nineteenth century Japan experienced her third cultural invasion.

There is considerable doubt and diversity of opinion among scholars today regarding the depth of Western penetration in Japan; in other words, while admitting changes in the surface, one may ask to what extent these changes were profoundly implanted in the Japanese people, their mode of politics, economics, justice, family life, and so on. This also raises a problem (and not merely a semantic one) about the extent to which 'modernisation', 'industrialisation' and 'Westernisation' are interchangeable terms. Thus, changes in the political or social structure, or the establishment of new institutions may appear as evidence of Westernisation but could also be interpreted simply as responses to a changing economic base. The point here, however, is that so far as Western observers of Japan in the nineteenth century were concerned there was no distinction to be made. The terms 'modern' and 'Western' were synonymous.

Westerners were in two minds about whether in fact Japan should attempt Westernisation. Kipling was very much against the idea:

> It would pay us to establish an international suzerainty over Japan: to take away any fear of invasion and annexation, and pay the country as much as ever it chose, on condition that it simply sat still and went on making beautiful things while our learned men learned. It would pay us to put the whole Empire in a glass case and mark it *Hors Concours*, Exhibit A.[4]

This was a view with which the Japanese totally disagreed. The Japanese became thoroughly indoctrinated with the Western belief in progress (Samuel Smiles's *Self Help* was a best seller in Japan for years). More significantly, Japan could not share Kipling's confidence that an international suzerainty over the country would guarantee it against invasion and annexation. All of Asia was either being annexed or exploited by various means – military, political and economic. For Japan's independence to be safeguarded strength was necessary and strength demanded radical reform of Japanese institutions.

There was another major problem that the Japanese had to confront. This had to do with the nature of the treaties Japan had entered into with the Western powers. These treaties were commonly referred to by the Japanese as the 'unequal treaties'. They were not peculiar to Japanese–Western relations, but were in the same form as the treaties that the Western powers had signed with (or imposed upon) all non-Christian nations. With regard to Japan the main features of these treaties were the following. They included the 'most favoured nation' clause, which meant that if any privilege were granted to one treaty power it would automatically accrue to all the others. The treaties stipulated the opening of a number of ports, known as the Treaty Ports, where foreigners were permitted to reside and conduct business but were not able to reside, carry out trade or travel beyond a determined radius from these ports without special government permission. The treaties included a clause of extraterritoriality – which in time became the most controversial issue in Japan – whereby subjects of treaty powers could not be tried by Japanese magistrates, as they were solely answerable to the jurisdiction of their own consuls. Finally, Japan was not allowed to regulate unilaterally the amount of her tariffs; in general these were restricted by treaty at 5 per cent *ad valorem*.

The consequences of the various 'unequal' clauses of these treaties were considerable. The 'most favoured nation' clause imposed a straitjacket on Japanese foreign policy as bilateral negotiation could easily prove fruitless. Limitation on customs duties meant that, unlike Germany, France and the United States, Japan was not able to protect her infant industries, nor could she take full advantage of a potentially very valuable source of revenue. The question of the treaties in general quickly became a *cause célèbre* among the Japanese, perhaps the first issue in Japanese history to be influenced to a great extent by public opinion. The most emotional and delicate issue in the treaties, however, was that of extraterritoriality:

> That a Japanese who commits an offence in England should be tried and condemned by an English magistrate, while an Englishman acting in the same way in Japan cannot be brought before a Japanese magistrate, but is tried in an English court on Japanese soil, involves a partiality which to the Japanese spirit of independence is far from palatable.[5]

For extraterritoriality to be abolished Japan had to prove that she had reached a level of civilisation comparable to the Western powers – prove it, that is, to the Western powers themselves. There can be no doubt that a major factor in the westernising of many Japanese institutions was due to the vexatious problem of extraterritoriality and the need to assure the West that their criminals would be safe in Japanese magisterial hands. International relations during this period were, needless to say, very different from what they are today. The concepts of national sovereignty and the equality of states applied only to the West. Western states in general and their diplomats in particular could take *vis à vis* Japan an attitude of strict paternalism. For Japan to gain respectable recognition (i.e. a revision of the injurious clauses in the treaties), she was expected, so to speak, to pass examinations in Western disciplines, with the Western powers as examiners.

In many ways the history of the first three decades following the Meiji Restoration can be written in terms of treaty revision. The revision of the unequal treaties was not merely a matter of foreign policy, but had considerable domestic implications; it was not merely a matter of government, but aroused considerable popular passion and at times fanaticism. The first attempt by the Japanese government at treaty revision was in 1872; the treaties were not revised until 1899. During these twenty-seven years the matter was constantly discussed in one form or another (bilateral negotiations, multilateral conferences); as negotiations dragged on over the years and no progress was achieved or even seemed likely in the near future, the attitudes of the Japanese toward the West hardened, became bitter. As *The Times* pointed out in 1887, 'The ways of treaty revision are not ways of pleasantness, nor are its paths the paths of peace.'[6]

The foreign community in Japan was virtually unanimous in its opposition to any change in the *status quo*. This is understandable, for, until 1899, 'their settlements in Japan had formed . . . a sort of little republic, without political rights, it is true, but also without duties. They paid few taxes, carried on their business free of police inquisition, printed what they liked in their newspapers, and, generally, did what was right in their own eyes.'[7] But the reasons given by the West for refusing to renegotiate the treaties were couched in loftier terms than sheer convenience. 'In a matter of this kind, it seems impossible for a Christian nation to treat as its equal a nation which has not yet been leavened with the high moral ideas that Christianity alone can impart.'[8]

The future of extraterritoriality rested on the Japanese theory and practice of jurisprudence. The Japanese government had made determined efforts to develop civil and criminal codes which would meet Western requirements. To that end an eminent French professor of law had been invited to Japan where he spent almost twenty years in the government's service. (In the late nineteenth century the Japanese employed a good number of foreigners – referred to as the *O-Yatoi Gaikokujin* or 'honourable hired foreigners' – to help develop various aspects of the country's economy, industry, education, political apparatus, army, navy, etc.). The problem, however, or so some Westerners felt, was that there was considerable disparity between modern Western legal theory in Japan and its implementation, which, it was alleged, remained primitive and indigenous. In the matter of torture, for example, theoretically abolished, in 1879 a correspondent to *The Times* pointed out:

It is true that the law permitting this barbarous punishment has been abrogated and is no longer on the statute-book. Unfortunately, like too many other just laws in Japan, it exists only on paper; for residents are well aware that the practice, although, perhaps, only exceptionally resorted to, is still secretly carried on by the Government. The relations of Japan with the European powers can hardly be altered until this foul stain is removed in reality.

So much of real advancement has been achieved within the last few years that it is to be regretted that the enlightened ideas which are not wanting should not have fully ripened into action.[9]

There were, however, as on all matters regarding Japan, differences in opinion among Westerners. A Liberal MP, Sir Edward Reed, took a very pro-Japanese stance in a two-volume book, entitled *Japan* and published in 1879. In this work and in correspondence to *The Times* he expressed considerable criticism of Britain's diplomacy with Japan. A dispute between himself and the British head of mission, Sir Harry Parkes (who had by that time been the representative in Japan for sixteen years), took place in the correspondence columns of *The Times* in the summer of 1881. Reed's view was that Britain was unnecessarily delaying the fruition of a more equal relationship between Japan and the Western powers. In an obvious reference to Sir Harry Parkes, he accused British diplomacy of general pettiness and procrastination. Parkes countered that British diplomacy had been perfect, 'that the leading Japanese statesmen still gratefully remember the services rendered them by Her Majesty's Government or its agents' and that 'a very long share of the material progress made by Japan may be traced to British initiation'.[10] Reed responded with an outright personal attack on Parkes and concluded in expressing

> my strong desire that he might at length be relieved from further service in Japan. Where the treaties are so obnoxious to another and comparatively weak country as are our treaties with Japan in some very important respects and where our Ministers are inclined to be at all overbearing, it is a cruel thing, in my opinion, to keep the same Minister at the foreign Court for so many years together. The practical effect is to convert our representative into a master, and possibly a tyrannical master, over the Government to which he is accredited, and to work much secret mischief of which our own Government and people know and can know nothing.[11]

Parkes left Japan in 1883, but British policy in the matter of treaty revision remained consistent, that is consistently negative. *The Times* correspondents to Japan in the late 1880s, however, favoured revision.[12] One of the elements of this question that *The Times* believed was sufficient cause for alarm was possible rivalry from other Western powers:

> More than once England had the opportunity of solving this problem, to her own as well as Japan's great advantage. More than once she neglected it. Germany, more complaisant, then stepped in as a friend, and is now making the best of her initiative.... [Never] did the Cabinet in Downing Street rise to the level of the situation and come to appreciate the important fact, that, whenever it condemns its representative to an illiberal policy or obliges him to hesitate over concessions which cannot ultimately be withheld, it actually creates opportunities of which Germany never fails to take adroit action.[13]

Britain's policy in Japan, argued *The Times*, was indicative of decline:

> England may be betrayed by sheer inadvertance into for-
> feiting her chances of winning the grateful reward of 39
> millions of the first people of the Orient, as well as of opening
> up to her merchants and others a new and promising field of
> enterprise and trade. Such opportunities were not neglected
> in the days when Great Britain laid the foundations of her
> huge Empire. Their neglect at this epoch will assuredly be
> remembered with surprise and regret in the future.

The article concluded in exasperation by asking: 'What conceivable reason is there . . . for excluding such a nation from
the comity of civilized States, and condemning it to the stigma
of semi-barbarous isolation?'[14]

Not all the newspaper's readers were convinced by its argu-
ments. One letter writer pointed out that 'it is too often forgot-
ten that Japan is the first Oriental State which has claimed the
abolition of Consular jurisdiction; Turkey has acquiesced in
the system for centuries; it exists in China, Morocco, Siam, and
elsewhere; it is about to be created in Persia'. Although admitting that Japan's claims were not entirely unjustified, that her
progress 'during the short period of her intercourse with us has
been unexampled in the history of the world', it was nevertheless a fact that 'it is a long jump from babyhood into manhood':

> Amongst all the reforms of the last three decades in Japan,
> the most necessary essential for her present claims on foreign
> Powers has been lamentably neglected. The Japanese, if
> they have thought at all about it, seem to have formed the
> idea that Judges, like poets, are born, not made. It is no
> exaggeration to say that the administration of justice, as
> understood by us, is wholly foreign to them, to their habits,
> their traditions, and their modes of thought.[15]

Regardless of whatever Western reservations may have
lingered, a new treaty was signed with Britain in 1894, the
other nations quickly followed suit, and in 1899 Japan's long

struggle for treaty revision had at last borne fruit. In the end, however, the Western conscience could rest at ease, for all the delays, frustrations, vexations had been for Japan's own good:

> this public proclamation of Japan's disability to be admitted to the comity of civilized states [i.e., the unequal treaties] constituted an incentive to which a great part of her modern progress is attributable. . . . after close scrutiny of her doings during the past thirty years, we have a right to say that, had not the spur of her impaired sovereignty been constantly forced into her side, her rate of advance would have been much slower. . . . Thus, when we come to cast up the final account, we find that if Japan had been subjected to somewhat harsh discipline, the advantages that accrue to her more than outweigh the pains she has suffered.[16]

Westernisation had to a degree been forced upon Japan. Without radically altering her institutions to Western tastes, there was little likelihood that the treaties could be revised other than by means of force: for Japan in the nineteenth century to have taken on the Western world was inconceivable. Japan learned many lessons from the West, not the least of which was the art of diplomacy. In the matter of treaty revision, the Japanese

> by talent, perseverance, patience, tact, exercised year after year, – in a word, by first-rate diplomacy . . . gained a complete victory over their adversaries, and at last avenged on the West the violence which it had committed in breaking open Japan a generation before.[17]

Rapid Westernisation had been essential for Japan to improve her position in international relations. But what, wondered many Western observers, would be the implications of this rapid change? Was the Europeanisation of Japan a desirable or undesirable end? Indeed was it really feasible? Having dealt with the concrete problem of treaty revision, we now leave it to consider more abstract, philosophical speculations on the part of Westerners in regard to Japan's changing destiny.

Japan's first tentative steps toward modernisation had taken place before the Meiji Restoration, especially under the rule of the last shogun. Following the Restoration the process was greatly accelerated. 'The Japanese are the only nation in the history of the world that had ever taken five centuries at a stride,' commented the *Edinburgh Review* as early as 1872.[18] In the same year *MacMillan's Magazine* remarked:

It seemed as if a sudden passion had seized upon the people to pull down and abolish everything that was old, and to adopt unhesitatingly and without enquiry whatever came into their heads or their hands smacking of Western usages. What, however, is to be the end of all this? and is there no danger to Japan? Is not the pace too great to last, and is there no fear that the speedy horse may break down when pressed too hard.

At the time the article was written an important Japanese mission (the Iwakura mission) was visiting Britain. *MacMillan's* advised steady progress, rather than undue speed. Careful study of Britain's civilisation would give the Japanese the opportunity to

learn the source of England's greatness. Let them profit by the results of perseverance and hard toil, the fruits of which will be before their eyes, and, pondering upon them, return home convinced that such violent and sudden changes as have befallen Japan are not without danger; that it is unsafe for a country but yesterday steeped in feudalism to adopt without mature reflection a constitution based upon the newest system in Europe, or upon the republican principles of the United States; that such changes to be durable must be the work of time, and that it is unwise to remove the old landmarks without due consideration of what it is best to substitute for them.[19]

The dangers, many argued, were great. One writer evoked a rather haunting metaphor in questioning the wisdom of Japan's race to civilisation:

In a city of New Brunswick, among a clump of cypress trees, one finds a small granite pyramid with six names inscribed on it which the sculptor could not understand. They are the names of six Japanese students who came there to instruct themselves in the midst of their American brothers. Having bitten into the fruit of science without being able to digest it, they died for their efforts. Is this the melancholy image of the destiny which awaits Japan? Must it perish after having tasted of this strong nourishment, or, in the manner of its ancient goddess Amaterasu, emerge brilliant and prosperous, to the united acclaim of all nations, from the obscure retreat where, like the goddess, it had hid itself. The future will tell; until then Europe cannot watch the germination on this new soil of the seed which it has sown without emotion.[20]

Another cause of suspicion regarding the course of Japan's modernisation was that she was not following the tutelage of any one particular nation, but seemed to be attempting to assimilate a sort of Occidental goulash. For example, 'the instruction of the army is in French, that of the navy in English, the school of medicine will be in German and that of agriculture in American'.[21] Similarly as Japanese students went abroad, 'each youth will naturally be prejudiced in favour of the particular country where he has studied; those from America will be republicans, those from England monarchists, and so on – a pretty medley. If in the future the nation is to be governed by these raw students, Heaven help it!'[22]

Equally criticised was the contradictory nature of many of the ideals espoused; thus a Frenchman complained:

In Japan . . . Napoleon has his admirers, but Rousseau and indeed even Emile Zola also have theirs; Catholicism counts a sizeable number of faithful, but none of the Protestant sects are deprived of theirs; postivism and free thought have numerous disciples without the ancient national religions having had to witness the desertion of their temples; conquering imperialism has its enthusiastic supporters, and pacifist socialism has no trouble in recruiting fervent followers.[23]

Here, however, one finds an illustration of the double standard that was frequently exercised, consciously or unconsciously, by Westerners when judging Japan: surely the same could have been written about France.

Yet another source of concern was whether in fact European institutions could be transplanted into Japanese soil. Was it not possible that the appearances of Western civilisation in Japan were 'merely deceptive coruscations, like the blue-lights of a theatrical transformation-scene – not wholly without danger to the surrounding properties and actors, perhaps, – and destined, like them, speedily to disappear and be exchanged for dirty oil-lamps and a state of darkness and squalor?'[24]

On a somewhat different level it could be asked whether Western influences in Japan had been for the country's good or not. Lafcadio Hearn was of the strong opinion that the West had a corruptive influence: 'through contact with Europeans . . . [the Japanese] lose their natural politeness, their native morals, – even their capacity for simple happiness'.[25] To Kipling the Japanese 'are, so to speak, drunk with Western liquor, and are sucking it by the hogshead' and he greatly lamented 'this wallowing in unloveliness for the sake of recognition at the hands of men'. Kipling singled out one major culprit:

> There are many American missionaries in Japan, and some of them construct clapboard churches and chapels for whose ugliness no creed could compensate. They further instil into the Japanese mind wicked ideas of 'Progress', and teach that it is well to go ahead of your neighbour, to improve your situation, and generally to thresh yourself to pieces in the battle of existence. They do not mean to do this; but their own restless energy enforces the lesson. The American is objectionable.

Kipling's view of Westernising Japan was particularly jaundiced by what he saw as the greatest sin of all, the sartorial revolution.

> 'Did it hurt his feelings very much to wear our clothes? didn't he rebel when he put on a pair of trousers for the first

time? Won't he grow sensible some day and drop foreign habits?' These were a few of the questions I put to the landscape and the Professor.

'He was a baby', said the latter, 'a big baby. I think his sense of humour was at the bottom of the change, but he didn't know that a nation which once wears trousers never takes 'em off. You see "enlightened" Japan is only one-and-twenty years old, and people are not very wise at one-and-twenty.'[26]

Kipling was not alone in his great objection to Western apparel. A correspondent to *The Times* complained: 'The most disagreeable impression I have experienced has been caused by hats. The most pronounced form of the foreign mania which has attacked the intelligent classes finds expression in head gear. All the hat shops of Europe must have been ransacked and all the accumulated stocks of bygone fashions bought up to supply the marvellous head coverings one sees in a Japanese crowd.'[27] Indeed, to another observer of the new Japan, Western dress seemed to symbolise everything taking place in the country: 'You can write a chapter "On Hats", and it will be, if you like, a study of their politics, of their ministries, of their administrations, all *à la européenne*. . . . And your second chapter will be entitled "On Shoes", and you will show us how our ideas of liberty and individualism have been trodden upon by the feet of that mass which has begun to wear them.' The same author, noting the omnipresence of the bowler, suggested that it might be to the Japanese the Phrygian bonnet of their revolution.[28]

More worrying was the view of the Dutch novelist Louis Couperus, who believed that the tragedy of the new Japan was that she had lost her national identity: 'Oriental refinement has been lost in Western aspirations. It is meet that a people should keep its nationality – that which forms its nationality – unsullied. The Japanese people has not done this. It has become a hybrid, something amphibious, half way between East and West.'[29]

Some of this criticism was justified, but not entirely. Although it was true that the Japanese had not 'always shown due discrimination' in their absorption of Western culture, as a Scottish professor of English in Tokyo pointed out: 'To do so was hardly possible in the dazzlement produced by the sudden influx of light. The brilliancy of the nineteenth century flashing upon eyes accustomed to the glimmer of the fourteenth! No wonder that some indiscretion resulted; the marvel is that the mistakes were not both more numerous and more serious.' Nor was he unduly pessimistic about the future: 'A period has now begun when, with their eyes better accustomed to Western light, the people may make steady progress, an important step in which will be to atone for the excesses of their first enthusiasm.'³⁰

There can be no doubt that in the seventh and eighth decades of the nineteenth century a rather indiscriminate infatuation with things Occidental had taken place in Japan. It is quite understandable of course that for a generation used to the strictures of a still isolated society the gust of fresh air brought about by the opening of Japan's doors proved intoxicating. For a time at least everything Western was held to be inherently superior to what was Japanese; any object or custom emanating from the West which could be acquired was a symbol of sophistication, of enlightenment, of civilisation. This was as true of the possession of watches, bowler hats or umbrellas as it was of eating meat, drinking wine, adopting Western interior decoration, and embracing, at least temporarily, Western religions, though on that score the Japanese were more circumspect. With time, however, the Japanese became more selective. By the late 1890s Curzon accurately assessed the situation:

> It should not be inferred, because Japan has recognised that Europe is ahead of herself in many branches of knowledge and resources of civilisation, and that she must go to Germany for her guns, to France for her law, to England for her railways – that she is, therefore, an indiscriminate admirer of that which she imitates, or that the Western man is an idol in her social pantheon. On the contrary, the more she has assimilated European excellence the more critical she has become of European defects; whilst the at times

precipitate rapidity of her own advance has produced a reactionary wave, which occasionally assumes serious proportions.[31]

In reply to doubts expressed by a number of Europeans regarding either the wisdom or feasibility of transplanting foreign institutions into Japanese soil, Leroy–Beaulieu (a French politician, economist and propagandist of French imperialism), underlined two important factors. 'Let us, to begin with, remember that the Japanese have already afforded precedents proving that they possess powers of assimilation in a rare degree,' he wrote, reminding his readers how in previous centuries 'they introduced Chinese civilisation into their dominions'. Furthermore, he discerned a certain smugness in the attitude of many Europeans who seemed to believe that the sources of European civilisation were geographically and racially exclusively European: 'there is one point which we should not overlook. Our own civilisation is not the monopoly of one race, but was constructed by the concurrence of many people.' He proceeded to enumerate not only the Romans and the Greeks, but also the Egyptians, Phoenicians, the Hamites and the Arabs. 'The whole history of our civilisation, therefore, protests against its having ever been monopolised by the Aryan branch of the white tree.' The Japanese, he continued, were of course further from the Europeans than even the Arabs, 'but once the unity of the human race is admitted, this becomes a mere question of degree of parentage. Must we, therefore, draw a line of degree between peoples beyond which the transmission of the civilisation of the one cannot penetrate to the other? . . . For that matter, the phenomenon is constantly taking place before our eyes, and if there be a people who might attempt it with hope of success, it is surely the Japanese, who to exceptional intelligence and remarkable powers of assimilation add a great spirit of enterprise and an uncommon energy.'

The primary motivating factor behind Japan's remarkable progress, according to Leroy–Beaulieu, lay in her desire to gain a 'military and economic position equal to that of any European country' and consequently 'she was obliged to undergo

immense changes in every department of her national existence, and she unflinchingly faced her new position, resolved to
accomplish every sort of transformation in order to place herself on a firm footing'.[32] An English employee of the Japanese
government saw the country's greatest asset in terms of the
qualities of its people, 'an intensely painstaking, hard working,
frugal, and thoughtful people, imbued with a resolve to succeed
in whatever they undertake, and with the innate conviction
that nothing is beyond their powers of attainment'.[33] Japan's
wise and selective borrowing from the West was further underlined by the popular French newspaper the *Petit Journal*. 'Here
again we see one of the characteristics of Japanese civilisation.
In borrowing our sciences, our inventions, everything which
constitutes our strength, Japan has been careful not to borrow
our scepticism, which is what constitutes our weakness.'[34]

Another 'Japan expert', Henry Dyer, believed that it was
'their ardent patriotism ... [which has] enabled them to
work what is admitted to be the political miracle of the nineteenth century'. He also rejected out of hand earlier criticisms
that Japan's course for the future lacked, if not vision, at least
clarity of vision:

> Early in their career they formed very clear ideas of what
> they wished to attain. They made their plans with delibera-
> tion, they carried them out with skill, and by their adapta-
> tions of Western methods to their national institutions they
> created a new Power which will influence conditions in all
> parts of the world and especially in those countries bound by
> the Pacific area.[35]

Accepting, as one had to by the end of the nineteenth
century, that Japan had achieved remarkable progress, that
she had been, if not completely Westernised, at least transformed from a backward, feudal country into a major industrial
and military power, how much of 'old Japan' had in fact disappeared? *The Times* as early as 1876 had remarked that 'the
change going on in these far eastern islands is not mere external
imitation, but an absolute transformation'.[36] Later, however,
opinions on the matter tended to be somewhat more sober.

Those (such as the novelist Couperus) who held the view that modern Japan had become a bit vulgar, a hybrid, neither fish nor fowl, neither Occidental nor Oriental, were answered by others who saw great strength in Japan's ability to juxtapose old and new, of indigenous and Western. 'While they are permeated by Eastern ideas they have been able to appropriate much that is best in Western thought, and thus they unite many of the best qualities of the East and the West.'[37]

At times, however, this East-West *mélange* did not necessarily produce the best of both worlds. In 1889 there occurred an assassination attempt on one of Japan's leading statesmen, Okuma Shigenobu, then Minister of Foreign Affairs (over a problem relating to treaty revision). A correspondent to *The Times*, after remarking that 'Dynamite was the explosive used', continued: 'It is a curious example of the way in which the old and the new are so often juxtaposed in Japan, that from the hands of a murderous youth, fired by the ancient feudal instincts of this far-off corner (as some would call it) of the round world, should have hurled one of the most civilized, if at the same time savage, instruments of death known to Western science.'[38]

To what extent a changing, Westernising environment altered the national character remained a matter of controversy. Hearn was adamant on the matter:

Emotional life . . . can no more be altered suddenly by a change of *milieu* than the surface of a mirror can be changed by passing reflections. All that Japan has been able to do so miraculously well has been done without any self-transformation; and those who imagine her emotionally closer to us to-day than she may have been thirty years ago ignore facts of science which admit of no argument.[39]

Equally controversial, however, was whether retaining the national character was a good or a bad thing. Was the Westernising influence also a civilising one? The Australian journalist and resident in Yokohama, John Black, had no hesitation in his judgement: 'It is sometimes thought that Japan was a paradise before foreigners came to it.' This, he asserted, was very much contrary to the truth. After listing a number of the more blatant evils of pre-Perry Japan, he concluded by saying that 'if the exclusion of foreign intercourse was productive of ignorance, that ignorance was – anything but innocence, and certainly not – bliss'.[40]

Leroy–Beaulieu stressed that, so far as the future development of the Japanese people was concerned, 'Their principal danger . . . seems to me to consist in their attempting to isolate themselves too much, and to believe that they have learnt everything that can be taught them, and consequently have no further use for their masters. . . . It is not belittling the extraordinary progress so rapidly accomplished by the Empire of the Rising Sun to say that it can only be perfected if the people of that wonderful country remain in contact with the inhabitants of Europe and America.'[41]

All things considered, however, perhaps it was Basil Hall Chamberlain who managed to produce the most perceptive combination of epitaph regarding Old Japan and prophesy *vis à vis* her progeniture, New Japan:

> Yes, we repeat it, Old Japan is dead and gone, and Young Japan reigns in its stead, as opposed in appearance and in aims to its predecessor as history shows many a youthful prince to have been to the late king, his father. The steam-whistle, the newspaper, the voting-paper, the pillar-post at every street-corner and even in remote villages, the clerk in the shop or bank or public office hastily summoned from our side to answer the ring of the telephone bell, the railway replacing the palanquin, the iron-clad replacing the war-junk, – these and a thousand other startling changes testify that Japan is transported ten thousand miles away from her former moorings. She is transported out of her patriarchal calm into the tumult of Western competition, – a competition active right along the line, in diplomacy and war, in industries, in shipping, possibly even in colonisation. Nevertheless, as Madcap Hal, when once seated on the throne, showed plainly, despite all individual difference, that the blood of the prudent Henry IV ran in his veins, so it is abundantly clear to those who have dived beneath the

surface of the modern Japanese upheaval that more of the past has been retained than has been let go. . . . the national character persists intact, manifesting no change in essentials. Circumstances have deflected it into new channels, that is all.[42]

WESTERN ENCOUNTERS WITH JAPAN – ENCHANTMENTS AND DISENCHANTMENTS

Does it not seem to you, who have a sensitive mind and love to dream of the fitness of things, that the gentle moon is distinctly a Japanese orb, whose especial pleasure it must be to shine on a gentle land, through the graceful stems of bamboo; to kiss the snowy brow of Fuji-yama, cold as chastity; to glimmer in the dusky rice-fields, where the sleeping heron stands like a huge dark flower on its slender stalk?[1]

With the passing of the decades the Japanese landscape, in some respects, began to resemble more and more that of the Western industrial nations: factories, barracks, dockyards, trams, telegraph wires, railway tracks, brick government buildings, and so on. Nevertheless, in spite of the changing topography, much remained that was completely new, completely different and very exotic to the recently arrived Westerner. Everywhere he turned he would see objects and people that must have intrigued him immensely. Here we shall look at some of the many aspects of Japan, both objects and people, which Westerners commented on.

It should be remembered that when the first treaties with the Western states were signed in 1858 (they remained operative until 1899), in theory foreigners could only reside within certain stipulated treaty ports, the most populous of which was Yokohama. Foreigners were not permitted to travel in the interior without a special pass issued by the Japanese authorities. In fact as the years passed it became easier for foreigners to obtain these passes, and more and more seized the opportunity to do so; and, of course, as the decades passed more Westerners came to Japan either to reside temporarily or to travel. So the

visitor in 1860 would have had great difficulty in seeing anything beyond the treaty ports – indeed his life would be in
danger – while the visitor in 1890 would have had much
greater access to the Japanese inland, and after 1899 any
Westerner could travel freely in the country.

It should also be noted that Westerners in Japan, depending
on their business, tended to make acquaintance with their
Japanese equivalents. Thus a diplomat would know mainly
government officials, a businessman would meet and deal with
Japanese businessmen, though he might not have much social
contact with them, and a teacher would get to know his colleagues and, of course, his students. As access to the country
became easier so did access to its people. In 1860 the chances of
a Westerner knowing any Japanese people at all intimately
were very remote indeed, whereas by 1890 he could enjoy a
wide circle of friends. Of course contact with Japanese depended on one's inclination. Many Westerners probably concentrated their social activities in the various clubs which were
to be found inside the Western settlements in the treaty ports.
The treaty ports attracted a large number of Japanese who
could find employment there; they could set up shops, for
example, catering to the Western craze for Japanese curios;
they could work as servants, dockers, porters, or as *jinrikisha*
drivers. The *jinrikisha* (literally man-powered vehicle), more
often called and written rickshaw by Westerners, consisted of a
covered seat on two wheels, pulled by a half-naked man in
wooden shafts. It is safe to assume that for perhaps most
Westerners contact with the Japanese was only with those
employed in the various occupations in the treaty ports.
Japanese male manual workers (including, of course, *jinrikisha*
drivers) were generally referred to as 'coolies'.

A feeling common among Westerners, regardless of situation
and interest in life, was that things in Japan were certainly very
different from what they were at home. For example, Sir
Rutherford Alcock, first British head of legation in Japan, noted:

Japan is essentially a country of anomalies, where all – even
familiar things – put on new faces, and are curiously reversed. Except that they do not walk on their heads instead

of their feet, there are few things in which they do not seem, by some occult law, to have been impelled in a perfectly opposite direction and a reversed order. They write from top to bottom, from right to left, in perpendicular instead of horizontal lines; and their books begin where ours end, thus furnishing good examples of the curious perfection this rule of contraries has attained. Their locks, though imitated from Europe, are all made to lock by turning the key from left to right. The course of all sublunary things appears reversed. Their day is for the most part night; and this principle of antagonism crops up in the most unexpected and bizarre way in all their moral being, customs and habits. Their old men fly kites while the children look on; the carpenter uses his plane by drawing it to him, and their tailors stitch from them; they mount their horses from the off-side – the horses stand in the stables with their heads where we place their tails, and the bells to their harness are always on the hind quarters instead of the front; ladies black their teeth instead of keeping them white, and their anti-crinoline tendencies are carried to the point of so seriously interfering not only with the grace of movement but with all locomotion, so tightly are the lower limbs, from the waist downwards, girt round with garments; and, finally, the utter confusion of sexes in the public bath-houses, making that correct, which we in the West deem so shocking and improper, I leave as I find it – a problem to solve.[2]

The exotic was a theme which appeared and reappeared in all the general books written about Japan. Other Japanese idiosyncrasies and characteristics unfamiliar in the West, from public nudity and mixed bathing to the Japanese concept of death and ritual suicide (*seppuku* or *harakiri*), were also frequent subjects of description and analysis. Some of these appear in different sections of the book, others must be omitted.

One fairly constant theme was the smallness of everything. Lafcadio Hearn remarked how one found oneself 'suddenly in a world where everything is upon a smaller and daintier scale than with us – a world of lesser and seemingly kindlier beings, all smiling at you as if to wish you well, – a world where land, life, and sky are unlike all that one has known elsewhere – this is surely the realisation, for imagination nourished with English folklore, of the old dream of a world of Elves.'³

Kipling was also struck by the toy-like quality of Japan:

'What sort of mental picture do you carry away?' said the Professor. 'A tea-girl in fawn coloured crepe under a cherry tree all blossom. Behind her, green pines, two babies, and a hog-backed bridge spanning a bottle green river running over blue boulders. In the foreground a little policeman in badly-fitting Europe clothes drinking tea from blue and white china on a black lacquered stand. Fleecy white clouds above and a cold wind up the street,' I said summarising hastily. 'Mine is a little different. A Japanese boy in a flat-headed German cap and baggy Eton jacket; a King taken out of a toyshop, hundreds of little Noah's Ark trees and fields made of green painted wood. The whole neatly packed in a camphor-wood box.'⁴

Japan in the mid-nineteenth century was a country much admired in certain artistic circles in the West. It was reputed to be a land of great beauty and much was written extolling this beauty. Few travel books on Japan failed to relate in detail the tremendous variety of both flora and fauna; and in flowery detail the charms of rural villages were described. Japanese houses and gardens found praise of the highest degree:

I have spoken of simplicity. The domestic architecture is as simple, as transitory, as if it symbolised the life of man.

It is possible that when I return I shall feel still more distaste for the barbarous accumulations in our houses, and recall the far more civilised emptiness persisted in by the more esthetic race.⁵

In an age acutely conscious of race, however, and much given to defining the characteristics, qualities and faults of the different races, a telling indication of the Western image of Japan was the attitudes Westerners displayed towards the Japanese as a people. Naturally it is impossible to provide a unified picture as opinions varied a great deal. Generally

45

speaking, however, the Japanese received much more favourable treatment than would appear to have been meted out to most other non-Western peoples. No doubt part of the reason for this is that Japan was neither colonised nor defeated in a humiliating war (as the Chinese had been in the Opium war). Also, comparatively speaking, Japan had achieved a degree of prosperity and progress unparalleled in most non-European countries. Comparisons with China (numerous in view of the proximity of the two countries) tended to favour Japan. A correspondent to *The Times* in 1876 remarked:

> Japanese cleanliness as opposed to Chinese filth; Japanese roads as opposed to Chinese mud tracks; Japanese neatness and order as opposed to Chinese decay and confusion, are all elements of pleasure. Chinese children call you names; Japanese children either say nothing or salute you; Chinese dogs are imbued with the spirit of mandarins and bark in chorus after every foreigner who passes; Japanese dogs are inspired with the courtesy of their masters, and are incapable of such insolence. A Japanese tea house positively attracts you to stay, in order to enjoy the cleanliness, the tastefulness of its little garden, and the courtesy of the servants. A Chinese inn repels you by a diametrical contrast. Is there a yard of spare ground alongside a cottage in Japan, there will be a tiny shrub or two, a few tastefully arranged pebbles, and probably a little fountain; in China there would be a rubbish heap.[6]

Kipling too was perplexed by the Japanese:

> 'The Chinaman's a native', I said, 'that's the look on a native's face, but the Jap isn't a native, and he isn't a Sahib either.'[7]

An article which appeared in the *Edinburgh Review* two years before Japan was opened to the West, at a time when very little information about the country was available, was, by mid-nineteenth century European standards, quite eulogistic:

> They are Asiatics, it is true, and therefore deficient in that principle of development which is the leading characteristic

of those ingenious and persevering European races which have impressed the traces of their footsteps on the fervid deserts of the tropics, and moored their ships to the blue icebergs at either Pole; but amidst Asiatics the Japanese stand supreme. Can the tribes of India, or the teeming swarms of China, for a moment contest the palm with the chivalrous Japanese? We refuse to accept the architectural monuments of India as tests of civilisation. They are proofs of superstition and slavery – nothing more. With regard to China, again, the Japanese have held the inhabitants of the Celestial Empire at arm's length through many a long century, and esteemed them, not without reason, to be an inferior race. They think of them and speak of them as Brian de Bois Guilbert would have thought and spoken of Isaac, the Money-changer, in Scott's romance. We can find no nation or tribe in history with whom we might compare the Japanese but by an effort of misplaced ingenuity. They are warlike and yet adverse to conquest; they are as lavishly obedient to authority as a bourgeois of Nanking, and yet as turbulent and unmanageable if that authority should over-step the limits which public opinion has affixed to its exercise, as a Flemish burgher of the Middle Ages; they will select a wife from a place which might have astonished a boon companion of the Regent Orleans, but they judge a violation of conjugal faith as severely as a Scotch Puritan, and punish it with the inexorable sternness of a Spanish hidalgo; they are not religious in sentiment, but devout worshippers in practice; they are most cruel in their punishments, but most reluctant to inflict pain; they are gentle and courteous in their social intercourse, but more tenacious of a vindictive purpose than a Corsican mountaineer; they are most eager to extend the bounds of their knowledge in the arts and sciences, yet they have shut themselves out from all intercourse with those nations from whom alone they could expect to receive that information which they most desire to obtain.[8]

If to this writer the Japanese was an amalgam of a Flemish burgher, a Scotch puritan, a Spanish hidalgo and a Corsican mountaineer, to others the very thought of comparing a Japanese to a Westerner was preposterous. Baudelaire's laconic comment was that 'The Japanese are monkeys.'[9] Ruskin's impression after witnessing a display of Japanese acrobats 'was that of being in the presence of human creatures of a partially inferior race, but not without great human gentleness, domestic affection, and ingenious intellect; who were, nevertheless, as a nation afflicted by an evil spirit, and driven by it to recreate themselves in achieving, or beholding the achievement, through years of patience, of a certain correspondence with the nature of lower animals'.[10]

In an age when geography and climate were believed to have profound influence on the characteristics of the various races, it is not surprising to find that at least in some quarters it was felt that Japan, due to her extreme distance from Europe, must thereby be deprived of the more positive features of the European races:

> Trace on a map of the world two parallel lines between the twentieth and sixtieth degree of the north latitude, and you will observe, to begin with, that you will have encompassed in this narrow zone all the nations, which, to this day, have played an important role in the history of humanity; then, as you progress eastwards, human personality decreases. It reaches, in our days, its maximum of intensity in the great republic of the United States; more temperate and better balanced in Europe, it weakens in the Levant, diminishes even more in Persia and India, barely subsists in China, and seems to disappear in Japan. Impersonality is the distinctive trait of the inhabitants of the Empire of the Rising Sun.[11]

Comments on the Japanese as a race were of course not always laudatory, and at times they were very much the contrary. The most frequent criticism was that the Japanese were compulsive liars. Still, generally speaking, in the nineteenth century, as pointed out earlier, European attitudes to the Japanese were favourable. Part of the reason for this may lie in the extremely positive image of Japanese women in the West, as shall be seen in the next chapter; another reason may have been the childlike qualities which Occidentals ascribed to the Japanese. Kipling's explanation for this phenomenon was that children in Japan had a very good influence on their elders:

> Can the people help laughing? I think not. You see they have such thousands of children in their streets that the elders must perforce be young lest the babes should grieve. Nagasaki is inhabited entirely by children. The grown-ups exist on sufferance. A four-foot child walks with a three-foot child, who is holding the hand of a two-foot child, who carries on her back a one-foot child, who – but you will not believe me if I say that the scale runs down to six-inch little Jap dolls such as they used to sell in the Burlington Arcade. These dolls wriggle and laugh. They are tied up in a blue bed-gown which is tied by a sash, which again ties up the bed-gown of the carrier. Thus if you untie that sash, baby and but little bigger brother are at once perfectly naked. I saw a mother do this, and it was for all the world like the peeling of hard-boiled eggs.[12]

It is impossible to reproduce adequately the extensive range of attitudes towards Japan and the Japanese in the course of the nineteenth century. On the whole one can say, however, that although Japan was praised for her beauty and the charms of her people the country was not taken very seriously. As will be seen in the final chapter this attitude had changed fairly dramatically by the beginning of the twentieth century. It was one thing to be a dream-land of cherry blossoms, geisha and temples, it was quite another to be a non-white country with a formidable army and navy and a competitive economy. Those who saw Japan in the mid-nineteenth century as a toy country, a country of doll-like Lilliputians, and wanted to preserve it in a glass case or camphor-wood box, were to be disappointed by future developments. There were some who had from the very beginning of renewed contact between Japan and the West realised to some extent what the future might hold. As early as 1859 one visitor commented:

> Our day's observation led us to a conclusion which every hour in Japan confirmed – that the people inhabiting it are

a very remarkable race, and destined, by God's help, to play an important *role* in the future history of this remote quarter of the globe.[13]

In this meeting of Japan and the West, needless to say, one of the greatest obstacles was the problem of communication. A number of scholars learned Japanese; so did a few diplomats and missionaries. So far as the bulk of the Westerners in Japan were concerned, however, the linguistic hurdle was generally by-passed.

English, or a form of English, was fairly quickly established as the *lingua franca*. On Japanese attempts to speak English much was written – some of it amusing, some of it compassionate, much of it ridiculing. One of the problems the Japanese faced in attempting to speak English was that

there is no true L-sound in Japanese, and, consequently, no sign to represent such a sound, just as there is no true R-sound in Chinese. Curiously enough, the Japanese attempt to pronounce our L results in an R-sound; they say 'Rondon' for London, whereas the Chinese, in trying to articulate a foreign word containing an R, pronounce it as an L, and inform you quite calmly that their staple food consists of 'Lice'. A Japanese would remark conversely, that 'Rice are very unpreasant insects'.[14]

Laughter at the expense of Japanese attempts to speak or write English was common. A few Westerners, however, had the good humour to put the shoe on the other foot and laugh at their own attempts to speak Japanese.

While I am on the subject of Japanese philology there are two stories worth telling. The Japanese salutation 'Good-morning', is *Ohayo*, pronounced *O-hie-O*. Now when the former American Minister Judge Bingham arrived at Japan and alighted in state at the pier at Yokohama, the crowd greeted him with cries *Ohayo, Ohayo*! 'Durned clever people these.' remarked the flattered judge; 'how the deuce did they know I was from Ohio?' The other story was told to me by one of the Tokyo editors who speaks English very well. 'How do you say "Good-morning", in Japanese, Mr. Fukuchi?' an American lady asked him. '*Ohayo*, Madam', he replied. 'Ah', she said, 'that is very easy to remember, because it's the name of one of the States of my own country.' Next morning he was walking along, and the lady passed him in a *jinrikisha*. 'Mr. Fukuchi', she cried, 'Illinois, Illinois!'[15]

On a more serious level the Japanese language itself was seen by some Western observers as an impediment to progress. A Frenchman, Bousquet, early adviser on legal matters to the Japanese government, concluded after a lengthy dissertation on the language:

. . . the Japanese can easily assimilate our industrial knowledge and learn the functioning of our machines, the use of our mechanics, but they are incapable of mastering our sciences of reason, our higher mathematics, law and philosophy, and our analytical methods are inaccessible to them as long as they are dependent on their own language. They can without difficulty become masters of all the material side of our civilisation; but as to the intellectual and moral baggage which are the honour of the Aryan races, they must leave them aside, due to an improperly educated brain and a language incapable of assimilating them.[16]

The spoken language was criticised, but the real villain, so many Westerners felt, was the written language.

Educated as we now are, and living as we do, it is difficult to think with toleration of any language, whether spoken or written, which cannot be fairly mastered in a year or two, and it is with impatience that we read of Japan that 'at the lowest estimate a schoolboy was required to learn one thousand different characters'; that 'in the government elementary schools of the present time, about three thousand characters are taught'; and that 'a man laying any claim to scholarship knows eight or ten thousand characters, while those who pass for men of great learning are expected to be aquainted with many tens of thousands'. . . . Now that Japan has entered upon the modern period, she must, so far, discard her ancient forms of language so as to furnish her sons with readier means of acquiring knowledge.[17]

Japan's reliance on the use of the Chinese script dated back over a millenium, yet many Western observers felt that now that a new Western dawn had come unto Japan 'it was evident that the want of a simple and easy script would stand very much in the way of that complete communication between Japan and the Western world which was earnestly desired by both sides; also that, from the same cause difficulties would arise in incorporating the new ideas and new terms of Western learning into the language of Japan'.[18] Japan, in the past the child of Chinese civilisation, must in the modern age become completely the child of Western civilisation.

It must not be thought, however, that all Japanese were necessarily unresponsive to Western advice on the need for abandoning the complicated Chinese script. In the intoxicating years of almost slavish admiration for and imitation of Western things in Japan (roughly the 1870s and 80s), a number of language-reform societies were formed. One of these, the *Romajikai* (society for the romanisation of the written language), was founded in 1885. As news of this new organisation reached London, debate on its merits and demerits took place in the correspondence pages of *The Times*. Welcomed by most, it was nevertheless viewed with very strong reservations by others, notably the artist, one time resident in Japan, Frank Dillon, who wrote in a letter to *The Times*:

I venture to think that the hasty adoption of any fundamental change in the written language of the people would not conduce to the healthy growth of their old civilisation, and is, moreover, open to the grave objection that it would delay the carrying out of other reforms far more conducive to the welfare of the people. . . .

The Chinese ideographic method of writing, imported into Japan in conjunction with the peculiar form of civilisation suited to the wants of the people, took root naturally and enabled them to emulate, and in many instances improve upon, the culture of their teachers. The change in question must be classed with such chimeras as phonetic spelling, whereby the genius of our language would be corrupted and its history and continuity marred. As a minor objection to the scheme . . . I may mention that much of the marvellous facility in free hand drawing evinced by the Japanese may be traced to their early training in the formation of letters, difficult, indeed, in our eyes, but acquired by them with facility. Hand-in-hand with the adoption of Western habits, a rapid deterioration in the arts of the country is clearly noticeable. There is not, or rather there was not until recently, the marked line of demarcation between the art that lent itself to designs for manufacture and fine art properly so called as it exists in Europe. Permeated with the love of nature and the desire to imitate the forms and varied hues of the objects by which he was surrounded, the Japanese workman brought his innate taste to bear upon the design and decoration of the work he was entrusted with. The wave of pseudo-civilisation that has swept over the land may bring it to the level of a minor European state, but if it carry with it the decay or the abandonment of native art, the true lovers of progress will look with dismay upon the wreck and regret the introduction of ideas unsuited to the habits and traditions of the people.[19]

We find here, and indeed fairly consistently throughout this book, the interesting tendency of most Westerners to be either in favour of complete transformation of the country, or complete conservation. Those on the side of conservation seemed to fear that were Japan to become Westernised in one area, the dam would burst and Westernisation would flood traditional culture out of the country. The transformation 'lobby on the other hand, presumably more interested in 'progress' than in 'culture', seemed persuaded that Japan could not advance unless she completely abandoned her heritage. The point is, of course, that the Japanese neither conserved nor transformed their society entirely, but developed by a subtle combination (in most instances harmonious) or juxtaposition of the two, tradition and modernity. They kept their language, both spoken and written, but invented new words as the need arose – as in the development of Western languages. Indeed the parallel with Western languages is interesting, for, just as we depended on Greek or Latin roots for modern contraptions and concepts, so the Japanese turned to Chinese roots in order to coin modern scientific, political and philosophical words. Many interesting examples of the marrying of tradition and modernity can be found. For example, the government abolished *samurai* military privileges and formed a modern army, but sought to imbue its ranks with the *samurai* spirit and code of conduct. The system and syllabus of education were revised in order to cater to modern needs, but the relationship of pupil and teacher remained basically in the old Confucianist mould. Many other such examples could be cited, but the point is that this modern-traditional blend seems to have escaped the attention of most Western writers on Japan. They tended rather to see Japan as backward and Oriental or progressive and Western.

Nevertheless, Frank Dillon's fears in regard to the future of Japanese art amidst the furore of modernisation were bound to touch a sensitive chord in the West. In the early part of the mid-nineteenth century, Japan, above all, was praised for her artistic qualities and her artistic productions. The Japanese colour woodblock print, the *ukiyo-e*, of such painters as Hokusai, Hiroshige and Utamaro, was perhaps the main inspiration behind the development of the school of impressionist painting in France. A fashion gripped Europe – essentially, though not exclusively, in France – which was generally described as *Japonisme*; Japanese *objets d'art* were known as *Japoneries*.[20] In the nineteenth century it could be confidently stated that 'There is hardly a drawing-room in London or Paris or New York in which there are not objects of Japanese art.'[21]

One of the most admired features of Japanese art was its communion with nature. John LaFarge noted how in Japan

The lovely scenery reminds me continually of what has been associated with it; a civilisation which has been born of it, has never separated from nature, has its religion, its art, and its historic associations entangled with all natural manifestations. The great Pan might still be living here, in a state of the world which has sanctified trees and groves, and associated the spirit-world with every form of the earthly dwelling-place. I feel as if I were nearer than I can be through books to the world we try to rebuild by collation of facts and documents.[22]

Lafcadio Hearn saw in the colours of Japan an explanation for the beauty of Japanese textiles:

There are no such sunsets in Japan as in the tropics; the light is gentle as a light of dreams; there are no furies of color; there are no chromatic violences in nature in this Orient. All in sea or sky is tint rather than color, and tint vaportoned. I think that the exquisite taste of the race in the matter of colors and of tints, as exemplified in the dyes of their wonderful textures, is largely attributable to the sober and delicate beauty of nature's tones in this all-temperate world where nothing is garish.

The Japanese love of nature also explained the exquisite purity of their flower arrangements:

For the Japanese do not brutally chop off flower-heads to work them into meaningless masses of color, as we barbarians do: they love nature too well for that; they know how much the natural charm of the flower depends upon its setting and mounting, its relations to leaf and stem, and they select a single graceful branch or spray just as nature made it.[23]

But to others, although they did not necessarily deny this close rapport with nature, the reason, nonetheless, was less romantic:

They do not have a clear perception of their personality, they do not know how to distinguish themselves from their environment: they get lost in it, charmed by the smallest detail which meets their eye. The view of the world throws them and maintains them in a sort of permanent drunkenness.[24]

More damning, however, was another interpretation:

> Impassioned admirers of nature, they do not know how to 'add man' to it, to give it life as Bacon would say; they only know how to imitate it with unintelligent zeal or to defy it with a puerile naivety. This thorough but trivial art only speaks to the eyes, rejoices only because of the peculiarity of its subjects or the novelty of its methods, it does not elevate the soul; it is, in a word, simply 'amusing'.[25]

To the lovers of Japanese art, however, apart from its close harmony with nature, another source of admiration was that art in Japan seemed far more alive than in the West, far more part of the daily existence of all Japanese people and not, as in the West, secluded in the drawing-rooms of the wealthy:

> Art in Japan is living as art in Greece was living. It forms part and parcel of the very life of the people; every Jap is an artist at heart in the sense that he loves and can understand the beautiful. If one of us could be as fortunate as the man in the story, who came in his voyages upon an island where an Hellenic race preserved all the traditions and all the genius of their Attic ancestors, he would understand what living art really signifies. What would be true of that imaginary Greek island is absolutely true of Japan to-day. Art is in Europe cultivated in the houses of the few, and those few scarcely know either the beauties or the value of the plant they are cultivating. That is the privilege of a class rather than the rightful inheritance of the many. The world is too much divided into the artist on the one hand and the Philistine on the other. But it is not so in Japan, as it was not so in ancient Greece. In Japan the feeling for art is an essential condition of life.[26]

Comparisons with classical Greece were fairly frequent, yet not always necessarily to Japan's advantage. To an art critic of the Chinese and Japanese exhibits at the Paris World Exposition of 1878, there was little question as to which was superior:

> One could say that in Chinese art there is something of the patience, of the effect and of the magnificence of Egyptian art, and in Japanese art something of the grace, of the movement of liberty of Greek art. But, as it seems necessary to stress in these days of fanaticism for Japanese things, Chinese art and Japanese art have no conception of the beautiful; they are as far from the grandeur of Egyptian art and the beauty of Greek art as the Hottentot Venus is from the Venus de Milo.[27]

Although Japanese art tended to be greatly appreciated in the West, this was not necessarily a unanimous view. On the question of Japanese art, as on practically all aspects of Japan, Western views could be quite diametrically opposed. One English journalist expressed very strong views on the matter:

> The possession of a taste for Japanese art goods of whatever description is a sure sign of vulgarity. They are not really anything like so beautiful as the tawdry Austrian and Swiss goods which all men abhor. They are much cleverer truly – fiendishly clever on occasion, indeed – but cleverness is no art, and very clever work can be most unbeautiful. A people with the ideals of art which obtain in Japan is bound in the nature of things to be ugly of temper and intention.
>
> English art is always said by its practitioners to be in a parlous way, but at its worst it has not been anything like so cheap, so feeble, and so squalid as is the best art of Japan. . . .
>
> Hundreds of men have spent thousands of pounds on Japanese stuff when the craze was on them, and been glad to get rid of it for an old song when their sanity came back to them.
>
> There is no graciousness, no kindness, no humanness in anything that a Japanese carves, or panits, or otherwise produces. The work, no doubt, has its minor merits; it is neat and tricky and skilful, and as who should say cunning.

57

It is also cheap and flimsy and conventional, and fundamentally undesirable.

I do not believe for a moment that Japanese art has ever had, or ever will have, any appreciable influence on the English mind. If it did have such an influence we might be quite sure that the time of our utter and final decadence had set in.[28]

The French writer and diplomat, Maurice Paléologue was equally unreserved, though in an opposite direction; Japanese art, he claimed, was 'the most refined, the most sincere, the most imaginative and the most passionately in love with life and reality, which human thought has ever translated'.[29]

Reactions to Japanese art were mixed, but, as pointed out earlier, on the whole very favourable. The most intense fashion for Japanese art was undoubtedly in Paris. The Impressionists as we have seen, were greatly inspired by Japanese wood-block prints and particularly by the use of colour. Although Japanese art was for obvious reasons most accessible to those who visited Japan, nevertheless, as the years following Japan's opening passed, more and more opportunities to become acquainted with it were made available to those living in the West and unable or unwilling to travel to the country. Japan first participated in a world exposition in Paris in 1867; following that there were frequent Japanese art exhibitions in the major cities of Europe and the United States. Also, national museums and private collections in the West began acquiring both greater quantity and a wider selection of Japanese wood-block prints, scrolls, ceramics and so on. Of interest here, for example, are the origins of the Musée Guimet in Paris. Edmond Guimet was a silk merchant who travelled extensively in China and Japan and in the course of his business acquired a large and precious collection of Chinese and Japanese art. It became the trend for people of substance to acquire Japanese *objets d'art* and curios. Émile Zola can be seen painted by Manet (in the Jeu de Paume) surrounded by Japanese things. *Japoneries* were to the end of the nineteenth century, though perhaps to a more limited extent, what *Chinoiseries* had been to the eighteenth. What is interesting is that, at the time of the development of great admiration for Japanese art in the West, in Japan the trend was the reverse. In the period of Western intoxication, referred to earlier, native expressions of art were not well favoured, while imitations of Western painting triumphed. But that is a different story.

Appreciation of the Japanese visual arts by the Western public demanded, perhaps, a certain amount of imagination, but no great erudition was necessary. The problem of literature was, for obvious reasons, rather different and so knowledge of Japanese literature, let alone appreciation, was necessarily rather limited. The number of Westerners capable of reading Japanese was infinitesimal. Certainly pioneering work of translation and adaptation of Japanese literature was begun in the late nineteenth century, notably by Lafcadio Hearn and Lord Redesdale (A. B. Mitford). In 1899 a true milestone in the development of Western knowledge of Japanese literature appeared in the form of William George Aston's *A History of Japanese Literature*. Then an important breakthrough for Western appreciation – and, indeed, assimilation – of Japanese literature occurred in 1913 when Ezra Pound made the acquaintance of Mary Fenollosa in India. Ernest Fenollosa, as noted in the Introduction, had been mainly involved with painting in Japan, but had also taken copious notes on Japanese literature. Fenollosa died in 1908 before Pound had a chance to meet him. Having acquired his notes, however, he proceeded to adapt Japanese poetry into his own work and produced under his and Fenollosa's posthumous names *The Chinese Written Character as a Medium for Poetry*.[30]

Before that the *haiku* (seventeen-syllable poem) had greatly impressed a number of French poets, especially José-Maria de Heredia and Paul Louis Couchoud. What captivated the Western mind here was the simplicity in both form and content of the *haiku*, the instant atmosphere that it conveyed. Perhaps, however, it was not surprising that to an ordinary English reader, reared on such poetry as Milton's and Tennyson's, the Japanese variety might appear superficial.

Japanese poems are like the leaves of the Sibylline books, or the prophesies of Old Moore; they are Sphinx-like remarks, with an air of wisdom, which are capable of meaning anything, but to the European mind generally mean nothing.[31]

The question of religion in Japan will appear as a *leitmotiv* throughout this book. This is not because of any desire to strike a religious theme, but simply because, parallel with consciousness of race, Europeans of the nineteenth century were equally obsessed with religion. Just as one distinguished between the white (Caucasian or Aryan) and other races, so one distinguished between Christian and pagan or heathen.

The case of Japan, in so far as religion was concerned, was of particular interest because of the contact and later confrontation of Christianity with that country in the second half of the sixteenth and early seventeenth centuries. Iberian missionaries (mainly Portuguese Jesuits and later Spanish Franciscans) had enjoyed a considerable amount of influence and had made conversions at a time when Japan was in the upheaval of constant civil wars. Although anti-Christian sentiments and proclamations had already appeared by the end of the sixteenth century, it was only once peace and order were re-established under the new shogunate, the Tokugawa dynasty, that persecutions began in earnest. Eventually the Catholic Church was able to count a number of martyrs, both European and Japanese; from the middle of the seventeenth century onwards the Christian faith seemed to have been effectively wiped out from the Japanese islands and the situation remained the same throughout the country's long period of isolation.

As the inexorable advance of the Western powers across the East began in the early nineteenth century, however, hope was renewed among Catholics that Japan would soon again be open for missionary enterprise. With Britain's victory over China in the Opium War (1841), the outlook for missionaries brightened considerably and, as one Frenchman commented, 'It was not only a new era in the relations between Europe and the Far East that the English guns inaugurated, they opened the way for the preachers of the Gospel.'[32]

The first treaties with the Western powers included relatively few provisions regarding the Christian religion; much to the disappointment of missionary societies the Western foreign ministries felt that they should not push the matter too far as they were aware of Japanese susceptibilities on the matter. Missionaries were permitted to reside in the open ports and build churches, but only in order to officiate to their own nationals; so far as the Japanese were concerned, no proselytism was permitted. Such a situation was extremely frustrating for the missionaries. When in 1863 relations between Japan and the Western powers reached a dangerous pitch an early French missionary (and later bishop) in Japan, Petitjean, expressed the view (or hope) that 'if there is a war, idolatry will at last give way to the holy faith'.[33]

No war took place, only a bit of gunboat diplomacy. The latter significantly altered the nature of relationships between the *han* (fiefs) more openly hostile to the foreign presence, Satsuma and Chôshû, and indeed indirectly helped to precipitate the Imperial Restoration; but the situation of the Catholic missionaries in Japan was by no means improved. Two years later, however, Petitjean was amazed to discover that there were Japanese who, from father to son and mother to daughter, had secretly continued practising the faith during the centuries of isolation and Christian proscription. In time, however, the Japanese government also discovered the existence of these *Kakure Kirishtan* (or clandestine Christians) and imprisonment rapidly followed, beginning in 1867. There was an outcry in the West, but initially at least to no avail. Then on the occasion of the Iwakura mission to the West in 1872 – a mission concerned with proposals regarding the revision of the unequal treaties – so much pressure was brought upon the Japanese mission, both official and unofficial, that the Japanese leaders realised that their policy of religious intolerance could no longer be practised in view of its harmful effects on the country's attempts at improved relations with the West. In 1873 the government lifted the ban on Christianity. In theory missionaries were still not permitted to engage in any sort of religious activity outside the treaty ports, but with the passing years the situation improved. Many missionaries found openings as teachers in the new Japanese schools and used these positions in the hope of winning converts to the Christian religion. In 1889 the principle of freedom of religion was embodied in the country's new constitution.

It is difficult to generalise, but perhaps one can say without too much hesitation that Westerners in the late nineteenth century were less dogmatic about religious matters than they had been in the sixteenth and seventeenth centuries. So, apart from the missionaries, there was a greater interest in Japanese religions *per se* without an accompanying desire to denigrate or convert. Indeed in some Western circles interest in and even adherence to Oriental religions was by no means extraordinary. Jesuit missionaries in China in the seventeenth century had evinced a strong interest in Confucianism, but this resulted in Vatican disapproval and excommunication of some and was one of the pretexts, if not an outright reason, for the temporary suppression of the Society of Jesus. In the more tolerant – indeed, increasingly secular – atmosphere of the nineteenth century, Eastern religions could be studied in a more detached and appreciative manner.

Curiosity regarding the nature of Japanese religions was revealed in most of the books written about the country. But there were a number of obstacles which the Westerner had to surmount. Not only were Christians monotheistic, whereas Japanese religions were not, but also it was difficult for the Westerner to understand how the Japanese could belong to more than one faith. A Christian was a Christian; similarly a Jew was a Jew; and even in other parts of the East a Muslim practised only Islam and a Hindu only Hinduism. The Japanese, however, did not feel that adherence to one religion necessarily excluded belonging simultaneously to another:

> On more than one occasion we have heard a Japanese asked by a European traveller what his religion was, – whether Buddhist or Shintô, – and have been amused at his look of blank perplexity. He could not, for the life of him, make out what the enquirer was driving at. It is the established custom to present infants at the Shintô family temple one month after birth. It is equally customary to be buried by the Buddhist parish priest. The inhabitants of each district contribute to the festivals of both religions alike, without

being aware of any inconsistency. They do not draw the hard and fast distinctions with which we are familiar.[34]

As another Western writer explained, 'The combination of Shintôism, Buddhism and Confucianism which constituted the Japanese religion and philosophy was therefore not a mere mechanical mixture; it was of the nature of a chemical compound.'[35] The problem that arose, however, was whether, given the impressive panoply of religions in Japan, the Japanese were religious. An early Swiss traveller and watch salesman commented that 'the Japanese are in religious matters the most indifferent people I have ever come across'.[36] Lafcadio Hearn, though agreeing with this view, found it to be a cause of considerable admiration for the Japanese:

> What has most impressed me is the seeming joyousness of popular faith. I have seen nothing grim, austere, or self-repressive. I have not even noted anything approaching the solemn. The bright temple courts and even the temple steps are thronged with laughing children, playing curious games; and mothers, entering the sanctuary to pray, suffer their little ones to creep about the matting and crow. The people take their religion lightly and cheerfully; they drop their cash in the great alms-box, clap their hands, murmur a very brief prayer, then turn to laugh and talk and smoke their little pipes before the temple entrance. Into some shrines, I have noticed the worshippers do not enter at all; they merely stand before the doors and pray for a few seconds, and make their small offerings. Blessed are they who do not too much fear the gods which they have made![37]

But, just as with the language, a question Western observers debated was to what extent the Japanese would be able to hold on to their religious heritage in the course of modernisation. This is a theme which will reappear frequently in sundry considerations of the modernisation of Japan; a theme also on which there was much controversy. A sample of this can be given from two diametrically opposed views. W. G. Aston, the great specialist of Japanese literature, wrote:

The process of absorbing new ideas which has mainly occupied the Japanese nation during the last thirty years, is incomplete in one very important particular. Although much in European thought which is inseparable from Christianity has been freely adopted by Japan, the Christian religion itself has made comparatively little progress . . . There are some considerations which tend to show that important results in this direction may be expected during the century which is nearly approaching us. The previous religious history of the nation has prepared Japan for the acceptance of a higher form of faith. Buddhism did not a little towards fostering ideals of holiness, humanity, and detachment from worldly things. Confucianism provided high, though it may be somewhat distorted, standards of morality, and a comparatively rational system of philosophy. Shintô taught a reverence for the Divine powers which created and govern the universe and man. But none of the three sufficed by itself to meet the heart, soul, and mind want of the Japanese nation. Can it be imagined that when a religion is presented to them which alone is adapted to satisfy far more completely all the cravings of their higher nature, the Japanese with their eminently receptive minds, will fail in time to recognise its immense superiority? They have already accepted European philosophy and science. It is simply inconceivable that the Christian religion should not follow.[38]

Lafcadio Hearn treated the same question very differently:

That the critical spirit of modernized Japan is now indirectly aiding rather than opposing the efforts of foreign bigotry to destroy the simple, happy beliefs of the people, and substitute those cruel superstitions which the West has intellectually outgrown, – the fancies of an unforgiving God and an everlasting hell, – is surely to be regretted. More than a hundred and sixty years ago Kaempfer wrote of the Japanese: 'In the practice of virtue, in purity of life and outward devotion, they far outdo the Christians'. And ex-

Samurai and servant. Pre-Restoration Samurai privileges included the right to carry swords; they were often referred to (and feared) by Westerners as 'the two-sworded men'. Following the Restoration, Samurai privileges were abolished and by the late 1870's the Samurai had ceased to be part of the landscape.

The Japanese. A Western artist's impression of the various types of Japanese to be found in the pre-modern period: 1 Officer of the Taikoon; 2 Mendicant Bonze; 3 Bonze of a superior order; 4 Military dress; 5 & 6 Japanese women; 7 Japanese soldier; 8 Man of the lower classes; 9 Coolie of the fish market; 10 Pilgrim.

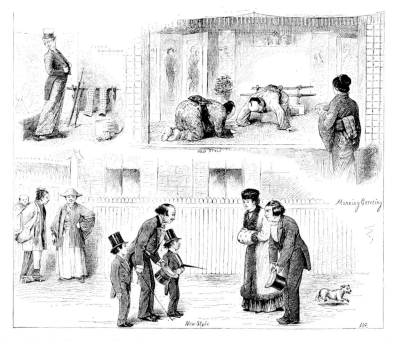

'New Year's Day'. A drawing, by a Western artist, contrasting the 'old style' with the new, European influence.

cept where native morals have suffered by foreign con-
tamination, as in the open ports, these words are true of the
Japanese today. My own conviction, and that of many
impartial and more experienced observers of Japanese life,
is that Japan has nothing whatever to gain by conversion to
Christianity, either morally or otherwise, but very much to
lose.[39]

Aston was wrong. In spite of fairly numerous Christian
missionaries of many denominations in Japan, the impact of
Christianity and the number of converts remained small.
There are a number of reasons for this, but it is not the purpose
here to go into them in any detail. Perhaps one might rather
summarise, even at the risk of over-simplification. The major
reason presumably was that the bulk of the Japanese remained
content with their own religions and saw no need to change. It
is true, however, that in the period of Western intoxication a
number of leading Japanese officials and intellectuals did
wonder whether encouraging their compatriots to embrace the
Christian faith would not be in order. Apart from the numerous
cases of genuine conversion, one can detect, nevertheless, two
motivations for contemplating such a course. First, Japanese
government officials perhaps felt that were the country to become Christian relations with the Western powers – namely
treaty revision – would be improved. Secondly, the new intellectuals, namely those influenced by Western thought and
aspiring to modernise Japanese society in order to reach
Western standards, doubted whether their aims could be
achieved by adopting Western science, technology and political systems without the religious tradition that lay behind
these. Soon, however, they were able to discover that many
circles in the West were strongly secular and indeed in Japan
herself not only had Western missionaries come, but also
Western atheists and agnostics who sought to counter the
Christian influence.

In fact by the end of the century indigenous religious sentiment remained strong, in spite of Western influences. Percival
Lowell, an early scholar of religion in Japan, illustrated this
phenomenon:

. . . in the nation's heart the Shintô sentiment throbbed on as strong as ever. A Japanese minister found this out to his cost. In 1887, Mori Arinori, one of the most advanced Japanese new-lights, then minister of state for education, went on a certain occasion to the Shrines of Ise, and studiously treated them with disrespect. It was alleged, and apparently on good authority, that he trod with his boots on the mat outside the portal of the palisade, and then poked the curtain apart with his walking-stick. He was assassinated in consequence; the assassin was cut down by the guards, and then Japan rose in a body to do honor, not to the murdered man, but to his murderer. Even the muzzled press managed to hint on which side it was, by some as curious editorials as were penned. As for the people, there were no two ways about it; you had thought the murderer some great patriot dying for his country. Folk by thousands flocked with flowers to his grave, and pilgrimages were made to it, as to some shrine. It is still kept green; still to-day the singing-girls bring it their branches of plum blossoms, with a prayer to the gods that a little of the spirit of him who lies buried there may become theirs; that spirit which they call so proudly the Yamato Kokoro, the heart of old Japan.

For in truth Shintô is so Japanese it will not down. It is the faith of these people's birthright, not of their adoption. Its folklore is what they learned at the knee of the race-mother, not what they were taught from abroad. Buddhist they are by virtue of belief; Shintô by virtue of being.[40]

In relation to the question of the national foundations of Shintô, others observed how religion and politics tended to become blurred in Japan. Thus one writer suggested that 'The only belief firmly implanted in Japan is respect due to hierarchy, to authority, to human grandeur. The fanatical devotion of the subjects to their suzerain is the most explosive proof.'[41]

Writing in 1904, the year Japan embarked on war against Russia, the scholar Basil Hall Chamberlain noted a paradoxical effect of Westernisation. Japan, as a result of European influences, had not become Christian; rather indigenous religious beliefs had greatly contributed to the process of modernisation:

> It has often been alleged of late that patriotism and loyalty to the sacred, heaven-descended Mikado amount to a religion in Japan. If we are to accept this statement, one important qualification must be made, which is that the fervour of patriotism and loyalty to the throne, which we see to-day at white heat, is no legacy from a hoary antiquity, but quite a recent development, – one of the many indirect results of the Europeanisation of Japanese institutions . . . It is no ingrained racial characteristic; it is a phase, comparable in some ways to the Puritan fervour which blazed up in England two or three centuries ago, and for a season moulded everything to its own temper. Like the stern enthusiasm of Cromwell's Ironsides, like the fiery zeal of the French revolutionary hosts, like all partly moral, partly political enthusiasms, it arms its votaries, and in fact the whole nation, with well-nigh irresistible might for the time being. It is a highly interesting phenomenon, – admirable in the fearless self-abnegation which it inspires, grotesque in the misrepresentations of history and even of patent contemporary facts on which it partly rests, vastly important in the concrete results which it achieves. New Japan could never have risen and expanded as she has done without some ideal to beckon her onwards; and this Imperialistic ideal was the only one within reach. It has been the lever that has raised her from Oriental impotence to her present rank among the great powers of the world. Whether it should be called a religion is a mere question of how we may choose to define that word.[42]

The aspects of Japanese life which we have looked at are but some of the many that Westerners commented on. It is hoped that they will help illustrate the general tenor of Western attitudes to Japan.

3

THE WOMEN OF JAPAN –
IN REALITY AND FANTASY

> *In no regard, perhaps, is the contrast between the East and the West*
> *more striking than their respective ideas concerning women and*
> *marriage.*[1]

> *The Japanese woman is the crown of the charm of Japan.*[2]

The perception of woman's status and fate in Japan tended to
influence Westerners' views of the level of civilisation – or
barbarity – of Japanese society as a whole. This is the element
of reality we shall be dealing with – albeit a reality embellished
or sullied according to the eye of the beholder. Secondly, we
will need to consider the image, or indeed the ideal, of Japanese
women in the West. This image transcended reality; it was a
source of dreams, certainly of fiction. In the period we are
dealing with, no aspect of Japan captivated the Western male
imagination as much as Japanese woman.

Even though the status of woman varied considerably in
Western European countries, travelling to the East the Westerner was bound to come across customs associated with the
female sex, which, by nineteenth-century European standards
at least, appeared inhumane. It was not simply that polygamy
was widespread, that female infanticide was not an uncommon
practice, but worse still: in India widows could be burned alive
at the pyre of their deceased husband (*suttee*, though abolished
in British India in 1829, was still practised in territories outside
British jurisdiction until the end of the nineteenth century),
while in China girls' feet were bound.

When reaching Japan, judgement on the status and fate of
woman depended on the models used for comparison. The
influential American missionary and teacher, William Griffis,
commented:

68

The student of Asiatic life, on coming to Japan, is cheered and pleased on contrasting the position of women in Japan with that in other countries. He sees them treated with respect and consideration far above that observed in other quarters of the Orient. They are allowed greater freedom, and hence have more dignity and self-confidence. . . . An amount of social freedom prevails among womankind in Japan that could hardly be expected in a country at once Asiatic, idolatrous, and despotic.[3]

There was general agreement that Japanese customs were more benign towards women than those of other Oriental countries. This may well have been one of the reasons why, as we saw in the previous chapter, Japan tended to be regarded by Westerners as a society of somewhat higher standing when compared to the rest of Asia. Yet in judging the status of woman in Japanese society most Western observers naturally tended to apply their own standards and values. As another American missionary, Sidney Gulick, remarked, 'the lot of woman as a whole is considerably inferior in Japan to what it is in America or England'.[4]

The question which many Western writers attempted to answer was why woman's position in Japan should be so inferior to what it was in the West. Investigations into many different aspects of Japanese culture yielded a number of interesting results. For example, there were possible implications to be derived from the teaching of early Japanese mythology:

We may pause a moment longer with the children to hear the story they are taught concerning the creation of the world – which means Japan. The beautiful islands were made by the gods themselves, two of whom came down to live there, becoming the progenitors of the present inhabitants, who are thus the 'sons of heaven', as they literally call their Emperors to this day. The advent story of these divine progenitors is certainly interesting, and suggestive of several things. Izanagi the god and Izanami the goddess each took a walk round the borders of the newly-created realm, going in opposite directions. At length they met. Instantly Izanami exclaimed, 'Oh, what a beautiful man!' But Izanagi was disappointed that a woman should precede him in anything, even in the matter of flattering speech; so this literal lord of creation commanded that they walk around the islands again, and that the goddess keep silent upon their meeting, thus giving him his divine right of precedence. Izanami meekly obeyed him, and when next they met she held her nimble tongue, while her liege lord sluggishly ejaculated, 'Oh, what a beautiful woman!'[5]

Far more popular than ancient mythology as an explanation for the apparent low esteem woman was held in in Japan, however, were the various religions. Confucianism is an example.

Confucianism, which moulds the morals of Japan . . . conceives of womanhood with infinite contempt. An eminent Japanese Confucianist, in his famous treatise on 'The Whole Duty of Woman', delights in deliverances such as these:
The five worst maladies that afflict the female mind are: indocility, discontent, slander, jealousy, and silliness. Without any doubt, these five maladies infest seven or eight out of every ten women, and it is from these that arises the inferiority of women to men. The worst of them all, and the parent of the other four, is silliness. Woman's nature, in comparison with man's, is as the shadow to the sunlight. Hence, as viewed from the standard of man's nature, the foolishness of woman fails to understand the duties that lie before her very eyes, perceives not the actions that will bring down blame upon her own head, and comprehends not even the things that will bring down calamities on the heads of her husband and children. Such is the stupidity of her character that it is incumbent on her, in every particular, to distrust herself and to obey her husband.
The teachings of Confucius, as recorded by this same disciple, state these 'Seven Reasons for Divorce':
1. A woman shall be divorced for disobedience to her father-in-law or mother-in-law.
2. A woman shall be divorced if she fail to bear children,

the reason for this rule being that women are sought in marriage for the purpose of giving men posterity.
3. Lewdness is a reason for divorce.
4. Jealousy is a reason for divorce.
5. Leprosy, or any like foul disease, is a reason for divorce.
6. A woman shall be divorced, who, by talking over much and prattling disrespectfully, disturbs the harmony of kinsmen and brings trouble on her household.
7. Stealing is a reason for divorce. It is little wonder that the disciples of such teaching hold women in unutterable contempt.[6]

Shintô, it was believed, was reasonably tolerant towards woman and in primitive times (before the introduction of Buddhism) she had been accorded a higher place. Subsequently, however, through Buddhism she was cast into a very inferior position, in view of the fact that

the notions and ideals presented by Buddhism in regard to women are clear, and clearly degrading. She is the source of temptation and sin: she is essentially inferior to man in every respect. Before she may hope to enter Nirvana she must be born again as man.[7]

The study of history also pointed to possible clues for an understanding of the low regard women were held in in Japan; for example, there appeared striking differences in the European and Japanese attitudes to women during their respective feudal periods. Japan, it was asserted, lacked the European tradition of chivalry. Basil Hall Chamberlain remarked, ' "God and the Ladies!" was the motto of the European knight. But neither God nor the ladies inspired any enthusiasm in the *Samurai*'s breast. . . . A Japanese knight performed his valiant deeds . . . out of loyalty to his lord or filial piety towards the memory of his papa, taking up, maybe, the clan vendetta and perpetuating it.'[8]

As to woman's role in contemporary society, it was noted how 'the whole sum of excellencies and defects of the Japanese female character arise from one all-including virtue, and the biography of a good woman is written in one word – obedience.'[9]

The consequences of this extreme dominance of the male in Japanese society were numerous and were the cause (or so it was believed) of certain outstanding differences between Japanese and Western social and moral customs. One of these was the question of female chastity:

> . . . it is certain that chastity represented much more the idea of a capital to be conserved than the sentiment of a defilement of one's honour to be avoided. This capital belongs to the father before marriage, to the husband afterwards; and it is robbing the proprietor if one alienates it without his approval. With his authorisation, however, the action becomes highly praiseworthy.[10]

This view was confirmed by another source, in that

> the young girl who gave in to a seducer *without the consent of her parents*, was punished with sixty lashes of the whip, not because she had violated the laws of decency, but because she thus deprived the owners of a good only they could dispose of.[11]

This idea of the Japanese woman as a good which males (fathers or husbands) could dispose of at will found illustration in numerous anecdotes. An example was provided by an American missionary:

> There was in Tokyo a native Christian pastor who asked permission of his missionary employers to come to America for study. They were about to accede to his request, when it occurred to someone to inquire how he intended to obtain the means. Imagine the amazement of his questioners when he replied that it was his intention to secure the money by renting out his wife to a temporary life of shame! 'Morality' still meant to him little more than the 'filialism' of a subordinate to a superior authority; and the obedience of his wife to her husband's behest would thus have been an act of 'righteousness'.[12]

The females thus disposed of, or so it was alleged, accepted their plight with serenity:

The Japanese maiden, as pure as the purest Christian virgin, will at the command of her father enter the brothel to-morrow, and prostitute herself for life. Not a murmur escapes her lips as she thus filially obeys. To a life she loathes, and to disease, premature old age, and an early grave, she goes joyfully.[13]

A problem, however, which preoccupied some of the more objective Western observers of Japan was to what extent these differences between Japan and Western countries were more apparent than real. In regard to prostitution, for example, a British doctor in Japan, J. E. de Becker, wondered whether

the majority of the unfortunate girls of the same class in other countries are not nearly in the same predicament as their sisters in this country with regard to the exercise of free will in the choice of their profession, the only difference being in the nature of motives that influence their decision. If misery, starvation and vicious habits constitute the principal influences that drive women to the immoral calling in other countries, the determining motive is here, in many cases, a mistaken idea of filial piety. In either case, the choice is equally free or otherwise, according to the way in which one likes to understand the meaning of the expression 'freedom of will'.[14]

The tenor of the remarks so far cited indicate that it was certainly believed by most Westerners (there were a few exceptions) that Japan was sexually a far more permissive society than the West, at least so far as Japanese males were concerned. The way prostitution was practised in Japan seemed to offer positive proof. Although various forms of prostitution existed, that which most intrigued, amused or scandalised the Westerner was the so-called *Yoshiwara* system.

Originally 'Yoshiwara' was the name of a district on the outskirts of Edo (the city eventually renamed Tokyo in 1868) exclusively reserved for carrying on the business of prostitution. The Japanese themselves used the term 'Yoshiwara' only when referring to the 'red light district' of Tokyo; most foreigners, however, adopted it as a generic term for all comparable places in Japanese cities. The Yoshiwara dated back to the early years of the Edo period (1603–1867); the system, interestingly enough, was comparable to that practised in ancient Athens where prostitutes had been segregated in the Solon.[15] The theory behind the 'Yoshiwara system' was that by secluding and specifically defining limits for prostitution the authorities could control what was going on in the brothels, who was coming and going, and, furthermore, areas outside remained (theoretically) free of prostitutes and those soliciting for their trade. Although 'the Yoshiwara' quickly entered into the vocabulary of foreign residents in Japan there was little likelihood that more than a handful actually knew very much about them.

In 1899, however, a mild sensation was caused among foreign residents by the publication in English of a book entitled, *The Nightless City: or the History of the Yoshiwara Yukwaku*. Originally published anonymously, it later transpired that the author was one of Japan's more eminent and distinguished foreign residents, the English doctor J. E. de Becker. In fact (and in spite of the titillation it aroused) it was a most scholarly work and remains to this day the most complete and authoritative account of the Yoshiwara in a Western language.

De Becker went into considerable detail in explaining the various traditions of the Yoshiwara, the different types of houses and the services they provided, the manner of dress and *coiffure*, the numerous festivals held every year, and the role the Yoshiwara had played in Japanese cultural life over the last few centuries. Indeed, in this book the Western reader could have learned a great deal about Japanese history, customs, art and literature.

The Yoshiwara may have been deeply implanted in Japanese tradition, but it did not entirely escape the tendrils of Westernisation. In the matter of architecture, for example, de Becker noted that since the beginning of the Meiji era changes have been introduced into the architecture of brothels and several magnificent and commodious houses have been built in a hybrid European style.

Similarly in respect to fashion and food Western influence was felt:

The adoption of foreign costume by prostitutes was first introduced by the Yamada-ro of Ageya-machi in 1886, and later on this example was followed by the *Shin-Inahen-ro* and several other houses, but before long the new fashion fell into disfavour and was abandoned. When the 'foreign craze' was at its height, the Yamada-ro provided foreign bedsteads for the women, and served up food in foreign dishes; but they never got so far as knives and forks, and although the plates were of a Western pattern one was expected to eat the viands with the cedarwood chopsticks provided ! ! !

It was the practice in lower grade brothels to expose the employees in rooms open to public view from the streets. In this manner the client could pick his companion and indicate his choice to the proprietress. The presence of foreigners, however, seemed likely to alter this practice:

In view of the approaching 'mixed residence' of foreigners in the interior, it is said that the authorities are contemplating the advisability of interdicting the present custom of exposing *yujo* (courtesans or prostitutes) in 'cages' to public view . . .

In the higher class establishments technological progress helped settle the question of public exposure:

. . . albums containing portraits of the women belonging to first and second-class houses are provided . . . for the convenience of guests. These books are called '*Shashin Mitate-cho*' (albums of photographs to facilitate the selection of women) . . .

75

So far the Western reader may have doubted whether his influence had been salutary; the following, no doubt, would have reassured him:

In September 1867, a hospital for the treatment of venereal diseases of prostitutes was established in Yokohama for the first time in the history of Japan, and subsequently similar institutions were established at Kobe and Nagasaki. This measure was adopted ... owing to the representations made by an Englishman – Dr Newton, R.N. – who, in spite of much opposition from prejudice and ignorance, succeeded in converting the authorities to his views after a long struggle.[16]

De Becker's book was a work of considerable erudition and objectivity. Apart from very few passages, he refrained from passing any moral judgement – favourable or unfavourable. In this he was the exception. The majority of Westerners commenting on the Yoshiwara indulged in remarks ranging from extreme condemnation to considerable admiration. Whereas a Scottish professor in Japan remarked that 'The most crying of the national vices is undoubtedly licentiousness',[17] a French naval officer, after having explained some of the more beautiful festivals of the Yoshiwara, protested: 'The Japanese, some say, honour vice. Why not rather admit that in the manner of the ancient Greeks they render hommage to beauty?'[18]

The American missionary Griffis saw at least one positive feature of prostitution in Japan when compared to the West:

... the social evil in Japan is shorn of some features so detestably conspicuous in other countries. The street-walker is unknown. The place set apart for the vile business is rarely inside the city, but in the suburbs. A man may live for years in a Japanese city, and see none of the moral leprosy, such as nightly floods Broadway, the Haymarket, and the Boulevard des Italiens.[19]

As a result of this, 'nobody in Japan can fall into temptation unwittingly: he must go in search of it'.[20]

Probably the feature of Japanese prostitution which most shocked Westerners was that the majority of the girls 'are virtually slaves, sold in childhood to the keepers of the houses in which they work, and trained, amid the surroundings of the *jorōya* (brothel), for the life which is the only life they have ever known'.[21]

When all was said and done on the subject, however, De Becker's view was 'that this Empire has by no means a *monopoly* of vice; and to foreigners who declaim against the "immorality of Japanese" I would say frankly – "You cannot afford to criticise this country too closely, for you certainly dare not lay the flattering unction to your souls that you, as a race, have any *monopoly* of virtue." '[22]

Even if morality (virtue or licentiousness) was basically the same in Japan and the West, customs were certainly very different. Some of the differences were encountered presumably at first-hand experience. An example is the discovery that 'The Japanese do not know how to kiss – if a Japanese girl knows how to kiss it shows the work of a foreign instructor; she does it as an accomplishment, not as an enjoyment'.[23]

Other peculiarities of Japan could be discovered through literature. Alice Mabel Bacon, author of an impressive work entitled *Japanese Girls and Women* (which first appeared in 1891), noticed how most Japanese romances were woven about the lives of the inmates of the Yoshiwara. No doubt an important reason for this was that 'in a country in which innocent romance has little room for development, the imagination must find its materials where it can'.[24]

Japan, even by Victorian standards, seemed to impose far more rigorous standards of behaviour on her 'non-professional' women:

Amateur flirting does not exist in Japanese social life. The accomplishments that ensure a woman's social success in the Occident are relegated to the Far East, to those who are paid to entertain the men; theirs are the wit and the power of the repartee, the interesting small talk on the topics of the day, the amusing little affectations – in short, all the delightful frivolities that go to make up the every-day conversation of the 'charming woman' of the West, but that are considered beneath the dignity of the Japanese lady, absorbed in the serious business of female life.[25]

Absence of flirtation also meant absence of courtship before marriage. Here again a striking difference from the West was perceived, namely in the respective societies' attitudes and customs in regard to marriage. Mrs Hugh Fraser, a writer and the wife of a British diplomat in Tokyo at the end of the nineteenth century, after expressing the view that 'marriage is not and never can be here, the supreme relation of life, as it is in Europe', nevertheless attempted to describe Japanese attitudes to marriage as objectively as possible:

As marriages are always arranged by parents or friends, the young people's consent only being asked at the moment when they have their first interview, a very small amount of personal feeling enters into the contract – at any rate in its early stages. An English bride would blush angrily were it hinted that she was not, as the phrase runs, in love with her new husband; that rarest of passions, pure love, is supposed to preside even at the most fashionable weddings. Not so in Japan. The young girl here would reply that such passion is for the women whom she need never meet; the very name of it is unknown to her, unless she has seen it illustrated in a play at the theatre; who would think of mentioning such a low feeling, where the solemn duty of wife to husband, and husband's father and mother is concerned? Her marriage is the passing from childhood's happy careless life to the responsibilities of reason. Body and soul, mind and spirit, must all tend to one thing – the giving entire satisfaction to the new master and his family. This seems very dreary and cold to us; and the best European woman, educated in the full consciousness of her own value, would feel that she lost her integrity by entering such bondage. That it is done by hundreds of girls every year without any thought of love or duty either, but simply for the sake of having a luxurious home and plenty of fun, does not touch the case at all. Our typical high-minded English maiden despises these weaker sisters, is ashamed for them as for some blot on womanhood itself. The best of her gods is still naughty Cupid; and if he is to be shut out of her life, she would rather give up the struggle at once.

Mrs Fraser further conceded:

> It seems to me that the common amusement called 'falling in love' has absolutely nothing to do with the affectionate and careful fulfilment of the duties of married life, and that the crown of an all-absorbing worship of one human being for another may be, and often is, granted without that passing preliminary ailment having been contracted at all.

And she certainly found numerous examples both in Japanese history and contemporary society to claim that 'all English history can show no record of higher, stronger love than the Japanese wife has again and again laid at her lord's feet'.[26]

Such dispassionate observations were not necessarily the rule. The American missionary Sidney Gulick saw Japanese customs in regard to marriage as inherently inferior to those of the West, since 'There are few experiences in the West so ennobling as the love that a young man and a young woman bear to each other during the days of their engagement and lasting onward throughout the years of their lengthening married life'.[27] Similarly, to many it was not simply the absence of love that relegated Japanese marriages to a very different and inferior moral status compared with the West; for in Japan 'the conjugal relation is without that sacredness with which Christianity alone can invest it'.[28]

If customs and institutions excluded love in marriage, this did not mean that 'love' did not exist in Japan. Yet the consequences of 'falling in love' appeared far more dramatic than was generally the case in the West (or comparable only to Western drama of the Romeo and Juliet or Tristan and Isolde variety):

> Instances are not rare ... of young people plighting their troth spontaneously, and resolving to die together when they

despair of obtaining the parental consent to their union. These double suicides through love . . . sometimes terminate a clandestine *liaison* that has been, or is in danger of being, discovered; much more frequently they are pure 'Bridals of Death', sealing for eternity the hitherto platonic affection of two young hearts – the victims are often mere boys and girls – despairing of the fulfilment, in this world, of their yearning. In such a case the lovers will plight their troth to each other, sometimes, 'for three, or more, successive existences' . . . sometimes 'for ever and ever'. They then, in many instances, partake together of a little feast and die, by their own hands, clasped in a last – often in a first – embrace. They invariably leave a written statement of their motives. Occasionally, they commit suicide separately, and in places distant from each other, but as a rule, they die clasped in each other's arms, by dagger, or poison, or, more frequently by casting themselves, tightly bound together with the girl's under girdle, into a river.[29]

Industrialisation, however, had its impact on love suicides:

The introduction of railways has added an additional method of consummating the Nuptials of Death, and the Tokyo express, thundering along the line, has sent more than one couple of unfortunate lovers to seek blissful reunion 'for ever and ever' in the Mei-do, the World Hereafter.[30]

Marriage and death somehow always seemed inseparable, if not literally, at least figuratively. Indeed the ordinary wedding ceremony itself was not lacking in funeral overtones;

on the wedding day the bride dressed all in white, the colour of mourning – to signify that she dies to her own family, and that she will never leave her husband's house but as a corpse – is borne away at nightfall to her new home, escorted by the middleman and his wife. The parental home is swept out on her departure, and in former days a bonfire was lighted at the gate – ceremonies indicative of the purification necessary after the removal of a dead body.[31]

Caged girls outside a brothel. While meandering down the streets of the Yoshiwara, potential clients could select their companion from the 'displays' offered by the various establishments.

The brothels of Tokyo's Yoshiwara district – and similar 'red light districts' in other Japanese cities – were by no means solely for the more obvious business of the trade; they were places for meeting and entertaining friends, for drinking and eating in a warm, relaxed and amusing atmosphere. Note two aspects of 'Westernisation' – the bowler hat and the handle-bar moustache.

A high-class geisha. Traditionally a good geisha – literally 'a person of artistic accomplishment' – would become renowned not so much for physical beauty, as for proficiency in singing, dancing, recitation and quick, witty repartee. Few Westerners could appreciate this, however, and the term geisha among the foreign community quickly became a generic term for prostitute. In this, as in many other things, they were mistaken perhaps not so much in fact as in nuance.

On the subject of married life, Lafcadio Hearn – himself married not only to a Japanese, but to a woman of *samurai* stock – warned his readers not to jump to premature conclusions. Family life in Japan, he explained, 'is much less open to observation than in any country of the West, not excepting Spain. It is a life of which foreigners see little, and know almost nothing, all the essays which have been written about Japanese women to the contrary notwithstanding.' Even if one had the opportunity of being invited into the home of a Japanese family,

of the relation of those souls to each other you will know nothing. Behind the beautiful screens which mask the further interior, all is silent, gentle mystery. There is no reason to the Japanese mind, why it should be otherwise. Such family life is sacred; the home is a sanctuary, of which it were impious to draw aside the veil.

Social behaviour, Hearn acknowledged, was different and therein arose some of the Western misconceptions on the matter:

To speak of one's affection for wife . . . to bring into conversation anything closely related to domestic life, is totally incompatible with Japanese ideas of good breeding. Our open acknowledgement, or rather exhibition, of the domestic relation consequently appears to cultivated Japanese, if not absolutely barbarous, at least uxorious. And this sentiment may be found to explain not a little in Japanese life which has given foreigners a totally incorrect idea about the position of Japanese women.[32]

Hearn's view was echoed in the work of a Japanese publicist, Inazo Nitobe, who wrote a number of books in English at the turn of the century, attempting to explain the nature and virtues of Japanese society. Nitobe wanted to put the record straight about the relationship of husband and wife in Japan:

I have found a rather superficial notion prevailing among

half-informed foreigners, that because the common expression for one's wife is 'my rustic wife' and the like, she is despised and held in little esteem. . . .

To me it seems that our idea of marital union goes in some ways farther than the so-called Christian: 'Man and woman shall be one flesh'. The individualism of the Anglo–Saxon cannot let go of the idea that husband and wife are two persons; – hence when they disagree, their separate *rights* are recognised, and when they agree, they exhaust their vocabulary in all sorts of silly pet-names and nonsensical blandishments. It sounds highly irrational to our ears, when a husband or wife speaks to a third party of his or her other half – better or worse – as being lovely, bright, kind, and what not. Is it good taste to speak of one's self as 'my bright self', 'my lovely disposition', and so forth? We think praising one's own wife is praising a part of one's self, and self-praise is regarded, to say the least, as bad taste among us, – and I hope, among Christian nations too![33]

The weight of Western opinion, however, tended to be against Hearn's rather romantic and favourable view of the wife's lot in a Japanese family. Sir Edwin Arnold – also married to a Japanese woman, the first to gain the title 'Lady' – had a somewhat less sanguine impression:

The Japanese wife . . . has nothing whatever intervening between her gentle head and this suspended Damocles' sword of easy divorce, except the good will of her lord, a certain social sentiment, and her daily power to please. Where unions endure the husband was a good fellow, and as for the wife, *elle a su plaire*![34]

Similarly Chamberlain cast aside all illusions on the matter:

When it is added . . . that a Japanese wife is not only supposed to obey her husband, but actually does so, that the husband, if well enough off, probably has a concubine besides and makes no secret of it, and that the mother-in-law, with us a terror to the man, is not only a terror but a daily and hourly cross to the girl – for in nine cases out of ten, the girl has to live with her husband's family and be at the beck and call of his relations – when due consideration is given to all these circumstances, it will be seen that marriage in Japan is a vastly different thing, socially as well as legally, from marriage in Anglo–Saxon countries.[35]

Here again, not only the 'topsy turviness' of Japanese society but also the miserable destiny of Japanese womanhood found expression in the scourge of the mother-in-law, the victim being the wife, not the husband. Indeed, 'So exacting is the old lady, at times, so exasperating does her continual "nagging" become . . . that wives have been known to seek release in death.'[36]

In family matters regarding the wife, the mother-in-law's power was absolute:

A very amiable friend of mine, an officer of the Imperial Household, told me, without much self-blame or hesitation, that he had sent a wife away, to whom he was much attached, and who was faultless of character, because she did not get on well with her mother-in-law![37]

A marital (or rather extra-marital) institution which received far more attention than the mother-in-law was that of concubinage:

Strictly speaking polygamy is not practised in Japan at present. Indeed, it has never been legal; the law acknowledges only one wife. But concubinage is not uncommon. In many respectable households there is a concubine – perhaps two or even three – in addition to the wife, a miserable state of affairs, degrading, unhappy, and mediaeval.[38]

Nor, according to the missionary Gulick (writing in 1903), had modernisation brought about any decrease in the keeping of concubines by married men; on the contrary, there had been in the last decades 'a marked increase of concubinage . . . The

83

simple and uniform explanation is that multitudes of merchants and officials, and even of farmers, can afford to maintain them to-day who formerly were unable to do so.' He further quoted a Japanese newspaper which for the year 1898

published an inventory of 493 men maintaining separate establishments for their concubines, giving not only the names and the business of the men, but also the character of the women chosen to be concubines. Of these 493 men, 9 are ministers of state and ex-ministers; 15 are peers or members of the House of Peers; 7 are barristers; 3 are learned doctors; the rest are nearly all business men. The women were, previous to concubinage, Dancing girls, 183; Servants, 69; Prostitutes, 17; 'Ordinary young girls', 91; Adopted daughters, 15; Widows, 7; Performers, 7; Miscellaneous, 104.

There was fairly widespread Western condemnation of the practice of concubinage in Japan. Gulick claimed:

Those nations which insist on valuing human life only by the utilitarian standard, and which consequently keep woman in a degrading place, insisting on concubinage and all that it implies, are sure to wane before those nations which loyally adopt and practice the higher ideals of human worth. The weakness of heathen lands arises in no slight degree from their cheap estimate of human life.[39]

The hardships which the ordinary Japanese wife had to put up with in one form or another meant that 'at twenty-five or twenty-eight years of age, she is a used creature, aged, ugly, who can no longer pretend to the joys of maternity. She herself then presents her husband with a *mekake* (concubine), and successively another and another depending on the fortune and versatility of her lord and master'. The Japanese, this author, asserted, having successfully abolished 'from their lives the passions and storms of love, they have banished it from the home, inviting sensualism in its place; but in so doing they have destroyed the charm of life and banished the chaste god of marriage from the conjugal bed, where pale debauchery offers its impatient and oustretched arms'.[40]

Unqualified Western condemnation of the institution of concubinage was not, however, universal. Arthur Diósy, at one time Chairman of Council of the Japan Society, London, explained – and here disagreed with Gulick – that in fact concubinage was on the wane in Japan. He pointed out, however, that a number of Japanese were apprehensive, and he had some sympathy for their reasons:

> They shake their heads ominously and express the fear, based on their observation of Occidental life, that the disappearance of the *Mekake* [concubine] as a recognised institution may lead to evils of another kind. The husband, they say, may seek variety in his sexual relations in other, and less open, and therefore more pernicious, ways; he may lead a double life, squandering his means on a clandestine establishment with a mistress, perhaps raising an illegitimate family, and thus creating a class, happily hitherto almost unknown in Japan, of those unfortunate innocent beings who suffer so cruelly in the West for the transgression of their parents; he may frequent the *Yoshiwara*, or he may cast lustful eyes on his neighbour's wife or daughter.[41]

Mrs Fraser was also ready to admit that under certain circumstances comparison between Japan and Britain was not necessarily to the former's disadvantage:

> ... where a man is no more a Christian than the ordinary society man in London; where he has taken no vows, however flippantly, binding him to one woman; where every day humanity does not take the sacred name of love in vain, – there I think that decency, order, and the family ties are less outraged by the existence of the quiet faithful concubine and her children than by the revolting arrangements resorted to in Europe, where men, who as the saying goes 'are not straight to their wives', are brought without shame or regret into the society of women from whom the poor Japanese *mekake* would shrink with horror.[42]

In this apparently extremely male-dominated society of Japan, with woman relegated to a position of seemingly unbearable inferiority, dependent on every whim of the male, having to endure such unendurable hardships, Western observers were nonetheless almost unanimous in their praise of the qualities of the Japanese female sex. Sir Edwin Arnold exclaimed, 'It is still a mystery to me how the Japanese woman has developed her gracious sweetness and bright serenity in the atmosphere of unchivalrous malestimation surrounding her from early times.'[43]

Most Western residents in Japan expressed the view that, since Japan was aspiring to reach levels of civilisation comparable to Europe's, woman's status and fate must be dramatically improved. A Frenchman in Japan in the 1870s gave vent to what Westerners now expected of the Japanese:

Now that the more intelligent Japanese are educated and instructed in the ideas and sciences of the Occident, they cannot allow the continuation of a gulf between them and their fair companions which deepens daily; if they persist, one would rightly accuse them of only playing a hypocritical comedy and not taking seriously the civilisation which they are trying to assimilate in every way. Would there not be something revolting in seeing half the nation wear our clothes, read our books, praise our philosophers and copy our mores, while the other half vegetates in ignorance and continues to serve as a toy to their masters' pretence of regeneration? One progress demands another; to rebuff the second is to renounce the first. One has to remain barbarous, *or* cease to treat women as savages.[44]

There were again, however, exceptions to the Western rule in regard to Japanese woman's emancipation. In view of the universally acclaimed qualities of the Japanese female sex, a few wondered whether the end did not justify the means. Chamberlain, although not of this school himself, quoted a letter he had received from 'a well known author' (whose identity he did not divulge):

'How sweet . . . Japanese woman is! All the possibilities of the race for goodness seem to be concentrated in her. It shakes one's faith in some Occidental doctrines. If this be the result of suppression and oppression, then these are not altogether bad. On the other hand, how diamond-hard the character of the American woman becomes under the idolatry of which she is the object. In the eternal order of things, which is the higher being, – the childish, confiding, sweet Japanese girl, or the superb, calculating, penetrating Oriental Circe of our more artificial society, with her enormous power for evil and her limited capacity for good?'[45]

Japanese males may not have 'fallen in love' with their women; Western men certainly did. There arose in the course of the latter part of the nineteenth century a very special relationship between the Western male and his ideal of the Japanese maiden. This ideal was encapsulated in the word *musmée*. (The term *geisha*, far better known in the West today, was not often used by Westerners in the nineteenth century.) The Japanese word *musume* means daughter, though it is also used as a term for a young unmarried woman. It was in this sense that Western males appropriated the word and thereby enriched both their vocabulary and their imagination. (Although no longer in use in English, *une mousmée* is still common in colloquial French.) The images conjured up by the *musmée* leapt into the world of Western fantasy with romantic intensity. The Japanese girl served as an inspiration for countless poems, plays, novels, operas and operettas. That the imagination was given very free reign indeed is borne out by the absurdity of some of the writing on Japanese women. Thus Alfred Noyes, in 'A Japanese Love Song', enthused on the Japanese maiden: 'Though the great skies are dark,/And your small feet are white,/Though your wide eyes are blue [*sic*]/ And the closed poppies red . . .'[46]
   The ideal of the Japanese woman was not limited to Western men living in Japan. Indeed, she became celebrated throughout Europe. Reports from Japan, however, confirmed that the fame was well deserved. Sir Edwin Arnold, for example, set hearts to flutter with his poem, 'The Musmée'.

> The musmée has brown-velvet eyes,
>   Curtained with satin, sleepily;
> You wonder if these lids would rise
>   The newest, strangest sight to see!
>
> Yet, when she chatters, laughs, or plays
>   Koto, or lute, or samisen –
> No jewel gleams with brighter rays
>   Than flash from those dark lashes then.
>
> The Musmée has a small brown face –
>   Musk-melon seed its perfect shape –
> Arched, jetty eyebrows; none to grace
>   The rosy mouth beneath; a nape,
> And neck, and chin; and small soft cheeks,
>   Carved out of sun-burned ivory
> With teeth which, when she smiles or speaks,
>   Pearl merchants might come leagues to see![47]

And so on for four more stanzas.

Hearn wrote in no less eulogistic terms:

> For it has well been said that the most wonderful aesthetic
> products of Japan are not its ivories, nor its bronzes, nor its
> porcelains, nor its swords, nor any of its marvels in metal or
> lacquer – but its women.[48]

What was it that the Japanese girl had, which presumably
her sisters in other lands lacked? Attempts were made to
describe what the English M.P., Henry Norman, called the
'indefinable something' characteristic of Japanese women:

> Good looks are not enough to account for this; prettiness is
> the rule among Japanese women, but I think the charm lies
> chiefly – though to attempt a rough-and-ready analysis is
> like dissecting a humming-bird with a hatchet – in an in-
> born gentleness and tenderness and sympathy, the most
> womanly of all qualities, combined with what the Romans
> used to call 'certain propriety' of thought and demeanour,
> and used to admire so much. If you could take the light

from the eyes of a Sister of Mercy at her gracious task, the smile of a maiden looking over the seas for her lover, and the heart of an unspoiled child, and materialise them into a winsome and healthy little body, crowned with a mass of jet-black hair and dressed in rustling silks, you would have the typical Japanese woman.[49]

Even *The Times* had a go in an article entitled, 'A Japanese Damsel Described'; it concluded:

Japanese ladies are very accomplished, very beautiful, and bear high characters in all that constitutes charming women; and their admirers, touched with their many attractions, declare in Eastern metaphor, that for such love as theirs the world were indeed lost.[50]

In endeavouring to describe the fascination of the Japanese woman, as with Japanese art, analogies with the classical aesthetic beauty of antiquity were sought:

. . . in the little, girlish steps of a musmée, crossing the mats of the tea-house, or tripping down the street on her wooden clogs, there is oftimes a grace of special movement – a delicate, strange play of folds and feet – which no Western painter has thus far caught, and which is something midway between the pacing of fantail pigeons and of the musical gait of Greek maidens on the friezes of the Parthenon.[51]

Hearn also sought refuge in Greek metaphor ('Rather might she be compared to the Greek type of noble woman, – to Antigone, to Alcestis'), and added that the Japanese woman

has no more in common with the humanity of this twentieth century of ours – perhaps very much less – than has the life depicted upon old Greek vases. (Her) charm is the charm of a vanished world – a charm strange, alluring, indescribable as the perfume of some flower of which the species became extinct in our Occident before the modern languages were born.[52]

The reputation for charm, grace, beauty and femininity of Japanese woman had therefore utterly seduced the Western male imagination. Apart from her intrinsic qualities, however, there were certain aspects of the social mores which no doubt added a great deal to the attraction. Japan, to many, was a sort of paradise on earth, where its inhabitants knew no shame – the Japanese Eve had not yet tasted the forbidden fruit, or if she had, God had turned a blind eye. For in Japan, the interested Occidental would learn, women thought nothing of appearing naked in public. To have read about all the charm and graces of the Japanese woman, the idea of actually seeing them uncovered must have tantalised the Western male even more.

The Comte de Beauvoir, travelling in Japan in 1867, noted in his journal:

> . . . in Japan one lives in full daylight; modesty, or rather immodesty, is not known; it is the innocence of the earthly paradise, and the costumes of our first parents have nothing which shock the sentiments of these people who still live in a golden age.[53]

Western visitors to Japan were likely to encounter experiences which later they would not fail to publicise. John La Farge recalled how a visiting American friend of his could not

> get over the impression made upon him by the pretty young lady near whom he stood under the eaves of the bath-house, where he had taken refuge from the rain, and whose modest manners were as charming as her youthfulness, and had no more covering.[54]

Kipling, shortly after his arrival in Japan, found himself in a considerable predicament:

> Had I been sheltered by the walls of a big Europe bath, I should not have cared, but I was preparing to wash when a pretty maiden opened the door, and indicated that she too would tub in the deep, sunken Japanese bath at my side. When one is dressed only in one's virtue and a pair of

spectacles it is difficult to shut the door in the face of a girl. She gathered that I was not happy, and withdrew giggling, while I thanked heaven, blushing profusely the while, that I had been brought up in a society which unfits a man to bathe *à deux*. Even an experience of the Paddington Swimming Baths would have helped me; but coming straight from India, Lady Godiva was a ballet-girl in sentiment compared to this Actaeon.[55]

Westerners also marvelled at how small and dainty Japanese women were – more like dolls than humans. Alice Mabel Bacon expressed the fear that Westerners in Japan would 'see, to their own surprise, that their country-women looked ungainly, fierce, aggressive, and awkward among the small, mild, shrinking, and graceful Japanese ladies'.[56] Finally, the Japanese female national costume – the colourful *kimono* and *obi* (sash with a bow), elaborate hair styles, all complemented by parasol and fan – contributed both to the charm and mystique of the Japanese woman.

The Western ideal of the Japanese woman was pieced together by a number of the attributes described (charm, grace, beauty, femininity), an element of the unreal, the suspicion of tolerant – if not permissive – sexual morality due to certain customs, all in a setting so often depicted as beautiful and exotic – teahouses, gardens, cherry trees and stone lanterns. All this provided ample material for the romantically inclined, resulting in numerous literary and musical works, all with suitably exotic titles: *A Japanese Marriage*, *The Geisha*, *A Flower of Yeddo*, *The Lady of the Weeping Willow Tree*, *Mi-ki-ka*, *Poupée Japonaise*, and, by far the two most famous of all, *Madame Chrysanthème* and *Madame Butterfly*. (*The Mikado* does not fit into this category of *japoneries*, as its links with Japan, apart from the title, are really non-existent.) The popularity of these works in the late nineteenth century far outranked anything else written about Japan and they contributed enormously to the essentially feminine image Westerners had of Japan.

Pierre Loti's *Madame Chrysanthème*, on which Puccini's *Madame Butterfly* was based, deserves attention, partly because of its immense success all over Europe – it was first published in 1887 and went through numerous editions and translations – and also because it created a genre which was subsequently often imitated. The story of *Madame Chrysanthème* is a simple one: Loti, a French naval officer, comes to port in Nagasaki where he has already decided to contract a 'marriage' for the length of his stay. Eventually the right girl is found through a helpful procurer, and she is called O-Kiku san or Miss Chrysanthemum. They live together, attend festivals, go sightseeing, eat in restaurants, etc. . . . Loti, however, grows tired of her very quickly and is much relieved when the day comes for his ship to weigh anchor so that he can leave O-Kiku san behind. He came, he saw, he conquered, he left.

Loti's was not a romantic novel. He was not at all seduced by the charms of Japanese womanhood. On the contrary in the novel he occasionally alludes to a far fairer and kinder maiden left somewhere near the Bosphorus. He dislikes both Japanese women and Japanese men (comparing them constantly to monkeys). Although this was the most popular novel written about Japan, it did not blemish the reputation of Japanese woman's beauty, though it undoubtedly confirmed the suspicions regarding her loose morality.

Following *Madame Chrysanthème*, more plays, novels, poems, operas and operettas were written and composed about some O-Kiku, O-Hana or O-Haru – names which indeed were often not Japanese at all, but that did not matter as long as the exotic appearance was maintained. (Loti himself was not overly preoccupied about making the local colour always local; for example he named one of his male characters Monsieur Kangaroo!) Loti had created a popular theme. O-Kiku san became Cho Cho san, from Madame Chrysanthème to Madame Butterfly. The main difference (apart from the change of the nationality of the naval officer from French to American) was that whereas Loti last saw O-Kiku counting her money (which she had received as part of the 'marriage' contract), Cho Cho commits suicide; obviously the latter course had more operatic effect. Both endings, however, have one thing in common, namely the Japanese girl was forsaken; Loti returned to his ship, Pinkerton to his wife. This theme gave rise to a genre which has been described as 'the novel of desertion'.[57] This in turn created the popular Western image of the Japanese woman as something beautiful, exotic, of easy virtue, and frivolous; she was there to conquer, to enjoy and to abandon. At times she committed suicide – and hence was not necessarily so frivolous – but no doubt this final act of despair satisfied the Western male ego.

Fiction, by definition, is not reality. Yet it seems that Westerners in judging Japan were not always able to distinguish the one from the other. Loti's novel in particular may have been responsible for many of the misconceptions about Japan and the errors of judgement regarding her modernisation and military strength:

> Loti prophesies the opposite of the Yellow Peril. The importance of Loti's writings on Japan lies in their reiteration in exquisite language that the Japanese is a monkey, endowed with a grotesque and perverted refinement of taste, but without morals. He suggests that the Japanese women, the 'mousmes', have no honor, and that the race can have nothing in common intellectually with Europeans. I believe that the contempt for the Japanese expressed in Loti's books in some measure influenced the Russians to refuse Japan's requests and led to the war of 1904. The Russian Court was open to French influence, and many Russian naval officers of high rank, following Loti's example, had discovered *Madame Chrysanthème*. Like Loti, the Russian Court looked upon Japan with contempt, and chose to believe his stories because Loti shared their prejudices.[58]

Could this image remain intact as Japan burst into the modern world with full military colours? In fact it did remain for quite a long time, but there were also attempts to project a new image of Japanese women, one more compatible with the new image of Japan. It was noticed by Westerners residing in the country that the women were not necessarily any less patriotic or valiant than the men. A number of incidents illustrated this point well. One such incident arose as a result of the visit of the Tsarevich (later Nicholas II) to Japan in 1891; an attempt was made on his life while *en route* to Tokyo,

93

where he was to meet the Emperor. The visit was cancelled and the Tsarevich quickly sent back to Russia. The Japanese government and Emperor were mortified. Whereupon:

> A little *samurai* girl, a mere child of sixteen . . . travelled to Kyoto, dressed herself in her holiday robes, composed her poor little body for death by tying her sash tightly round her knees after the custom of *samurai* women, and cut her throat in the doorway of the great Government offices. They found on her two letters: one a farewell to her family; the other containing a message, which she begged those who found her to convey to the Emperor, saying that she gave her life gladly, hoping that though so lowly it might wipe out the insult and she entreated him to be comforted by her death.[59]

Japan's first major war in the modern era, the war against China in 1894, also gave the opportunity for the courage of women to manifest itself:

> in 1895, the tidings of Lieutenant Asada's death on the battle-field, were brought to his young wife, she at once, and with her father's consent, resolved to follow him. Having thoroughly cleansed the house and arrayed herself in her costliest robes, she placed her husband's portrait in the alcove, and prostrating herself before it, cut her throat with a dagger that had been a wedding gift.[60]

In 1905, the year of Japan's stunning and generally un-expected (in the West) victory in war over Russia, an American novelist, Sidney McCall, published *The Breath of the Gods*. In this novel, the Japanese heroine, by name of Yuki, can be said to have avenged the plight of Madame Chrysanthème and Madame Butterfly and all their sisters forsaken by Western seducers. It is also a novel of desertion, but here the Western male is abandoned by the Japanese girl. *The Breath of the Gods*, however, never reached as wide an audience as Loti's *Madame Chrysanthème*; indeed, in purely literary terms the two novels do not bear comparison. The plot is terribly contrived. A young Japanese girl, Yuki, has been partly educated in Washington

D.C., where she meets a young Frenchman, Pierre, whom she falls in love with. Yuki is warned by a visiting ex-*Daimyō* (feudal lord) to Washington, shortly before her return, that back in Japan great things are expected of her:

> Keep always to the thought that you are Nipponese, – that you guard, in yourself, an immortal spirit, powerful for good or ill. Let not the tendrils of your outreaching soul cling to alien ideals, for, if so, each in the twining means a wrench and a scar, and the unscarred soul is sweeter to the gods. Think nothing of the body, – of personal desires, of personal reward. Say to yourself always, 'It is enough to be a Nipponese'.

Upon returning to Japan, Yuki discovers that it is intended that she be betrothed to the ex-*Daimyō*. She is torn between her love for Pierre and her duty to Japan. Eventually she decides to opt for the latter, but Pierre is not at all pleased about this and refuses to leave the scene gallantly. Meanwhile the clouds of war between Japan and Russia are approaching. Pierre manages (as a result of an unbelievable series of circumstances) to steal some important Japanese state papers; the ex-*Daimyō* (a general in the Japanese army) offers Yuki in exchange for the return of the important papers. Yuki, who by now is very much in love with her Japanese husband, agrees; the scene is set for the exchange, Pierre hands over the papers, but only to find that the Yuki who is brought to him is dead – she has killed herself. Her husband goes off to war against Russia. At the end of the novel the war is over and has been won; now, his duty to the state having been performed, he can join his wife:

> ... on a rocky promontary across from the impregnable fortress of Liau Tung, a grim, quiet warrior sat alone, with field glasses dangling limply from his hands, and eyes that saw only a white, white face upturned to his, and lips that murmured, 'I know you now, my husband – and shall wait! Banzai Nippon!' while the cold steel crept nearer to a warm and shrinking heart. Banzai Nippon.[61]

Apart from fiction, however, there were also true stories going around the foreign community about the patriotism and courage of Japanese women in the course of the Russo–Japanese war.

A typical case is that of the grand old lady, bereft of all her male relatives, husband, brother, and sons, all killed, or carried away by sickness, at the seat of war, who received the successive tidings with stoical calm, until the sad news reached her of the death of her younger son, the last of the family to fall in defence of his country. Then the old mother burst into tears, exclaiming: 'I weep at last, but do not misunderstand the cause of my tears! I weep because I have no one left whom I can send out to die for our country, and because, were I to marry again, I am too old to give the Emperor more warriors to fight his battles.'[62]

On a less sombre note, a traveller in Japan remarked:

. . . it was always this dainty creature, the *geisha*, who made merry the last evenings of the officers ere they went forth to war; and she was always the last to cheer them on their way, pledging them, in tiny sips of sake, health, victory and a safe return. Truly it is almost as hard to imagine how Japan could survive without the geisha as without the army itself.[63]

4

POLITICS – ORIENTAL OBSCURANTISM TO OCCIDENTAL ENLIGHTENMENT

> *The civilisation of Japan differs entirely from that of any other country; and if we expect them to meet us half-way in the spirit of advancement and progression common to the West, we shall be grievously disappointed.*
>
> (Oliphant in 1858)[1]

> *I took the pamphlet and found a complete paper Constitution stamped with the Imperial Chrysanthemum – an excellent little scheme of representation, reforms, payment of members, budget estimates, and legislation. It is a terrible thing to study at close quarters, because it is so pitifully English.*
>
> (Kipling in 1889)[2]

When the representatives of the Western powers arrived in Japan in the mid and late 1850s they were confronted with a political system of diabolical complexity. The very terms used to denote functions or areas of administration were indeed of Oriental inscrutability: there were *Bugyō, Rōjū, Tairō, Shōgun* or *Taikun* with a *Bakufu, Daimiō* (*Tozama* and *Fudai*) and their *Han*, not to forget the *Gosanke* and of course the *Mikado* and his *Kuge*. The institutions were obscure enough; so were the hierarchies within them and the precise relationship of one functionary to another. Within a few decades all this was replaced by terms easily translatable as Emperor, Prime Minister, Ministers (of Agriculture, Commerce, Foreign Affairs), Cabinet, Privy Council, Parliament (or Diet as it was called), Constitution, and, in lieu of *Daimiō* and *han*, Governors and prefectures; the new nobility could also be addressed in terms meaningful to Europeans – princes, marquises, counts,

97

viscounts and barons. Japan, on the surface at least, had undergone a political revolution of great magnitude. From a situation compared by many Occidental visitors to darker, medieval Europe, Japan emerged as a modern state with all the trappings of a Western parliamentary democracy.

At the time Japan was opened Westerners realised that the political consequences would be considerable. They understood also that the Japanese rulers were aware that these changes would dramatically alter their position and jeopardise internal peace. Fear of the West as a harbinger of internal disaster was, as *Blackwood's Magazine* expounded, deeply entrenched in Japanese history:

> . . . these men remember the history of the first foreign invasion, of the dangers so narrowly escaped from Jesuit intrigue, of the violent and successful termination of the foreigner's residence in the country, which resulted in his expulsion, in the martyrdom of thousands of their countrymen, in the restoration of peace to Japan, and in the establishment of a perpetual law that the foreigner should henceforth be excluded, and the welfare of the Empire of the Sun should never again thus be risked.[3]

The Times in 1858 admitted that so far as the Japanese government was concerned, 'It is not to be wondered at that . . . [it] should not have experienced any great desire to establish an intercourse with other nations, which, in all probability, would carry in its train greater evils than could be compensated for than by its incidental advantages.' The rulers of Japan, *The Times* remarked, 'foresee that the changes now being effected will, in all probability, some day or other revolutionise the country'.[4] On the other hand, others argued that 'Many tokens would seem to indicate that the Japanese themselves – that is the population, not the Government – are prepared for the change, and anxiously desire to see themselves relieved from the spell which has hitherto kept them secluded from all intercourse with foreign nations . . .'[5]

Japan's resistance to intercourse with the West led the Western powers to the occasional use of gunboat diplomacy.

One such use of force by Britain followed the assassination of an Englishman, Richardson, by samurai of the Satsuma fief: the port of Kagoshima, capital of Satsuma, was bombarded by a British fleet. It is interesting to note how this act did not meet with universal acclaim at home. An English M.P., Charles Buxton, recounted in detail in a letter to *The Times* the terror which had been inflicted on the Kagoshima population of 180,000 civilians. 'The bombardment of a town . . . is looked upon by every people of Europe with horror . . .' he exclaimed, and added, 'and in the case of Japan, every principle of justice and of policy demanded gentleness and self-restraint.' He granted that 'the murder of Mr. Richardson was atrocious; no one dreams of palliating it'. The British were correct in demanding reparations from the Japanese government and even in destroying the fortifications of Kagoshima. 'But who will say that it was either right or wise to visit this vengeance upon the heads of the unoffending people of Kagoshima? They were no more responsible for the murder of Mr Richardson than the people of Birmingham.' He proceeded to explain the nature of Japanese politics and their foreign policy. Admitting that both were reprehensible in the extreme, nevertheless he concluded that 'as a matter of policy surely our wise course would have been to do all we could to win the hearts of the people, even if we assailed their princes'.[6]

If the 'people' may have been relatively easy to understand, the 'princes' were another matter altogether. There seemed to be a veritable plethora of princes of different sorts, and the complexity was by no means lessened by the apparent co-existence of two emperors. The relationship of shōgun to mikado (both of whom were generally referred to by Westerners as 'emperor') was, needless to say, far from clear. As early as 1852 the *Edinburgh Review* sought to clarify the situation for its readers by suggesting possible European analogies:

It is impossible to have any clear notion of the anomalous position of the two sovereigns of Japan without clearly understanding the sequences of events which led to the maintenance of the old, and to the establishment of a new dynasty by its side. The result might be stated, analogously,

99

pretty much as follows. Suppose that Napoleon Bonaparte, when First Consul, had thought it a stroke of policy, previous to his seizure of the imperial crown, to recall Louis XVIII from Hartwell to Versailles. Suppose that he had surrounded him there with all the pomp and state of a court, but carefully debarred him from all interference with the affairs of government, limiting his duties to the single necessity of wearing the crown of Saint Louis for a given number of hours every day in the Salle des Maréchaux, with the solemn condition attached that during the time of the ceremonial he should not move his head or turn his eyes one hair's breadth to the right or left, – then Louis XVIII would have been the Mikado of France, the idol of the Faubourg, the incarnation of legitimacy. He would have given himself up to literature, written longs and shorts, and quoted Horace on every occasion, and so he would have done his duty. All the *littérateurs* of France, from Chateaubriand down to Frederic Soulie, would have been forthcoming at the Court of this Roi Fainéant, or his successors. Meanwhile the Ziogoon [Shōgun] of the Luxembourg, – of the Tuileries and the Malmaison, – the son of his own works, – would have carried out his schemes of policy and conquest in his own way, placed the imperial diadem upon his head and contented himself with honouring the incarnate principle of legitimacy at Versailles with a complimentary deputation once a year at first, and then less frequently for economy's sake. Thus it was supposed that the honour shown to hereditary authority in the person of the Mikado would also be recognised for the benefit of the usurping dynasty which had possessed themselves of all the realities of sovereign power.

Our sketch, however of the position of Mikado would be incomplete did we not refer to his ecclesiastical authority. He is not altogether a fiddling Count René of Provence, he has in him a dash of the Pope, or rather of the Grand Lama.[7]

From the early period of intercourse, therefore, Europeans tended to speak of the shōgun (or Tycoon as he was more often called) as 'temporal emperor' and the mikado in Kyoto as 'spiritual emperor'. Laurence Oliphant (accompanying Elgin as his secretary when the latter was appointed to sign Britain's first treaty with Japan) noted how the mikado 'is in fact a mere puppet'; all negotiations, therefore, were to be entered into with the shōgun and his administration. The British mission had brought the shōgun a yacht as a gift from Queen Victoria, obviously in the hope of facilitating the success of the mission. Oliphant also discovered, however, that the shōgun was not necessarily as powerful as might be believed:

> The Tycoon [shōgun], on the other hand, is ostensibly the Administrator of the Empire; but he, too, has been exalted to so high a pitch of temporal dignity, that his lofty station has been robbed of all its substantial advantages, and he passes the life of a state prisoner, shut up in his magnificent citadel, except when he pays a state visit to Miako [Kyoto]. It was a cruel satire upon this unhappy potentate to present him with a yacht; one might as well request the Pope's acceptance of a wife.[8]

As the rivalry between the two camps became apparent the prospect of victory by the mikado's forces was met with alarm. There are a number of reasons for this attitude, which prevailed almost without exception until the Restoration had to be accepted as a *fait accompli*. Firstly, it appeared that the mikado's troops consisted mainly of the xenophobic fanatics urging the expulsion of all foreigners (and responsible for a number of assassinations and other acts of terrorism against foreigners). Secondly, the shōgunal government was the government which had signed the treaties, and was thus committed to observing them. Thirdly, in spite of the great and constant difficulties in treating with the shōgunal government, there undoubtedly was an attitude of 'better the devil you know...'. *Blackwood's Magazine* in 1862 was apprehensive at the prospect that the 'patriotic party . . . might invoke the sacred authority of the Mikado, and that he might, for once, in so exceptional a case, if successful intrigue had won his sympathies, condescend from his exalted position to sanction with his countenance those who professed to be upholding the sacred and exclusive character of that empire of which he was the sainted and sovereign lord'. It was to be earnestly desired on all sides that 'such a contingency will never arise'; while Japan's future and fruitful relations with the Western powers would be best served when 'a class will be created whose wealth will give them influence, while their interests will make it their policy to encourage foreign intercourse'.[9] In other words a bourgeois revolution should take place in Japan.

How likely was it, though, that such a revolution would take place? A member of the first official French mission to Japan, the Marquis de Moges, expressed the view that 'Japan had conserved only the shadow of feudalism'; and that over the centuries Japan had evolved into more of a modern state in view of the fact that 'political and administrative centralisation had been established in the Empire'.[10] Japan was theoretically divided into some two hundred fiefdoms (*han*), but divergence of opinion centred on the problem of whether the feudal lords (*daimyō*) had real power, or whether effective power was vested in the central authority of the shōgun.

Marx held a view diametrically opposed to that of the Marquis de Moges and indeed was struck by the similarity between Japan in the 1860s and medieval Europe: 'Japan, with its purely feudal organisation of landed property and its developed *petite culture*, gives a much truer picture of the European middle ages than all our history books . . .'[11] Marx's diagnosis was shared by Britain's first permanent diplomatic representative in Japan, Sir Rutherford Alcock, who was also struck by the similarity of the Japanese situation with that of medieval Europe:

> Japan appears to be actually governed, at the present day, by a sort of federal aristocracy, recalling in some respects that of the Lombard dukes; – and France under the Merovingian kings; of the early state of the Germans when their kings were elected out of particular families. A confederation of Princes and territorial Seigneurs possess the land, enjoying apparently very much the same kind of jurisdiction as our own barons in the days of the Saxon rule of the first Plantagenets.

Alcock, writing in 1863, believed it impossible for any significant progress to be achieved in Japan in view of the prevalence of 'rampant feudalism'. Were any modernising measures and an extension of foreign intercourse even attempted,

> ready to do battle to the death, stands feudalism in full strength and vigour – feudalism, armed *cap-à-pié*, with its nobles and their followers, . . . These feudal classes, with more or less intelligence as to cause and effect, but a true instinct, see the destruction of their privileges, and the subversion of their power in the progress of foreign relations and the full development of commerce. They see that we bring not only goods for sale, the purchase of which they believe will impoverish the nation, but new religions, new ideas of social order, liberty, and political rights, new customs and habits, all subversive to those now existing, and hostile to them and their order. In this farthest extremity of Eastern empire, Western civilisation is *aux prises* with feudalism, strong in its traditions and nationality, and defiant in its semi-chivalric and militant character.[12]

Yet within five years the Meiji Restoration had been achieved. The Charter Oath announced as its fourth principle that 'Uncivilised customs of the past shall be discontinued . . .'; and, as noted in Chapter 1, the new government rapidly set about instituting far-reaching and profound reforms. In the years following this 'glorious revolution', as some described the Restoration, there developed a tendency to see the pre- and post-Restoration periods in opposing terms of darkness and light, medievalism and progress; indeed this view of history lasted fairly comfortably until the Second World War. The reality of both periods was by no means so clear cut. John Black, the Australian journalist in Yokohama, was exceptional in desiring to give justice where he felt justice was due. In his opinion the last shōgun, Tokugawa Yoshinobu, deserved praise:

> He initiated many reforms for which the present government obtains the credit; and whatever advantages there

may be – and undoubtedly there are many – in having the Government in its present shape – he had foreseen them, and declared his hope of gradually bringing it about. It is my sincere belief that, had he been permitted to work in his own way, we should have seen Japan make as rapid progress as she had made, without all the horrors of revolution, and repeated outbreaks of internal strife, that have occurred.[13]

When political authority was restored to the Emperor, the actual incumbent of the Throne, Mutsuhito, was sixteen years of age. The name chosen for his reign (*nengō*) was Meiji, meaning Enlightened Rule; it was meant to embody the spirit of New Japan. The Charter Oath was the first public proclamation of the new and enlightened principles which were to guide the country. Yet it was not to be expected that with this particular stroke of the brush enlightenment would be achieved overnight. For example, the first article of the Charter Oath declared: 'Deliberative assemblies shall be established on an extensive scale, and all measures of government shall be decided by public opinion.' The government's first tentative steps at establishing such an assembly (the *Kōgisho* of 1869), however, showed some of the hurdles which enlightenment would have to face:

. . . great hopes were entertained of its usefulness. It was composed of persons representing each of the daimiates, who were chosen for the position by the daimyos. It was a quiet peaceful debating society, whose function was to give advice to the imperial government.

That it was a thoroughly conservative body is apparent from the result of its discussion upon several of the traditional customs of Japan. On the proposition to recommend the abolition of the privilege of *hara-kiri* [ritual suicide] the vote stood: Ayes 3, noes 200, and not voting 6. On the proposition to abolish the wearing of swords [a *samurai* privilege of feudal times] . . . the final vote was unanimously against it in a house of 213. After a short and uneventful career the *kogisho* was dissolved in the autumn of the same year it was summoned.[14]

The road to enlightenment was indeed not an easy one, as the American missionary Griffis vividly explained:

A mighty task awaited the new Government after the revolution of 1868. It was to heal the disease of ages; to uproot feudalism and sectionalism, with all their abuses; to give Japan a new nationality; to change her social system; to infuse new blood into her veins; to make a hermit nation, half blinded by a sudden influx of light, competitor with the wealthy, powerful, and aggressive nations of Christendom. It was a problem of national regeneration or ruin. It seemed like entering into history a second time, to be born again.

What transcendent abilities needed for such a task! What national union, harmony in council, unselfish patriotism required! What chief, towering above his fellows, would arise, who by mighty intellect and matchless tact could achieve what Yoritomo, or the Taikô, or Iyéyasu himself, or all, would be helpless to perform? At home were the stolidly conservative peasantry, backed by ignorance, superstition, priestcraft, and political hostility. On their own soil they were fronted by aggressive foreigners, who studied all Japanese questions through the spectacles of dollars and cents and trade, and whose diplomatists too often made the principle of Shylock their system. Outside, the Asiatic nations beheld with contempt, jealousy, and alarm the departure of one of their number from Turanian ideas, principles, and civilisation. China, with ill-concealed anger, Corea with open defiance, taunted Japan with servile submission to the 'foreign devils'.[15]

The most formidable problem confronting the new government came from the very group which had brought it to power. For it was certainly not the masses, nor was it the merchant class, who had fought for the Restoration, but the samurai. Inflamed by nationalistic slogans and an ideology harking back to an idealised and remote past, nothing, prior to the Charter Oath, seemed to indicate that the new government intended bringing about such fundamental reforms – reforms which made their position as a class precarious, indeed obsolete.

The government had abolished the fiefs (*han*), replacing them by prefectures (*ken*), thus depriving the samurai of their fealty. More unpopular measures followed; perhaps the most injurious was the decree of universal male conscription promulgated in 1873. The samurai was a warrior and his position in Japanese society hitherto had been recognised by the fact that he alone was permitted to carry arms.

Discontent among the samurai flared into open rebellion on a number of occasions. The severest blow, however, came in 1876 when the samurai instead of continuing to receive stipends (for doing nothing) found that these were commuted with the government offering them instead a once-and-for-all lump sum. The government, faced with serious financial problems, saw this measure as sound both politically and economically. The samurai could not just be abandoned to their own fate, they were too much of a threat. By supplying them with capital, it was hoped that not only would they be pacified, but that they might begin to learn the arduous task of becoming capitalists – by investing their money in banks and various other new projects either started or encouraged by the government.

It should be stressed that not all samurai were facing decline as a result of the Restoration. On the contrary, many samurai took ample advantage of the new circumstances and found careers in government, the new bureaucracy, the army and navy, industry, journalism, etc. Meiji Japan was a society which still discriminated in favour of samurai, but perhaps the effect of this discrimination was the 'survival of the fittest samurai'. The bulk of the samurai class (what has been described as a sort of lumpen-aristocracy) was indeed facing extinction. And, quite naturally, the prospect was far from appealing.

For the intransigent samurai the summary settlement of their stipends

> had unfortunate results. The lump sums which they received were often soon consumed, and they were left penniless and helpless. The traditions under which they had been trained led them to look down upon labor and trade with disdain, and rendered them unfit to enter successfully on the careers

of modern life. In many cases worry and disappointment, and in others poverty and want, have been the sequels which have closely followed the poor and obsolete samurai.[16]

The last great attempt by the samurai to reverse the course the government seemed so intent on pursuing came in 1877. In February of that year the Satsuma Rebellion erupted. Satsuma was one of the two fiefs which had been most involved in the carrying out of the Restoration (the other being Chōshū). Although Satsuma men played a prominent part in the government following the Restoration and indeed in the ensuing decades, a schism had occurred in their ranks. The opposition to government policy was led by Saigō Takamori, who had been one of the most prominent figures in the immediate pre-Restoration period; he had resigned from office in 1873, disgusted at both the foreign and domestic policies of the government. Saigō was not only the leader, he 'was the idol of the samurai'.[17] And, as was appreciated by an Englishman, Augustus Mounsey, geographer and adviser to the Japanese government at the time, he had all the necessary attributes to be a great hero and, after his death, a legend:

His fame no doubt rested on the services he had rendered as a general and a public man and on the prestige attaching to his position of chief councillor of the most powerful of the clans; but his popularity was due in a great measure to his personal character and qualities. Physically he was extraordinarily tall for a Japanese, being a full head above all his fellows; he was proportionately broad, had massive limbs, and would have been considered a well-built and powerful man in any country. His head was well formed, and in spite of his dark bushy eyebrows his face generally wore an expression of frank simplicity as well as of manliness. He was a good swordsman . . . Morally he had the reputation of being surpassingly intrepid and courageous; he was calm, resolute, and courageous at the same time, as well as sincere and true in his friendships. Wealth had apparently no attractions for him, and the money he had he spent with a liberal hand. . . . he appears to have been frugal and sober in his habits. His retirement from office, and the unostentatious manner of his country life led people to believe that he had no ambition for himself, and he was thus endowed in the imagination of his admirers with all the self-denial of a true patriot. In all these qualities his character contrasted most favourably in the opinion of large numbers of the samurai and people, with those of the Satsuma and, indeed, most other clansmen who had risen to high places in the government, and who were considered in many parts of the country, and especially in the south, as mere place hunters. Saigō's manner too, captivated the minds of all who came in contact with him, and this combination of prepossessing qualities endeared his name amongst the people, and made him appear as the beau ideal of a samurai to all the military class, who considered him the representative of their best interests.

The civil war lasted seven months. By September, however, the government forces had the Satsuma samurai in full retreat and the final encounter took place at Shiroyama, a hill overlooking Kagoshima, where Saigō met his end in true samurai fashion: 'Before dawn on the 24th of September a tremendous shower of shells was poured on the summit of the hill. . . . Saigō was amongst the first to fall, wounded by a bullet in the thigh. Thereupon Hemni Jiuroda, one of his lieutenants, performed what samurai consider a friendly office. With one blow of his keen heavy sword he severed his chief's head from his shoulders, in order to spare him the disgrace of falling alive in his enemy's hands.'[18]

With Saigō's death and the surrender of his troops (many of whom, like their leader, chose to commit suicide)

ended, it may justly be believed, the last struggle of feudalism against the centralised power of the Government of the Restoration. Few will doubt that if the rebel movement had been successful the country would have been thrown back in the path of progress, and become a prey to anarchy and internal dissensions that would have undone all the labour of ten years' careful and earnest administration.[19]

'Saigō is dead, Old Japan died with him.'[20]

With the subjugation of the 'reactionary' samurai the government had to turn its attention to another sort of opposition, namely self-styled progressive pressure groups. Various political clubs and parties began emerging in the 1870s which 'looked forward to a modification of the absolute form of government' of the early Meiji period; 'they recalled to themselves and others the solemn pledge which the emperor had given to his people in the charter oath, when he announced that a "deliberative assembly shall be formed, and all measures decided by public opinion" '.[21]

Japan was still in theory an absolute monarchy, but was in reality run by an oligarchy of samurai almost exclusively from the two ex-fiefs of Satsuma and Chōshū. Though the debate was allegedly political, it was also enflamed by the fief partisanship of other samurai especially those from the former Tosa fief, who had contributed to the Restoration but were excluded from important government posts. These organisations eventually merged in a fairly all-encompassing, though disparate, movement entitling itself the *jiyūminkenundō*, or movement for freedom and popular rights. Basically they demanded a constitution and the establishment of a parliament. Apart from that their ideology was not very clear, but expressed in slogans supposedly inspired by European political philosophers, with Jean-Jacques Rousseau perhaps the most popular. The movement could hardly be described as radical, but it had much nuisance value, and though its ideology may have been fairly primitive its political techniques were reasonably sophisticated, especially in the use of the quickly developing new press. Also in this period, numerous Western works on politics were translated into Japanese and voraciously read by a population becoming increasingly aware politically. This new political pressure group was the government's main adversary in the dozen years between the suppression of the Satsuma rebellion and the eventual promulgation of a constitution in 1889.

The government responded to these attacks by a combination of concessions, usually followed by repressive ordinances. The government, however, had to take into account 'the

constant agitation kept up by new engines in Japanese politics –
the press, the lecture platform, and the debating club'; and so
'the mikado, yielding to the irresistible pressure of public
opinion, expanded and confirmed his oath of 1868, in the
famous proclamation of October 12th, 1881: "We therefore
thereby declare, that we shall in the 23rd year of Meiji (1890)
establish a Parliament . . ." '22

The confrontation between the government and the so-
called progressive forces centred chiefly on the question of
timing; the progressive forces demanding the immediate establishment of parliament, the government insisting on the need
for a gradual approach. Generally, Westerners took the government's side. The Liberal M.P., Sir Edward Reed, approved
the government's intention 'to move forward neither too
swiftly for the peace and security of the nation, nor too slowly
for the rapid development of those representative institutions
which, as they know, form the surest basis for internal tranquility and external respect.' Reed observed that 'the government is at present [1879] necessarily of a very centralised
character, and must remain so while the country is being prepared for the adoption of a popular or representative system'.
And so he concluded 'that the passage from the close and rigid
feudal system of Japan . . . to a parliamentary system can only
with safety be made gradually, and those are enemies and not
friends of Japan who would urge the country to rush with heed-
less impetuosity along the path of political progress'.23

Another observer stressed that Japan's political development should not be viewed from a Western standpoint; for
'although there are many enactments against which the democratic ideas of Americans would revolt, the system is certainly
well adapted to the present needs and capabilities of Japan'.
Like Reed he believed that the people needed to develop
greater political maturity, that they 'are simply under the
necessity of growing up to political privileges that are gradually
bestowed upon them'. The Japanese government deserved
praise and not rebuke when seen in its proper perspective:

We should not find fault with Japan, because in only a few
years she has not leaped into the enjoyment of political

privileges which the English and American people obtained only after centuries of slow and often bloody development; but we should congratulate Japan, because by peaceful measures, she has gradually removed herself entirely out of the pale of Oriental absolutism, beyond even despotic Russia . . .[24]

Westerners clearly felt Japan's best course was to continue developing under the aegis of enlightened despotism. But even the government at times seemed too precipitate. *The Times* in an article in 1888 argued that 'the wonderful reforms that it has inaugurated and successively accomplished during the last 20 years . . . if judged by the ordinary canons of Western politics, would savour strongly of reckless radicalism'. The article went on to comment that if Western reaction to Japan was not without considerable apprehension

> it is not alone because her fleet strides are without precedent in the world's annals. It is also because a careful study of Japanese history reveals a deeper and graver cause for anxiety. For there was, and always had been a socialistic tendency among the Japanese people. All these things point an unmistakable moral, and may well inspire apprehensions that Japan needs the curb rather than the spur, and that when once set in motion her political progress may be too swift to be safe. Nothing, indeed, is more certain than that, while great and early changes are inevitable, any precipitate measures of enfranchisement in the immediate future would be fraught with the gravest danger to the country.

The Times noted with alarm the growing number and strength of agitators and that 'constituting their great majority were members of the student class'. In 1887 the government had passed the Peace Preservation Law, seen by most students of Japan today as evidence of an increasingly totalitarian and repressive régime. To *The Times* the act was a source of considerable relief: 'The Government had recourse to a measure which savoured only of charitable contempt. It simply issued a peace-preservation edict, under which the police soon ordered the hot-brained youths to remove themselves from the capital and return to their homes and their studies. . . . This action of the authorities made some stir at the time, but the sequel proved that no more humane and effectual means could have been chosen for putting an end to foolish agitation.'

Apart from the question of timing, the main source of controversy between government and opposition was over the Western model to be chosen for Japan's impending new constitution. Immediately following the Emperor's declaration in 1881 that a constitution and a parliament would be established, one of the country's leading statesmen, Itō Hirobumi, left for Europe where he stayed mainly in Germany; there he studied constitutional law under the tutorship of eminent German and Austrian constitutional theorists: Rudolf von Gneist, Herman Roesler and Lorenz von Stein. It was obvious that the government intended to adopt a Germanic model. The opposition favoured a more liberal model than the conservative German one. The more moderate wing of the opposition under Ōkuma Shigenobu strongly adhered to British constitutional principles, while the leader of the *jiyūminkenundō*, Itagaki Taisuke, was, while Itō was in Germany, in France studying French constitutional theory under Émile Acollas. It is a cruel irony, however, that the advocates of a liberal constitution found little sympathy in the countries which served as their inspiration. *The Times*, for example, after having once again raised the spectre of the people's 'socialistic tendencies', expressed satisfaction that 'Japan's statesmen must be well alive to the situation, and to the warnings which it inculcates. Already, indeed, they have given proof of their wariness and sobriety by a prudent choice of German models for Japan's future constitution, clearly recognising, no doubt, that, however admirable the British Constitution, for example, may be in the abstract, to transplant it into this country without fully preparing the soil for its reception would be only to invite, in their worst form, dangers from which even the Anglo–Saxon race itself is not wholly exempt in its political progress.'[25]

When the Constitution was finally promulgated it was met in the West with mixed feelings, though in general not without considerable approval. One of the features of the document which puzzled Westerners, however, was the deification it gave to the Emperor. Henry Norman, the English M.P., admitted that 'there is . . . in Japan a belief concerning the highest matters of interest, which will strike a European mind as . . . extraordinary'. He goes on:

When the Emperor has occasion to refer to the origin of his dynasty he is apt to refer to the time ten thousand years ago, 'when our divine Ancestors laid the foundations of the earth'. When His Majesty promulgated the Constitution he did 'humbly and solemnly swear to the Imperial Founder of Our House and our other Imperial Ancestors', and did 'now reverently make Our prayers to Them and to Our Illustrious Father, and implore the help of Their Sacred Spirits'. And he further declared that the Imperial Throne of Japan is 'everlasting from ages eternal in an un-broken line of succession'. The 'Illustrious Father' is Jimmu-Tenno, to whom Tensho-Daijin, the sun-goddess, gave a round mirror, her portrait, a sword, a seal, and a brocaded banner. Now, there seems a fatal want of harmony between these beliefs, which are devoutly held by every loyal Japanese, and the modern scientific spirit which is supposed to be actuating his country. Between the divine Ancestry of the Emperor on the one hand, and the telephone on the other, there seems an impassable gulf.[26]

The Times unequivocally declared in February 1889: 'from the dawn of history . . . the Government of the country has been a pure despotism down to Monday last' (date of the promulgation of the Constitution). It recognised that 'although for nearly twenty years past the present Emperor has moved among his subjects like an ordinary sovereign, the theory of his unbroken descent from the gods through thousands of years has been asserted again and again in Imperial decrees'; and that 'under these circumstances, the Constitution itself is treated as a free and gracious gift of sovereign to people; it is nothing to which the latter are in any degree entitled, or which the sovereign is bound in conscience or morality to grant'. Yet in spite of this the article boldly claimed that 'the representative principle is broadly and firmly established in the country; . . . the great leap in the dark has been taken'. And it hoped that the 'people will use with judgement, moderation, and success the new instrument of self-government which is now placed in their hands'.[27]

A month later, after *The Times* had had greater opportunity to study the document, it remained impressed, especially since 'the first plunge into Parliamentary representation will be made with befitting vigilance and caution'.

> Looking to the average means of the Japanese, the franchise is undoubtedly high – a piece of prudence to be much commended, seeing that any precipitate measure of enfranchisement at this epoch might result in a popular despotism fraught with danger to the country. It is evident also, not only from the broad outlines of the scheme, but from abundant internal evidence running through the text of the new laws, that, besides a careful avoidance of any definition of the responsibility of the Cabinet *vis à vis* the Diet, the whole intention is to follow the German principle of making the former responsible to the Crown alone, and to render the life of the Ministry independent, at least temporarily, of a hostile Parliament. At present certainly these tactics are wise, whatever Japan, like some other countries under constitutional Monarchy, may come to in the future.[28]

The constitution of 1889 was abolished after Japan's defeat in the Second World War.

The first election for Parliament in Japan was held on 1 July 1890, with an electorate of less than half a million out of a population approaching 42 millions. Before turning to Western evaluation of the parliamentary system in Japan, however, we must discuss an extraparliamentary political device resorted to by the Japanese which did not pass without comment; namely the apparently extensive use of assassination as a political instrument.

There had been quite a number of assassinations prior to the Meiji Restoration, notably, in 1860, that of the *Tairō* (Regent),

Ii Naosuke, for having signed treaties which were, in the view of Japanese xenophobes injurious to the nation. Following 1868, however, this political means seemed not to disappear in the new atmosphere of 'enlightened rule'. For example, there was the fate of Ōkubo Toshimichi, 'a statesman and patriot of the purest type', a Satsuma samurai who 'had from the beginning resisted the reactionary movements of his clan'. At the time of the Satsuma rebellion

he was Minister of Home Affairs and put forth all his exertions to suppress it. On May 14, 1878, Tokyo was startled by the news that Ōkubo, while driving through a secluded spot in the old castle grounds, on his way to the emperor's palace, had been murdered. The assassins . . . gave as the reason for their crime their desire to avenge the death of Saigo. Japan could ill afford to spare at this time her most clear-headed statesman and her noblest and most unflinching patriot.[29]

Just over a decade after this incident *The Times* remarked, 'Indeed, a record of statesmen who came to the front in 1868 and the years immediately succeeding would show that more died by the hands of the assassin than in their beds.'[30]

Basil Hall Chamberlain explained that as one of the consequences of liberalisation in the country 'there sprang up a class of rowdy youths, called sōshi in Japanese, – juvenile agitators who, taking all politics to be their province, used to obtrude their views and their presence on ministers of state, and to waylay – bludgeon and knife in hand – those whose opinions on matters of public interest happened to differ from their own'.[31]

The Times, interestingly enough, had no sympathy for the attempt on the part of the Japanese fourth estate to establish itself and its freedom:

Complaints have often been made against the Japanese Executive for not having long ago relaxed the present somewhat rigorous Press laws. Not only, however, do current events show that, as might be expected, they are the best judges of the way of dealing with their own people, but it will be surprising if henceforward, after a tragedy which has so nearly robbed the country of one of its most brilliant and devoted statesmen, they are not seen to come down with an iron hand on every journalistic effort to disturb the public peace.[32]

The article here was referring to the attempted assassination of the then Foreign Minister, Ōkuma Shigenobu.

Two questions arose; namely, whether political terrorists 'are commoner in Japan than elsewhere, or whether their surroundings are calculated to develop their dangerous propensities . . . a sombre and morbid character, with a strong attraction towards deeds of violence and bloodshed'. Both were answered in the affirmative, especially the latter:

A nation's character does not change radically in the course of a few decades, and one of the moral traits of old Japan was self-sacrifice at the shrine of loyalty. The records of avengers of blood fill a large space in Japanese history, and are taught to children from their infancy, are represented on the stage, and are glorified in song. These stories still stir the pulses of the bulk of the nation, and still challenge many a stout youth to write his name similarly in the page of history.[33]

On the day of the promulgation of the new Constitution, 11 February 1889, the Minister of Education, Mori Arinori, was assassinated. David Murray, an adviser to the Japanese Ministry of Education and close friend of Mori's, sadly reflected:

It would seem that no great advance can be secured in Japan without the sacrifice of a valuable life. As Ii Kamon-no-kami was murdered in 1860, and as Okubo fell by the assassin's hand at the close of the Satsuma rebellion, so now on the very day when the emperor was to promulgate this liberal constitution, Viscount Mori Arinori fell a victim to the fanatical hatred of one who looked with distrust upon the progress which his country was making.[34]

By 1905, however, Chamberlain was reasonably confident that the future would see a steady improvement in the political climate. These acts of terrorism, he claimed, are 'unhealthy symptoms, like others incidental to the childhood of the New Japan, [and] seem now to have passed away without any permanent ill effects'.[35]

Chamberlain was wrong. Assassinations of important political, military and industrial figures occurred with comparatively frequent regularity throughout the ensuing four decades.

The first parliamentary elections took place in 1890. In theory the Lower House had little power. The Cabinet, as pointed out earlier, was responsible to the Emperor and not the Diet. This and 'loyalty to the Emperor compelled all parties to accept as a tenet which was not to be disputed that the sanctity and inviolability of the Imperial prerogative was to be observed.' Very soon, however, 'the most radical among the Members of Parliament . . . showed that they were of opinion that a Cabinet not acknowledging responsibility to the Legislature was virtually impotent for law-making purposes.'

In spite of Japan's apparent constitutional advance towards Western style parliamentary democracy, 'the broad fact is evident that the government of Japan combines the features of an autocracy, an oligarchy, and a constitutional government. That the two former are still all-powerful has been made plain by recent events, when Parliament has been repeatedly dissolved while the same Ministry has continued to hold office.'

Nor was the political debate purely a matter of differing ideologies. To a great extent politics were heavily influenced by 'personal elements' in view of the fact that the constitutional provisions ensured 'the continuance in power of practically the same men as those who wielded it before the promulgation of the Constitution'. Therefore it was not surprising to learn that 'the opposition was directed against men, not measures, and obstruction of a very determined kind became the weapon of the political parties'.[36]

Most Western observers of the Japanese parliamentary struggle took the side of the government. Curzon noted: 'In three and a half-years of its existence, since its first meeting in November 1890, the Japanese Diet has passed through six sessions and three General Elections.' The government, however, was not to be blamed: '. . . considering how immature is the Lower House, and how inevitably . . . it is by its constitution afflicted with the vices of an irresponsible Opposition, it succeeded till lately in conducting its operations with a credible decorum.'

Japan in some respects was beginning to look more and more like her political models in the West. 'In the country we read of political clubs, of large meetings held in theatres and public places, of eloquent speeches, of cheering audiences, of the virtues and the wickedness of public men; and we realise that in Japan, as elsewhere, Demos, having found belated articulation is repeating, for the comfort of the scientific historian, the familiar and venerable accents.' Curzon argued that there were 'other evidences that Japan is in the bondage of a universal law', namely in the character of her new class of 'professional politicians'. 'These individuals are in a position of perpetual freedom and no responsibility; they can enjoy the luxury of attacking and paralysing every Government in turn; and, whilst by their votes they can neither form nor oust a Ministry, they can fetter its limbs with any number of Lilliputian cords.' In one way or another, 'the Japanese House of Representatives has rendered itself as disagreeable to successive Governments as it could, obstructing their measures, defeating their budgets, and generally betraying an attitude that might have been studied in Irish academies.'[37]

The parties resented the oligarchy's attitude towards them and insisted that for a government to be viable it had to secure a parliamentary majority. The Constitution was not on the side of the parties, but in time political realities and public opinion were. Most Western commentators, however, remained very conservative so far as Japan's parliamentary development was concerned. *The Times*, in 1905, argued: 'In truth, as all students of Japanese domestic affairs know, political parties had not yet shown themselves rich in the elementary qualities that office-holding demands – discipline, cohesion, and devotion to principles. They might be described as associations of agitators grouped about a central personality whose power was suggestive rather than directive, who knew that only the heat of attack would fuse his followers into working homogeneity, and who, even if he ventured to form an administration, would find himself in a minority in the Lower House.' In view of all this *The Times* judged that 'Party cabinets are plainly impossible in such conditions, and must remain impossible unless some powerful attraction, not now visible even in outline, brings the orbits of these unstable coteries into convergence, and thus creates a new association with cohesive principles and a working majority. At present nothing is more difficult to foresee.'[38]

While attempting to clarify Japan's present political situation and to hazard a guess as to its future, Curzon engaged in a fairly common Western device, namely, finding European analogies:

In reality the conflict is only a Japanese version of the familiar duel between a powerful and disciplined oligarchy and an ambitious but as yet imperfectly organised democracy. It is essentially the same historical phenomenon that was presented by the contest of the Gracchi with the Senate in the expiring century of the Roman Republic; and that was reproduced in our own country in the popular struggle against what is commonly called Whig ascendency in the first quarter of the present century. The Cabinet of Count Ito is in English political terminology a Whig Cabinet, composed of members of the great Whig families, the Cavendishes and Russells of modern Japan (though without their pedigrees), and sustained by the patronage which the Japanese equivalents to rotten boroughs afford. The system possesses that desperate tenacity which is the result of inherited ability and conscious worth. It has the authority which prescription and possession unite to confer, and it is undoubtedly in conformity with the history and the most cherished traditions of the people. A long time may yet elapse before it disappears; but ultimately, in face of an opposition which complains with some truth that it is being deluded by the mere semblance of liberty and outward form of change, it seems destined to perish, as did the influence of the Whig oligarchy in England.[39]

One of the frequent criticisms of the parties was that they lacked any coherent ideology. Leroy–Beaulieu, for example, said: 'If you question a Japanese about the programmes of these different parties he will give very vague answers, and, for that matter, they are hardly distinguishable one from another.'[40] The political parties in fact became the mouthpieces of rising Japanese big business. Since the end of the century, however, Western left-wing literature had seeped into Japan and a number of indigenous left-wing movements began to coalesce and attempts were made at forming their own parties. In fact until the end of the Second World War the left-wing movements were weak, mainly as a result of government harassment (at times persecution) and inherent weaknesses and doctrinal disputes within the movements themselves. The left-wing British weekly, *Justice*, however, in an article in 1897 appeared very confident of the future of socialism in Japan.

Socialism has recently gained another country, where it has already taken deep root. We mean Japan, where a Socialist Party has recently been formed. This country has proved one of the ablest in Asia to embrace our European Civil-isation with all its qualities and evils, but, above all, it has proved to be the most formidable ground for the develop-ment of the *bacillus capitalisticus*. It is not yet thirty years since Japan emerged from its 'grand revolution'; since it, in 1869, passed from the feudal system to our modern bourgeois régime, as this latter found the possibility of growing and developing in that country with an enormous rapidity and power unparalleled in any European country. Imported into Japan by England, the *bacillus capitalisticus* found there the most desirable conditions for its growth, magnificent geographical situation, mineral wealth of all kinds, and especially plenty of extremely cheap labour. And our bacil-lus went energetically to the work of decomposing such a marvellously nutritious ground, and of developing there all those products of that putrid decomposition which so distinctly characterises it, effective development; famine with tuberculosis, prostitution with syphilis, idleness with drunkenness, and overwork. But having brought into Japan the European civilisation with its capitalism, Europe imported there at the same time a germ of a new conception, which appears to spread rapidly in the minds of the Japanese, and which, growing and developing enough, will lead to another social constitution under which happy life will not be an airy word, but a real fact for all human beings, without distinction of race or colour.

The weekly went on to express satisfaction at the rapid development of trade-unionism in Japan – a very sanguine view not really in accordance with reality. It also noted how Western left-wing literature, and especially the *Communist Manifesto*, was welcomed and avidly read in the country, thus awakening the class-consciousness of the working people. *Justice* felt confident for the future in that 'although this Socialist movement is a very young one, it has already become so strong and it spreads so rapidly that the Japanese bourgeois and governmental classes are inspired with the most fearful alarm'. It predicted that in the not too distant future 'the *bacillus capitalisticus* will be killed by the *phagocitus socialisticus*' (the phagocitus being 'white blood corpuscles which possess . . . the property of passing through blood vessels, and to destroy all the bacilli which have penetrated into any part of our body').[41]

Justice's diagnosis and prophesy were both wrong. Apart from the two reasons given above for the unsuccessful career of socialism in Japan, there was another barrier against its fruition, as was noted by the French socialist paper, *Petite République*, namely that militarism and patriotism obscured the terrible social conditions of the country and diverted attention away from them.[42] This was also the view of one of Japan's leading early left-wing figures, Kōtoku Shūsui. In the West such an interpretation of Japan's decision to go to war with China in 1894 was not limited to the left; Curzon, for example, had no hesitation in declaring that 'hostilities had been deliberately started by the Japanese Government in order to deflect public attention from domestic troubles'.[43]

Contemporary evaluation of Japan's early parliamentary experiment is necessarily influenced by later developments, namely the totalitarian militarism of the 1930s and 40s. Parliamentary democracy never really took root in pre-Second World War Japan. Party government did come about (as forecast by Curzon), but the reservations expressed by a number of Western commentators on the parties proved to be true. The heyday of Japanese parliamentarism in the late teens and twenties of this century was marked by rampant corruption and also by continuous seemingly endemic violence. The economic crisis and the deteriorating international situation of the late 1920s and early 30s could not be handled, so many Japanese felt, by the irresponsible parties. If the situation had turned out differently, we may well have concluded this chapter with the optimistic view of an American missionary writing in 1903. Remarking that 'we often see and hear rather uncomplimentary statements about the Imperial Diet, political parties, cabinet ministers, and Japanese political affairs in general', he asserted that 'such criticisms result either from ignorance or from a wrong point of view'; and that, on the contrary, Japan 'seems deserving of the greatest credit for the progress of the first decade of constitutionalism'.[44] As it is, the anxieties expressed by Henry Norman seem more appropriate. He warned of 'certain signs of threatening dangers' and expressed grave concern for the future:

> ... if the Japanese politician ... does not realise that the difficulties ahead are infinitely greater and more trying than those which have been overcome, he may plunge into a bottomless pit of troubles. There are still in modern Japan all the elements for civil explosion, and serious economic and political difficulties would undoubtedly bring these into action.[45]

5

INDUSTRIOUSNESS, INDUSTRY AND INDUSTRIALISATION

The Japanese should have no concern with business. The Jap has no business savvy.

Kipling[1]

It is impossible to resist the belief that Japan is destined to become a factor of no inconsiderable importance in the world's commerce.

The Times[2]

The enormous industrial development of New Japan, and the competition, in many cases successful, it has entered into with the Occident – not only in Japan itself, but in markets hitherto considered as virtually reserved for the products of Europe and America – supply an object-lesson that teaches us what the Far East can do when thoroughly aroused.

Arthur Diósy[3]

Present-day writing about Japan is concerned mainly with the economic side of Japanese life. In newspapers, for example, articles dealing with Japan tend to appear only in the financial or business sections. Only occasionally, through incidents such as the Red Star Army occupying an embassy or the melodramatic suicide of one of her well-known authors (Mishima), is the 'non-economic' reader reminded that Japan exists. As a result the country today is often labelled as 'Japan, Inc.', its people as 'economic animals' and the national religion as 'GNPism'.

In the popular Western writing of our period there was less concern with the economic development of Japan than with other factors in her emergence into the modern world. This was for a number of reasons. The economic changes in Japan were less spectacular, less breathtaking, than the military conquests and perhaps less interesting than the political experiments. Secondly, Japan had not become by the end of our period a 'great' economic power and her competitive position *vis à vis* the Western powers remained relatively weak. Thirdly, and perhaps most important of all, the economic position of the Western powers seemed secure and although a few gloomy prophets of doom might raise the spectre of the economic 'yellow peril', it would be dismissed by the majority. The present-day obsession with Japan's economic strength is in great part caused by the West's economic weakness.

Finally, it should be noted that Japan's economy in the beginning of the twentieth century remained essentially agrarian: by far the greater part of the population was still occupied in the rural sector and the land tax was the country's chief source of revenue. Yet the new government had embarked on an ambitious programme of industrialisation as part of its *Fukoku-kyōhei* (rich country–strong army) programme. It is the Western appraisal of Japan's industrial and commercial development that this chapter deals with. It must be borne in mind that the question of treaty revision was of obvious importance in Japan's economic development. As has been pointed out earlier, one of the clauses of the unequal treaties imposed a 5 per cent *ad valorem* tariff on Western imports, thus, until 1899, making it difficult for the government to protect its infant industries from foreign competition. But as the matter of treaty revision has been dealt with at some length in chapter 1, little mention of it will be made here.

Besides the difficulties encountered in the treaty system and the great economic advance Western powers had on Japan, there were other apparent obstacles to the government's aspirations. In the first place Japan was a relatively poor country in mineral resources. She had little capital. And although in the course of the two and a half centuries of the *pax Tokugawa* Japan had developed a reasonably sophisticated economy with a number of wealthy merchants, profit and all activities associated with commerce were held in disdain according to the social values of the dominant samurai class. During the Tokugawa period the merchants were the bottom rung of the feudal caste system, below artisans, peasants, and samurai in that order.

'There is such a thing as trade,' said an old samurai to his pupil, 'see that you know nothing of it, for trade is the only game in which the winner is disgraced.' In a thoroughgoing feudal society, where personal gain was excluded, where men were to receive their daily portions and therewith be content, the man who sought gain was outside the pale of respectability. Merchants there must be, as there must be scavengers, but both are to be avoided and despised.[4]

To a certain extent the decades following the Restoration can be seen as a struggle between feudalism and emerging capitalism. The government was quite firmly on the side of capitalism and played a leading role in the development of Japan's economy. It initiated programmes, undertook the construction and development of industries, created financial institutions and generally laid the foundations of the new economic structure. However, just as Japan was governed by a group of men of great ability in both political and economic matters, so did a number of skilful and adventurous private entrepreneurs emerge; perhaps the best known in the West (and in Japan) was Shibusawa Eiichi. It is also in the last two decades of our period that one of the characteristics of the Japanese economy took shape, the *zaibatsu*. *Zaibatsu* (literally, financial cliques) were (and are) huge business concerns with interests in practically all fields of economic activity. The Mitsui *zaibatsu*, for example, was exceptional in that its roots went back far into the early Tokugawa period, but was comparable to the others (Mitsubishi, Yasuda and Sumitomo) in that it would eventually include light industry – especially textiles – heavy industries, mining, shipping, insurance, banking, etc.

There can be no doubt that Japanese commercial and industrial affairs were more than competently administered and developed by the country's political and business leaders. Japan was not the only non-European country attempting to industrialise in the second half of the nineteenth century. Indeed Japan's neighbour and century-old mentor, China, had embarked on a limited programme of industrialisation before Japan had even experienced the Meiji Restoration. After the crushing of the Taiping Rebellion in 1864 and during the so-called T'ung-chih restoration, the Chinese built arsenals, dockyards and textile factories. Yet there were four important factors which distinguished China's efforts at industrialisation from Japan's. Firstly, relations between the Western powers and Japan were very different from what they were with China. China was ruthlessly exploited by the Western powers and their merchants. With Japan the relationship was different both in nature and in degree; there was for example, no opium trade with Japan. Secondly, although the Chinese imperial government was victorious in crushing the Taiping Rebellion, the rebellion had lasted more than a decade, which, along with numerous other uprisings, exhausted the country politically, financially and militarily. Thirdly, not only was the Chinese government far less in control over the country's affairs than the Japanese government, but indeed Chinese government leaders were notoriously corrupt; the Empress Dowager, for example, embezzled funds from the construction of a naval arsenal in order to rebuild her summer palace (destroyed and looted by French and British troops in 1860). Finally, Japanese businessmen were fired by a spirit of nationalism which aimed at preventing Western encroachment on the country's economic independence and development, and were also determined to equal, indeed to outdistance, the West on its own terms.

Yet all this can be seen clearly with hindsight. At the end of the nineteenth century many Western observers were still more disturbed by the obstacles they believed Japan had to surmount in order to achieve her industrial revolution, than they were impressed by recent achievements. Apart from the obvious material obstacles to economic development, the moral or social ones appeared just as real. Even in 1890, over two decades after the Restoration, Leroy-Beaulieu noted that the transformation necessary to turn Japan into a capitalist nation was not inconsequential:

> Civilisation has as one of its characteristics the extension of human needs; one has to awaken in the Japanese masses the taste for satisfactions they do not possess. At the same time

one has to furnish them with new methods and new instruments of work. All this does not take place without a material and moral perturbation. The introduction of machinery was gradual in Europe: nevertheless, it created much suffering; in Japan it will be sudden, instantaneous, the people are not ready for it, and the harm done can have more intensity and be of longer duration. What is needed is a prodigious change not only in the material order of things, but also in Japanese mores, a complete transformation of the social ethics . . .[5]

Given Japan's lack of capital in the early stages of her industrialisation,* the human resources were obviously of great importance. Leroy-Beaulieu in the passage quoted above stressed the need for a revolution in social values. One positive aspect of the Japanese character which most Western observers seemed to agree on, however, was the frugality of the people. The English missionary James Scherer noted: 'Take, for example, the important question of *economy*. We simply do not know the meaning of the word. A Japanese can live and lay by a surplus where a Westerner would starve a dozen times over.'[6] Another important factor in terms of human resources on where there was scant agreement was on the capacity of the Japanese for hard and sustained work. A Frenchman remarked in 1878 that 'unfortunately, for the Japanese to succeed in exploiting by themselves their latent riches, they would need an accumulated capital, which they lack, a sustained energy and a fervour for work which they certainly do not manifest'.[7] Kipling and Scherer came to completely different conclusions, although using exactly the same example. Kipling claimed that 'Japan of my limited view is inhabited entirely by little children whose duty is to prevent their elders from becoming too frivolous. The babies do a little work occasionally, but their parents interfere by petting them. At Yami's hotel the attendance is in the hands of ten-year-olds

---

* It should be noted that Japan had one valuable product for export which did earn a considerable amount of foreign revenue, namely silk. Japan may be said to have been fortunate in being opened precisely at a time when silk-worms in France and Italy were ravaged by a blight, the *pégrine*.

because everybody else has gone out picknicking among the cherry-trees.'⁸ For Scherer, however, 'Another positive quality of the Oriental character is their untiring industry. No one can lodge at an Eastern inn without receiving the impression that the taverner and his help never go to bed. All night long the sleepless sounds of labour are rampant and furious. This habit of ceaseless occupation often extends to the very highest classes.'⁹

In regard to capital, one of the marked features of the early stages of Japan's industrialisation was the government's refusal to depend on foreign loans. The reason was that

> the face of the nation is firmly against having recourse to foreign capital as long as the present treaties remain in force. Japan has become gravely apprehensive lest the abuses which have grown up under the extra-territorial system should defy all efforts to prevent their gradual spread over the whole Empire.¹⁰

In fact the suspicions of the Japanese Government were not limited to the question of the treaties. Indeed the government feared that if it were to contract sizeable debts with the Western powers and if for some reason it was unable to meet a payment, the Western powers would not hesitate in demanding concessions which could seriously jeopardise Japan's sovereignty. The Japanese were too well aware of the grave difficulties China was facing and the constant Western infringements on both her sovereignty and territory to allow the same thing to happen in Japan. *The Times*, all the while praising Japan's heroic endeavours, noted with regret:

> If only the surplus funds of the West could be placed at the disposal of this spirit of enterprise, the prospects of Japan's commercial development would be immensely brightened, and a new and profitable field of investment would be opened to foreign capitalists.¹¹

The French weekly, *Le Moniteur des Soies*, argued in similar vein that just as the Japanese government had sought Euro-

A Western artist's impression of the inauguration by the Emperor of the first railway in Japan, 1872. While the artist has undoubtedly used poetic licence, some of the headgear being more in tune with Tibet than Japan, note the coexistence of Japanese and Western uniforms.

The Japanese Parliament opened by the Mikado, Tokyo, November 29, 1890.

The Mikado in procession at Yokohama, 1894.

The Imperial Office was rooted in both tradition and modernity. The Mikado, or Tennō was presented as a modern monarch, comparable to, say, the Kaiser in Germany and wearing military uniform. Yet, the legitimacy of his rule and his claim to divine status harked back to pre-historic mythology and Japan's oldest religion, Shinto.

pean expertise to develop the country's army and navy, so was it that economic progress could be achieved only by asking foreign merchants and capitalists to reconstitute its riches.[12]

The last few years of the nineteenth century and the first few years of the twentieth, however, witnessed spectacular changes (or culminations) in practically all fields. In 1889 Japan had a constitution, in 1890 her first election for Parliament; in 1894 the treaties were successfully revised, the revisions coming into operation five years later. And in 1895 Japan won a major war in defeating China. As a former principal of the Imperial college of Engineering in Tokyo, Henry Dyer, stated:

The war with China in 1894–5 marked an epoch not only in the political history of Japan, but also in its industrial and economic history, and its successful termination gave an impetus to every department of national activity; which had a great effect on industrial development.[13]

With Japan's victory it seemed that the sacrifices of the early stages of industrialisation and the struggle necessary to realise the aim of *Fukoku-kyōhei* (rich country–strong army) were justified. Not only did the Japanese gain confidence, they gained much needed cash in the shape of the massive war indemnity they obtained from the Chinese. Thus capital had been obtained through force and force would now permit the country to risk foreign loans. In the years just prior to the Russo-Japanese war, Japan borrowed heavily from the West for the first time, mainly from her ally after 1902, Great Britain, but also from the United States.

It is this period which marks the take-off of Japan's successful industrial revolution. As early as 1894 *The Times* gave an indication of how quickly material progress had been achieved:

. . . a moneyed mercantile class has come into existence. Co-operative enterprise has sprung up. The country is intersected with railways, full of work and paying well. No fewer than 700,000 spindles are now making cotton yarn in competition with England and India, and the number will soon be . . . a million. Steamers under native flag swarm on the coast and inner waters, paying handsomely. Every conceivable kind of manufacture is in a state of intense activity; the country is like a beehive. Steamers are built and engined without foreign help. Harbour improvements have been carried out at great expense; roads are made and kept serviceable everywhere.[14]

Henry Dyer, quoting a report on an industrial exhibition at Osaka in 1903, also proved to what extent Japan had become self-sufficient in many of her new requirements:

Considering that only thirty years ago Japan had no such institution as a factory, and knew nothing whatever of iron foundries or machine shops, the Japanese-made machinery display at the exhibition at Osaka is astonishing. There we find silk-weaving and mat-making machines, electrical motors and generators, gas and oil engines, locomotives, electrical fittings, tools, beltings, match-making machines, fire-brigade appliances, rice-cleaning machines, huge steam navvy oil tanks, soap-making machines, printing machines, massive hoisting engines, tea-refining machinery, heavy mining machinery, and many other smaller machines; all of Japanese manufacture, admirably made and well adapted to the purposes designed.

One of the best exhibits is in clocks, some of them very handsome and very cheap, made by one or other of the twelve Japanese clock companies. The porcelain exhibition is good, consisting of beautiful vases, artistic porcelain trays, basins, tea-cups, etc. The exhibit of Japanese-made shoes is quite creditable. Other native manufactures exhibited are bamboo furniture, whatnots, overmantels, fire-screens, shell buttons, paper lanterns, fine silken rugs, shawls, paper, camphor, oils, soap, all kinds of sauces and relishes, silks of every hue and description, silk lace, gold and silver thread, linen, duck, tent cloths, ivory work, hinges, lacquer and silver work, surgical instruments, pianos, organs, and other musical instruments, bicycles, gymnastic and athletic goods, microscopes, cameras, barometers and almost every kind of educational apparatus.[15]

David Murray, an American adviser to the Minister of Education, was one of the few to stress the greater importance of Japan's economic development in relation to other advances, and the possible danger arising due to British capitalists' ignorance of these achievements.

Japan's material and industrial progress since 1890 has been even more marked than that which she has shown in military and constitutional affairs, though even to this day what she has achieved in this respect meets with but scant recognition among the manufacturers and merchants of Great Britain, who have failed alike to recognise the already great and always growing importance of Japan as a market for their own products or the possibility of her becoming a formidable competitor with them, not only in the Far East, but even in Australia and India.

The internal transformation of Japan's economy was bound to affect her position in the world, and consequently that of the Western powers as well. As Murray noted, Japan's industrialisation was reflected in the changes incurred in her exports:

What may be called her indigenous manufactures, those of porcelain, bronze, lacquer, and basketware, of *objets d'art*, have always been exported to a fairly substantial value, but to these are now added many of the great and leading staples of English industry, and it is the latter which mainly contributes to form the bulk of all the manufactures exported. In that of cotton yarn, formerly the principal import into Japan, she has not only become her own self-supplier, but is steadily and surely becoming that also of Northern China. Matches, glassware, clothing, umbrellas, machinery, clocks, and lamps, made by her, are very largely sold throughout the whole of the East as far from her as Singapore, while there are few manufactured articles of daily necessity in Western life which are not produced in Japan to a greater or less extent and at a cost which compares very favourably with that in Europe. The total value of her manufactures exported to other countries has advanced almost by leaps and bounds, and now annually exceeds eight millions sterling.[16]

These industrial developments obviously altered the urban landscape of Japan. Thus a description of Osaka in 1905 revealed that 'hundreds of tall chimneys stand hard by its many canals, belching forth clouds of black smoke to disfigure the fair surroundings, and to gladden the hearts of Japanese holders of shares in cotton-mills earning, on average, dividends of twelve per cent'. It was not surprising, therefore, that 'Englishmen sometimes called it the Manchester, Scotsmen the Glasgow, Frenchmen the Lille, Germans the Hamburg and Americans the Chicago of Japan'.

The seriousness with which the Japanese undertook the business of economic development was perhaps nowhere as strikingly illustrated as it was in the efforts they put into commercial and industrial education. In the early post-Restoration period Japanese students were sent abroad to study in the great schools of political economy in the West and numerous Western specialists in all fields, theoretical and practical, were invited to teach in Japan. In time, however, the Japanese became increasingly self-reliant, to the extent that

> There is no better-organised, no better-equipped institution of its kind in the world than the Commercial High School in Tokyo, where a complete course of instruction, theoretical as well as admirably practical, is given. In one large hall of this School, that has counterparts in the chief commercial cities of Japan, a number of bays, or recesses, are labelled with the names of the principal mercantile centres of the world, and in each of these a number of students, who have been well grounded in theoretical knowledge, taking the parts, respectively, of bankers, importers, exporters, brokers, insurance agents, and shipping agents, carry on active, simulated international trade in strict accordance with the business usages of the places at which they are supposed to be dealing. The various steps of every conceivable commercial transaction are accurately gone through, from the comparison of samples, obtained from the School Museum,

to the giving and receipt of orders, the making out of invoices and bills of lading, of policies of insurance and freight-notes, and to the drawing, and sometimes the 'protesting', of bills of exchange, even to disputes as to quality and packing, giving rise to instructive correspondence in several languages, with the necessary dictation shorthand, and type-writing, and 'code' telegrams. When will London, the commercial metropolis of the world, have a Commercial School like that of Tokyo, or, indeed, a Commercial School of any kind worthy of the name?[17]

It must not be thought that the enthusiasm for Japan's economic development and confidence in her future as illustrated above represented the unanimous view of Western observers. T. W. H. Crosland, an Englishman writing just at the outbreak of the Russo–Japanese war (1904) and convinced of Russia's eventual victory, tried to discourage his compatriots from offering loans to Japan:

Japan is not, in any sense, a sound investment. She has been going too fast and too far for soundness. And she is not rich in the sense that a 'world power' should be rich.

Not only are the Japanese poor in the monetary sense, but they are largely without effects, that is to say, they possess no accumulations of valuables, furniture, works of art or other objects. The foreign army which, if we mistake not will one day have to go to Japan, may depend upon coming back lootless, inasmuch as there is nothing to loot. Nor are the natural resources of the country at all rich. Only a very small part of the land is under cultivation, the reason being that much of the land surface consists of mountains and volcanic tracts which cannot be made arable.

Again, Japan has comparatively little mineral wealth, and she is almost devoid of timber. Her whole dependence, therefore, lies in the development of her manufacture and of her carrying trade, and these are, as yet, in a distinctly embryo condition. So that, broadly speaking, Japan is scarcely the country to which one would desire to lend money. For solid wealth Russia is worth five hundred of her, and we have under our dominion in India princes who could buy her up lock, stock and barrel.[18]

One feature of Japan's commercial development which did not escape Western criticism and indeed at times Western anger was the country's reputation for slavishly – and some argued dishonestly – imitating Western products:

> In commercial matters the Japanese have exhibited their imitativeness in the most extraordinary degree. Almost everything they have once bought, from beer to bayonets and from straw hats to heavy ordinance, they have since learned to make for themselves. There is hardly a well-known European trade-mark that you do not find fraudulently imitated in Japan.[19]

A more benign suggestion was that 'The Japanese are assimilators rather than mere imitators',[20] while Valentine Chirol, former foreign editor of *The Times*, rather than criticising Japanese imitativeness, praised it:

> If George Eliot's definition of genius as an infinite capacity for taking pains cannot be altogether accepted as satisfactory, there is no people to whose genius it would seem so applicable as the Japanese. At first they no doubt applied themselves merely to copy the products of European industry, and, as with all beginners, their first attempts were often clumsy and imperfect, but with unswerving tenacity of purpose they kept on plodding away until they had in most cases remedied their defects, and in some improved even upon their models.

Part of the reason for Japan's ability to compete commercially with the Western powers was that Japanese products were generally far cheaper than the same products made in the West. But whether 'made in Japan' rightly deserved the connotation of cheapness of quality as well as of price was also a matter of some dispute. Valentine Chirol, writing in 1896, took the view that Japanese products were not substantially inferior in quality. After ranging over a wide variety of manufactured products available in Japan, he claimed:

> If for intrinsic quality and fashionable finish they [the Japanese products] cannot yet be said to stand comparison with the best articles of the same category in first-class London shops, it would be just as great a mistake to imagine that they are mere 'shoddy' imitations. In fact the relative inferiority of quality is in most cases trifling compared with the relative inferiority of price. Where the greatest delicacy of workmanship is most essential, the Japanese lightness of touch and precision of eye produce almost perfect results as in the manufacture of scientific instruments, mathematical, optical, photographic, and specially those for purposes of surgery and dentistry.[21]

Leroy-Beaulieu, however, was perhaps marginally more representative of Western opinion on the matter:

> This brilliant picture of Japanese commercial prosperity has, unfortunately, its shady side. Many complain that the articles manufactured in Japan are not up to the mark in point of excellence and finish. As is generally the case with Orientals, they start well and make their first batch of goods admirably, but the quality soon falls off, probably the result, not so much of negligence, as of over-hasty production, due to competition. There can be no doubt that these and other complaints are not unfounded, and many intelligent Japanese are the first to acknowledge and deplore them. As an instance in point, matches are not nearly so well made as they used to be. Many complaints have also been made as to the increasing inferiority of a certain class of silk goods known as *haboutaye* and of the silk pocket-handkerchiefs, of which an enormous quantity are exported, with the result that the export of these last-mentioned necessary articles fell from 1,855,000 dozens in 1895, to 1,157,000 in 1897.[22]

As we shall see shortly, the question of the quality of Japanese manufactured products was not the only subject of debate among Western writers; another was the effect of industrial-isation on the quality of the life of the people. Valentine Chirol, for one, however, was pleased to note not only that 'in all those branches which are indigenous to Japan, it has lost little, if anything, of its artistic originality and traditional pre-eminence', but that in its more modern manufactures as well the native talent was being properly exploited.

One of the sections [of the Kyoto Industrial Exhibition] which naturally claims the chief attention of an English visitor is that of textiles, for it includes those manufactured products which already compete only too successfully with those of Lancashire and India, viz., cotton yarns of every grade, and piece goods of every variety. Here, too, can be seen in its simplest and most striking form the ability of the Japanese not only to turn out the cheapest work possible where it is of a purely mechanical order, but to invest it whenever there is the slightest scope for their artistic feel-ing, as in the patterns of the commonest cotton fabrics, with a charm of grace and originality peculiarly their own.[23]

In regard to artistic originality in industrial design, Leroy-Beaulieu agreed with Chirol. Noting that the Japanese sought inspiration from nature in embellishing their products, Leroy-Beaulieu exclaimed, 'It is a country of craftsmen, rather than of workers.'[24]

While new Japanese manufactures and their producers may have received praise from Western quarters, this was far from being the general attitude towards the country's merchants. Commercial relations between Japan and the West were often far from harmonious, as 'every European merchant who deals with Japanese merchants tells you that, in matters of business, they are dishonest and untrustworthy'.[25]

Part of the problem seemed to be that whereas the old feudal samurai moral code had been rendered obsolete by Japan's adoption of capitalism and participation in the world of trade, the country had not yet found a new morality to suit its new society.

Nothing is more threatening to the future of Japan than its sudden development of commercialism. The old standards are gone, a new appetite for wealth has been aroused, and thus far no corresponding sense of commercial honour has been developed. Probably nothing so injures Japan as its want of a commercial code of ethics. Certainly commercialism in our own lands is far from impeccable, and one sometimes smiles when one hears the Japanese especially denounced; but when all allowances are made it remains true that the Japanese are in universal disrepute, in striking contrast to their Chinese neighbours on the continent, and to their own reputation in all other walks in life. But in a commercial age like our own it is the commercial code which after all finally determines position, and unless Japan reforms and brings to its commercial transactions the same intelligence and the same honour which characterise its other departments of life it will bear a stigma which its friends will be powerless to remove.[26]

In order to explain the ungentlemanly behaviour of the Japanese merchant, Basil Hall Chamberlain suggested a pattern of continuity from the feudal period:

Notice the place in which commerce stood [during the Tokugawa period], at the very bottom of the scale, below the very tillage of the soil. Traces of this contumely have survived modern changes; for men naturally become what the world holds them to be: – the hucksters or traders (we will not dignify them with the name of merchants) were a degraded class in Old Japan, and degraded their business morals remain, which is the principal cause of the difficulties experienced by European merchants in dealing with them.

How radically different one's impression of the Japanese could be depending on the purpose of one's visit became apparent:

. . . European bankers and merchants in Japan . . . complain, it is true, not so much of actual, wilful dishonesty –

though of that, too, they affirm there is plenty – as of pettiness, constant shilly-shallying, unbusinesslikeness almost
passing belief. Hence the wide divergence between the
impressions of the holiday-making tourist, and the opinions
formed by the commercial communities at the open ports.
Japan, the globetrotter's paradise, is also the grave of the
merchant's hopes.[27]

But apart from the vicissitudes of the European merchants
in Japan, a question which taxed the minds of observers of the
country's changing economic scene was the effect of these
changes on the Japanese people. Japan's attraction, indeed
fascination, for many, as we have seen, was that of the land of
the charming *musume*, of a pre-industrial paradise, innocent in
matters of factories, trade, banking, shipping; the country of
the 'living art'. It must have been disheartening to see the
chimneys of new factories belching out smoke over the beautiful
landscapes of rural Japan and brutally disfiguring the cities.
As often happens in such cases there was a marked tendency to
overglamorise the past, in this case the Tokugawa period.
Henry Dyer, for example, painted a very Utopian picture of
pre-industrial Japan:

During the Tokugawa period, extending over two hundred
and sixty years, Japan was in a state of perfect tranquility,
and the feudal chiefs did a great deal to encourage and protect manufacturing industry, especially that of an artistic
nature. The energy which was formally spent on internecine
war was expanded in friendly rivalry in the industrial arts,
and the consequence was that a very high standard of excellence was attained. The best work was not made for sale, but
for use or presentation; time was not money, and the arti-
ficers and artists threw their personalities and all their skill
into their work. Both artists and workmen were free to work
when they felt in the mood to do justice to their objects, and
equally free to seek repose the instant fatigue notified them
of their failing powers. They therefore had real pleasure in
their work, and each of the products was a distinct specimen
of skill, perfect, novel and idiosyncratic. . . . Skill passed

from fathers to sons or adopted sons, and surrounded by their own domestic circle they carried on their work under conditions which were almost perfect from an artistic point of view. Qualified critics and fellow-workers kept up a spirit of healthy emulation, and the worker unconsciously imbibed in a more or less degree some of the purity, poetry, and refinements of the motives which actuated his art.[28]

This is far too idealistic a view of Tokugawa society and those working under Dyer's suggested conditions would have been an infinitesimal privileged few, if indeed they existed at all. But this image of the Tokugawa period corresponded to the romantic Western dream of Japan. It is not surprising to find that Lafcadio Hearn was one of the more outspoken critics of industrialisation. He too sought comparison with the Tokugawa period, but contrasted not just the deterioration of the artistic element in Japanese life, but also a degeneration in social relationships:

Old Japan had never developed a wealthy and powerful middle class: she had not even approached that stage of industrial development which, in the ancient European societies, naturally brought about the first political struggles between rich and poor. Her social organisation made industrial oppression impossible: the commercial classes were kept at the bottom of society, – under the feet even of those who, in more highly evolved communities, are most at the mercy of money-power. But now those commercial classes, set free and highly privileged, are silently and swiftly ousting the aristocratic ruling-class from power, – are becoming supremely important. And under the new order of things, forms of social misery, never before known in the history of the race, are being developed.

Lafcadio Hearn's indictment against capitalism in Japan was one that strongly favoured the values of feudalism. The rulers of feudal Japan, in his opinion, were far more benign and evinced a genuine concern for the material and moral well-being of their subjects. With the decline of this form of benevolent, paternal despotism, therefore, numerous other admirable values of Old Japan disintegrated as well:

> in Japan it is hardly more than thirty years since the patriarchal system was legally dissolved and the industrial system reshaped; yet already the danger of anarchy is in sight, and the population – astonishingly augmented by more than ten millions– already begins to experience all the forms of misery developed by want under industrial conditions.
>
> But this immense development has been effected at serious cost in other directions. The old methods of family production – and therefore most of the beautiful industries and arts, for which Japan has been so long famed – now seem doomed beyond hope; and instead of the ancient kindly relations between master and workers, there have been brought into existence – with no legislation to restrain inhumanity – all the horrors of factory-life at its worst. The new combinations of capital have actually re-established servitude, under harsher forms than ever were imagined under the feudal era; the misery of the women and children subjected to that servitude is a public scandal, and proves strange possibilities of cruelty on the part of a people once renowned for kindness – kindness even to animals.[29]

Here again, however, the reality of the Japanese situation was interpreted differently and with a different emphasis according to the eye of the beholder. David Murray insisted that so far as the material well-being of the Japanese were concerned, there could be no comparison. Whereas the past had been severely austere and had witnessed constant hardships, in the decades following the Restoration

> Luxuries speedily became necessaries, and in every domestic detail, in food, clothing, lighting, lodging, the Japanese labourer has now the daily enjoyment of comforts that were unthought of a generation ago . . . It may be safely said that throughout the entire Empire there is neither man nor woman who has not a sufficiency of daily food and a lodging for the night.

Indeed the Japanese in some ways were more prosperous than people in the West. For although Japanese 'requirements are simple and less costly than those of the West ... they are always supplied, and no streets on the coldest nights are disfigured by the starving, shivering outcasts that are familiar sights in those of the great towns of the West.'[30]

David Murray's picture of industrial Japan was divorced from reality. There was real hardship, though admittedly less in urban areas – those most frequented by Westerners – than in the more remote rural and mining districts. On the other hand both Dyer and Hearn were misleading in attempting to bring out such stark contrasts between a combination of bucolic contentment and artistic excellence of the Tokugawa period and the infernal horrors of industrial Japan. Not that the situation in factories or mines was better than they portrayed, but the past was by no means brighter. Undoubtedly Japan did lose some things of value from the Tokugawa period, but it also stood to gain a great deal. Nostalgia for pre-industrial Japan was out of place in terms of realities, though perfectly understandable, perhaps, in terms of dreams and images. Nevertheless, whether the transition from feudalism to *Fukoku* (rich country) needed to be as brutal as it was must remain a matter for debate. Henry Dyer was undoubtedly correct in pleading for Japan 'to recognise that the inordinate pursuit of merely material ends will not lead to the highest national welfare'.[31]

Western writing on Japan, as we have noted previously, was not concerned solely with commenting on the Japanese situation – both in criticism and admiration – but was also directed at the West itself. As Japan rushed headlong into industrialisation with all its ramifications, there was – to the Western eye– a sense of *déjà vu*, an understandable heart-breaking sensation that in the future it was not only Japan but indeed the world that would lose something never to be regained. There was a feeling of desperation as one had to sit witness to a seemingly inevitable scenario. The gravest danger, it seemed, to Japan's future

springs from her very success in rivalling Western nations in their manufacturing industries. While we have succeeded, after many struggles, in mitigating the horrors of the old factory system, and are still occupied in devising fresh safeguards for the future, Japan is complacently allowing identical evils to grow up in her midst. It is time for her to realise that even though her army and navy become the most powerful in the world, the title of 'civilised' cannot properly apply to her so long as young children work twelve hours a day in her factories. The character of her people, to which is due in the last analysis every success that she has achieved, has sprung from the free development of individual character, and it is seriously threatened by the rapid growth of great manufacturing industries, which tend, when unrestricted, to reduce the individual man to a mere cog in the mechanism, and which eat up the lives of women and children. When Japan rings with the rattle of machinery; when the railway has become a feature of her scenery; when the boiler-chimney has defaced her choicest spots as the paper-makers have already obliterated the delights of Oji; when the traditions of *yashiki* and *shizoku* [mansion and samurai aristocracy] alike are all finally engulfed in the barrack-room; when her art reckons its output by the thousand dozen; when the power in the land is shared between the professional politician and the plutocrat; when the peasant has been exchanged for the 'factory-hand', the kimono for the slop-suit, the tea-house for the music-hall, the *geisha* for the *lion comique*, and the *daimio* for the beer-peer – Japan will have good cause to doubt whether she has made a wise bargain. Her greatest triumph will come, if ever, when she has shown that while adapting and even improving the western methods of influence and power, she is able to guard herself from falling into the slough of social and economical difficulties in which European and American societies are wallowing, and from which one may almost doubt whether they will succeed in emerging without leaving civilisation behind them for good.[32]

6

YELLOW HOPE – YELLOW PERIL

> *The repulsion of the gigantic Persian despotism had a similar effect on the tiny Hellenic people to that of the defeat of the Russian despotism on the Japanese. At one blow they became a world-power ruling the sea which surrounded them and with that commanding its trade.*
>
> (Kautsky)[1]

> *The battle of Trafalgar broke the power of Napoleon; the battle of the Sea of Japan sealed the fate of Port Arthur, and ended the war with Russia. Two big results, worthy of being put side by side.*
>
> (Lord Redesdale)[2]

The slogan the Japanese government adopted on the eve of its intensive modernisation programme was *Fukoku-Kyōhei*, 'rich country–strong army'. It is a matter for dispute to what extent the first part of the slogan, rich country, was in fact achieved by the end of our period – or for that matter whether it was really achieved until the 1960s. Industrialisation took place, but the bulk of the people remained poor by Western standards. On the second part of the slogan, however, there can be no debate. In the course of the three decades following the Meiji Restoration Japan became a formidable military power in the Far East.

Throughout most of Japanese history, military power and martial values have been predominant. In the Heian period, from the ninth to the twelfth centuries, Japan was governed by a civilian nobility. In the preceding and following centuries, however, actual power remained firmly in the hands of a military aristocracy. Japanese martial values are evident in numerous facets of the country's culture: in sport there is emphasis on the *budō*, or martial arts, *judō*, *karate*, *kendō*; in religion the flourishing of Zen Buddhism was closely allied with the social moral code of *Bushidō* (way of the warrior); in the arts, although both religion and nature remained important themes, in drama particularly stories of military prowess and duty were perhaps the most popular – notably the story of the 47 Ronin first translated into English by A. B. Mitford (later Lord Redesdale). The samurai was supposed to epitomise the most cherished values of Japanese society: mainly a combination of fearlessness and unqualified loyalty.

The reforms immediately following the Restoration were aimed at abolishing the samurai as a cast – thus opening the way for 'men of talent' – but not at abolishing the samurai spirit. Therefore after 1868 two parallel and complementary developments were instituted and encouraged by the government. The first was intensive military modernisation and the second was not merely the retention, but indeed the exaltation of the samurai spirit. So, while the government abolished samurai military privilege by establishing conscription in 1873, it ensured the maintenance of the proper samurai ethic among its new recruits by issuing a number of imperial decrees and proclamations which stressed both the importance of the military in general and the loyalty and fearlessness which was expected of every soldier individually.

Military modernisation had in fact begun before the Restoration. Even before Perry's visit a number of Japanese had been preoccupied at the weakness of the country's defences and urged drastic reforms. Following the opening of the country this desire for military modernisation intensified, with both *han* (fief) and shōgunal governments beginning, by the early 1860s, to seek Western arms and expertise. Just before the Restoration the last shōgun had succeeded in obtaining training missions from the French army and the British navy. The new Meiji government followed suit, though eventually the French military mission was replaced by mainly German tutorship.

In spite of Japan's military traditions, as noted in Chapter 1, Japan had very little experience of actually fighting a foreign power. The Kublai Khan's armada was defeated more by the elements than as a result of military encounters. Toyotomi Hideyoshi's grand plan for the conquest of Korea and China in the late sixteenth century had proved abortive. Apart from a few minor skirmishes in the 1860s between *han* armies and the Western fleets, no serious battle, let alone war, had erupted

The Yellow Peril.

The Russo-Japanese War. (Caran d'Ache in *Figaro*)

Two views of 'the Japanese menace'. The Kaiser's design for the 'Yellow Peril' pre-dated Japan's victory over Russia by ten years. With Japan's victory, however, the nightmare conveyed by the Kaiser's drawing seemed to many Westerners to be approaching reality. Note, among other things, that the peril appears in the form of the Buddha, whereas Buddhism is unquestionably one of the world's least militant religions. The famous French cartoonist, Caran d'Ache, is ridiculing miniscule Japan's challenging the great Russian bear.

Baron Kuroki, Commander-in-Chief of the First Japanese Army.

between Japan and the West. In the early Meiji period the army so far as the government was concerned was primarily for internal use. Trigger-happy military adventurers were frustrated by the government in their desire to seek foreign encounters. An expedition to Formosa in 1874 was seen by the government more as a means of getting rid of meddlesome fiery samurai than as a major military enterprise. The real test of the new army had come in 1877 when the government's conscript army had battled with Saigō's samurai army. Saigō's defeat had very profound military implications, apart from the purely political ones.

But, increasingly, a variety of factors were pushing Japan irrevocably in the direction of foreign war. It is not my purpose here even to attempt an analysis of Japan's imperialist motivations. Suffice it to say that relations with both China and Korea had been bad almost from the very beginning of the Meiji era. Perhaps one can add that a government which arms itself to the extent Japan did in the second half of the nineteenth century, which urges the population and particularly the soldiers to patriotic and martial frenzies, and which is equally beset by serious economic and political difficulties, cannot long stay on the path of peace. Japan's first major war – with China – broke out in 1894 and by the next year Japan had gained her first major victory.

Ten years later, however, in early 1904, the question was being asked: 'does Japan now make ready to unsheathe the sword?' This time the antagonist was not another Asian nation, but reputedly one of the mightiest European powers, Russia. As *The Times* commented in a leading article on the eve of the war, the consequences of this confrontation would be formidable: Japan

> stands on the threshold of a contest which must make or mar her as a Power among the powers. Other great conflicts have been entered upon in modern history which were fraught with great possibilities and felt to be of fateful import to the combatants; but never, perhaps, has one been imminent which so plainly involved the very existence of one of them as a powerful nation. If Japan were to be vanquished in this

struggle, she would have to . . . acquiesce in her permanent relegation to the rank of a third or fourth class Power – perhaps to her ultimate extinction as an independent people.

For Japan there could be no doubt that this was her greatest gamble. But the significance of this war, as the same leader noted, was not limited to the fate of Japan: 'In its determination even more than the fate of Japan's national existence is involved. The history not merely of the Far East, but of all Asia as well, must be incalculably influenced by the issue of the struggle.'

The beginning of the twentieth century had seen the crystallisation of the precarious balance of power among the imperialist nations extending from Argentina to the Philippines. In East Asia for the first nine decades of the nineteenth century Britain had been without any doubt *the* dominant power, the only possible serious rivals being Russia and to a far lesser extent France. However, during the last decade of the century a rapid and spectacular change took place. New powers appeared on the scene: Germany, the United States, Japan, and Russia – with renewed vigour as her Trans-Siberian railway, long a dream, became a reality. Japan too had embarked on a course of imperialism, her primary interest being the Korean question, forever a thorn in Japan's side (or a dagger at Japan's heart as a German military adviser in Tokyo had put it).

The war between Japan and China in 1894–5 had been waged over which country would have the predominant influence in Korea. Japan won a dramatic victory – taking many Europeans by surprise, as China, being so much larger than Japan, appeared the stronger of the two. Japan's victory over China had a number of important and rapid consequences. As noted in Chapter 1, Japan's unequal treaties with the Western powers were finally revised the year of the outbreak of war. But for the Japanese the Western 'anti-Japan conspiracy' did not end, revised treaties or not. One of the terms Japan had imposed on China in the peace settlement at Shimonoseki was that the latter cede the Liaotung Peninsula to Japan. This upset Russia, who, after manoeuvring France and

Germany to join her, intervened – in what was called the Triple Intervention – forcing Japan to relinquish this claim. As a compensation Japan's war indemnity from China was increased. The effect on the Japanese of the Western powers' 'ganging up' on them was immeasurable; riots broke out in Tokyo and elsewhere. The Japanese, so proud of their recently won victory, found themselves humiliated by the white powers and there was nothing they could do. For Japan alone to take on the combined forces of Russia, Germany and France was unthinkable. There was nothing left to do but, in the words of the Emperor Meiji, bear the unbearable and endure the unendurable.

However, two immediate consequences in Japan of the combination of the victory over China and the humiliation over the Triple Intervention were a greater and more accelerated military build-up and the realisation that diplomatically Japan should never again find herself in such an isolated situation as she had been in 1895. This need for a friend in Tokyo coincided with a similar realisation in London. Britain may still in 1895 have been the major power in the East, but the potential rivals were both stronger and more numerous. After failing to achieve successful negotiations for an alliance with Germany, Britain and Japan turned to each other and formed the Anglo–Japanese Alliance in 1902. Another consequence of the Sino–Japanese war was that, with China disposed of, Japan's main rival with regard to Korea became Russia. Russia's reasons for intervening in the question of the Liaotung Peninsula were based primarily on her ambition to dominate Northern China, Manchuria and Korea and to secure the ice-free port of Port Arthur at the tip of the peninsula. In the years following the Triple Intervention, Russian–Japanese antagonism grew till it exploded early in 1904.

Perhaps the most immediate consequence of China's defeat in 1895 consisted of a number of rapid developments which radically affected China's internal and external affairs. The internal developments need not detain us here, except to note that they helped precipitate the overthrow of the Manchu Ch'ing dynasty just over a decade and a half later. China's position *vis à vis* the powers changed dramatically as well. The activities of the Western powers in China had been based on an uneasy balance between cooperation on the one hand (the so-called Concert of Powers system) and mutual jealousy on the other. However, until the Sino–Japanese war, China's territorial integrity and sovereignty had been at least nominally respected by the powers, with a few exceptions – Hong Kong, Macao and European administration of the international settlements in the treaty ports. Following China's defeat at the hands of the Japanese, however, the last three years of the nineteenth century witnessed a scramble for concessions and spheres of influence, comparable in its rapidity and intensity to the earlier scramble for Africa. Thus, whereas for almost a century the situation had always been that of the European powers cooperating with one another at the least Chinese provocation, now the possibility of a clash between the main rivals – namely Britain, Germany and Russia, and to a lesser extent France and the United States – became less and less remote.

Although Japan had provoked the scramble, initially she was still not considered one of the major powers by the West, the Triple Intervention having served as ample proof of this. However, matters began to change in 1900 when Japan joined the Western powers in the crushing of the Boxer uprising in North China. (The 'Boxers' were members of a xenophobic secret society – in fact named 'The Society of Harmonious Fists', hence dubbed the 'Boxers' – who staged a violent rebellion directed both against Westerners and Westernised Chinese. They were unmercifully crushed by the combined forces of the Western powers and Japan.) Increasingly it became apparent to the West that Japan was not prepared to rest on her laurels, but that her victory only encouraged her to greater exploits. Japan thus contributed to this international rivalry when in 1904 she attempted to stake an important claim for herself in East Asia. The main obstacle to Japan's ambitions in 1904 was Russia. Japan's victory over Russia, however, fundamentally altered the balance of power in the Far East and ultimately in the West. To say that the outcome of the Russo–Japanese war caused the outbreak of the First World War and later the Russian Revolution would be a gross exaggeration; that it precipitated these two events would appear indisputable.

Finally, *The Times* had noted one more significant feature of this war: 'It is really the contest of two civilisations, and in this lies, perhaps, its profoundest interest to the observer. For the first time an Asiatic Power confronts a European Power on equal terms and with equal weapons . . .'[3] At the time, especially so far as other Asians were concerned, this was its profoundest significance. That a yellow people could defeat a white people in a major war was contrary to all accepted laws of nature and of history. The Japanese victory was to give a great boost to the morale of nationalist movements in India, Vietnam, China, and elsewhere in the colonised world. But to many Europeans as well, the racial factors in this war had very grave implications.

Attitudes to race were fraught with emotion. As a result racial theories harboured numerous contradictions and inconsistencies, but they were nevertheless there, nevertheless real and widely accepted in the West. The Japanese, as has been seen, escaped the crueller denigrations suffered by most other Asians. Yet the condescending, paternalistic attitudes to the Japanese were obviously not untinged with feelings of white racial superiority. Japan's rise as a formidable military power was bound to provoke racial instincts. This Western obsession with race was based partly on unquestioned premises of white superiority, but these premises were in turn based on rising feelings of insecurity. Nothing gave greater credence to this view than the emergence of the concept of the yellow peril. For a race which unquestionably believed in its own superiority over others, the message here, nevertheless, seemed to stress vigilance. And it is no doubt with this thought in mind that Kaiser Wilhelm in 1895 sent his cousin Tsar Nicholas II a drawing by H. Knackfuss from a design by the Kaiser: the title was the 'Yellow Peril'. What precise form this yellow peril was to take was not quite clear. But the evocative image both catered to the emotion-ridden fears of many Westerners and stimulated them.

The drawing enjoyed wide circulation, being reproduced in numerous newspapers throughout Europe and serving as an illustration to numerous books. The 'peril' meant different things to different people: to some it was especially economic; to others it was more of a military peril, at its worst conjuring up dreams of hordes of Asians descending upon Europe ready to pillage, burn, rape – in other words, the destruction of European civilisation and the killing or enslaving of its populations. These are the sorts of nightmare that were conveyed in the Kaiser's allegorical drawing. Ten years after its first appearance, however, the prophesy of the drawing became much closer to a reality. To those who interpreted the defeat of Russia by Japan in 1905 as the fall of the first bastion on the periphery of European civilisation, the haunting spectre of the yellow peril had definitely begun its inexorable march to the centre of Western civilisation.

As we shall see, however, the yellow peril – prophesy-of-doom neurosis – was not a unanimous response in the West to Japan's victory. The impact of and response to Japan's war against Russia reflected in some measure the changing political situation in Europe; to the more politically, rather than racially, inclined, 'it is part of the irony of the situation that in this controversy the Asiatic Power represents the forces of civilising progress, and the European Power those of mechanical repression.'[4] For some, therefore, and particularly for the rising socialist, social-democratic and other progressive European political movements, Japan was seen not as the yellow peril, but as the yellow hope. Both reactions were, needless to say, based on false assumptions. That the Japan of 1905, for example, could be seen as a force for political progress, as a hero of the left, was absurd. Apart from political considerations, however, there were also preoccupations of national interest which varied from country to country. On the whole the 'establishments' of continental European countries favoured Russia, while their left wings either remained neutral or sided with Japan. In Britain sympathy for Japan transcended partisan political considerations. Japan, after all, was Britain's ally.

Indeed, *The Times*, which remained consistently pro-Japanese throughout the war, rarely missed an occasion for congratulating itself – and Britain – on having judged the situ-

ation in Japan accurately. According to its correspondent in
Tokyo the root of the problem lay in the world's ignorance of
Japan, as he explained in an article shortly after the outbreak
of the war:

The story of the last ten days must have fallen upon the
Western world with the rapidity of a tropical thunderstorm
– the whole world fair and smiling, except for the leaden
apprehension lurking in the atmosphere and the pillar of
dark cloud hovering above the horizon; that cloud which
the weatherwise refused to recognise as portending of the
coming storm. That is the trouble at the root of the present
situation – the past inability of the West to take Japan
seriously. . . . All this is due to the superficial study of Japan
which has characterised Western contact with it. We as a
nation alone appear to have formed a shrewder estimate of
the Power which had in Eastern waters a naval strength
superior to our own, and which at a pinch can put half-a-
million of men into the field. But for the rest, they still were
pleased to look upon the Japanese through the eyes of the
aesthetic penman, and thought of the nation as a people of
pretty dolls dressed in flowered silks and dwelling in paper
houses of the capacity of matchboxes. Even while Admiral
Togo was steering a given course in the Yellow Sea these
opinions were to be heard in the centres of the European
communities in Japan. The professional guide and the
tourist are responsible for much – they are responsible for
the fictitious picture which caricatured Japan until the 10th
of the present month [February 1904], when the truth
became known.

The correspondent dwelt in his concluding remarks on a
theme which did attract a considerable amount of attention
from Western observers: that the strength of Japan was due to
a fairly great extent to the patriotic fibre of her people.

I do not believe that there is a single home, shaded though it
may be with the proverbial cherry-tree, constructed as it
may be of tissue and tinder, but has made its monetary

sacrifice, over and above the forfeit of its manhood, to the national war chest. Such spontaneous and universal patriotism is extraordinary; up to the present the immediate requirements to supply the sinews of modern warfare have been found within the cluster of islands which in the East are topographically analogous to our own little cluster in the West. Yet there have been people – more, there have been nations – that have been foolish enough to believe that these people should not be taken seriously; that Japan is but one stupendous doll's house – a people to be toyed with, humoured when they are peevish, subdued by threats when they are disobedient. Little has Japanese patriotism been understood.[5]

Those who had long predicted the emergence of Japan as a rising power, and who had felt ignored, returned to the theme of the West's misconceptions of the country with increasing satisfaction as the war went on. Another theme, however, that some Westerners were clear-sighted enough to understand was that the yellow peril was but a speculation in Europe, whereas its converse, the 'white peril', was a reality in Asia. Sidney Gulick wrote a book entitled *The White Peril in the Far East: An Interpretation of the Russo–Japanese War*, in which he claimed that Japan's war against Russia was historically justifiable:

We talk about the possibility of Japan's arming and leading the yellow race in a conflict with the white, and we shudder over the woes which might come to us, should she do this. But do we consider the actual woes which the white man is today inflicting on the yellow man by his presence and by his methods, by his armies and his commerce?

Examples of the white peril were numerous and reaction against it perfectly understandable:

A conspicuous instance of this was the so-called opium war. England's opium trade with China today is but one form of the white peril. In Europe or America what people would view with indifference such treatment of its territory and its capital by an alien race as has been inflicted on China by the white man? And the danger to China is not past. It is but now reaching its culmination. For are not the nations of Europe definitely planning the division of China among themselves? . . . If the conclusions reached are true, are we not justified in calling the white man's presence in the Far East the 'white peril'? This, indeed, is the scourge of today. The white peril is the cause of the present war. The 'peace of the Far East', about which European diplomats have loved to talk, is not their real aim. They themselves are the cause of the turmoil and of the ruin, wrought by war at Port Arthur, and on the plains of Manchuria.

Such a view was naturally based on the assumption that Japan's interests in the East were altruistic in comparison with the wicked mercantile and military ambitions of the European powers. Gulick, and others like him, stressed, as a result, how normal it was for the Japanese to be inspired with a sentiment of revenge:

In all the treaty ports of Japan and China, the stories of the relations of the white man to the yellow are sickening and disheartening. The white man relying on the force of his fists and his guns, stirs the Asiatic into fierce desire for revenge.

The consequences of Japan's victory, according to Gulick, would stem the white peril:

Japanese victory in the present war will have weight. Those white men whose supreme ideal is might, will be inspired with respect for the Japanese, and respect modifies conduct. Japanese victory will also tend to restrain the white peril in its particularly aggressive form today.

On the question of the yellow peril, he was quite candid:

It is sometimes said that Japan's victory spells the imme- diate rise of the yellow peril. She will reorganise China's military power; and raising her to the standard of her own efficient financial, educational and governmental attainments, will make those four hundred million people invincible. And then combined, China and Japan will exploit the world. Victorious Japan, they say, means bumptious Japan, swaggering Japan, Japan with a 'big head'. All of which would signify discomfort and immediate danger to America and Europe. This in truth is the yellow peril feared by some. What of these fears and charges?

In the first place, if might makes right for the white man, why not for the yellow man? If Japan and China have the might, why should they not swagger and burn and kill and rule? We who are white have had the 'big head' badly for several centuries. Surely turn about would be but fair play.[6]

The well known and widely read French socialist novelist, Anatole France, echoed similar sentiments in his novel, *Sur la Pierre Blanche*. In the course of a discussion between the principal protagonists of the novel on the 'state of the world', one of them explained the Russo–Japanese conflict:

What the Russians are paying for at this very moment in the seas of Japan and in the gorges of Manchuria is not just their avid and brutal policy in the Orient, it is the colonial policy of all the European powers. What they are atoning for is not just their crimes, but the crimes of all military and commercial Christianity. I am not suggesting here that there is justice in this world. But one does witness strange turnabouts; and might, still the only judge of human actions, at times makes unexpected jumps. Its sudden turns upset a balance we thought stable. And its games, which are never without some hidden rule, bring about interesting matches. The Japanese cross the Yalu, and with precision beat the Russians in Manchuria. In the same way, their navy annihilates a European fleet. At once we discern a danger threatening us. If it exists, who has created it? It was not the Japanese who came looking for the Russians. It is not the yellows who sought the whites. Today we discover the yellow peril. The Asiatics have been living with the white peril for quite some time. The sacking of the Summer Palace, the massacres of Peking, the drownings of Blagovetchensk, the slicing up of China, were these not cause for worry to the Chinese? And had the Japanese any reason to feel secure from the guns of Port Arthur? We have created the white peril. It is those sequences of age-old Necessity which give to the world an impression of divine Justice and one cannot help but admire that blind queen of men and gods, when one sees Japan, so cruel to the Koreans and Chinese in the past, Japan, accomplice to European crimes in China, become the avenger of China and the hope of the Yellow Race.

It would not appear to be the case, however, that the yellow peril terrifying European economists is comparable to the white peril hanging over Asia. The Chinese do not send to Paris, Berlin or St Petersburg missionaries to teach Christians the *fung-chui* and cause general chaos in European affairs. A Chinese expeditionary corps has not gone down the bay of Quiberon to extract from the Republic the right of extraterritoriality, i.e. the right to have a case between Chinese and Europeans brought before a tribunal of mandarins. Admiral Togo did not come with a dozen battleships to bombard the roadstead of Brest in order to help Japanese commerce in France. The flower of French nationalism, the elite of our Trouble-mongers, have not laid siege to the Chinese and Japanese legations and marshal Oyama has not, as reprisal, brought the combined forces of the Far East down our boulevards demanding the execution of our xenophobic trouble-mongers.* He has not burned down Versailles in the name of a great civilisation. The armies of the Asiatic powers have not taken to Tokyo or Peking the paintings of the Louvre or the china of the Elysée.

Anatole France was writing before the end of the war and, though not certain of its outcome, he was confident of Japan's 'mission':

I do not know what will be the outcome of this war. The Russian Empire uses its indeterminate forces, compromised by the ferocious stupidity of its government, wasted by the

* The reference here is to the Boxer Uprising.

dishonesty of its administration, lost by the ineptness of its military command against the methodical energy of the Japanese. It has shown the extent of its impotence and the depth of its disorganisation. Nevertheless its financial reserves, fed by rich creditors, are almost inexhaustible. Its enemy on the other hand has no other resources than difficult and onerous loans, which their very victories will deprive them of. For the English and the Americans intend to help Japan weaken Russia, but not to help her become a great and formidable power. One cannot predict the victory of one of the belligerents over the other. But if Japan makes the yellow race respectable to the white race, she will have greatly served the cause of humanity and as a result paved the way, albeit against her own wishes, to the peaceful organisation of the world . . .

One fears that 'grown-up' Japan will educate China; that it will teach her to defend herself and exploit her riches. One fears Japan will make China strong. One should not fear this, but positively hope for it for the sake of universal peace. Strong nations contribute to the harmony and richness of the world. Weak ones, like China and Turkey, are a perpetual source of trouble and danger.

Japan's mission of revenge as the great yellow hope against the white peril would extend to the European colonies in Asia:

'But if the Japanese were victorious,' he said, 'they would eventually take Indo–China away from us.' 'It would be a great service they would be offering us. Colonies are the scourge of the masses.'[7]

Opposition to colonialism on moral or political grounds was rising in some quarters in Europe. One of the most outspoken organs of anticolonialism was the weekly *Justice*, edited by Henry Hyndman– founder of the British Social Democratic Federation – which among other things had actively campaigned against the Boer War. In an article published a few days after the outbreak of hostilities, *Justice*'s position in regard to the conflict and the expectations it derived from it were made abundantly clear:

All who hold, therefore, as we hold, that Asiatics have a perfect right to work out their own destinies untrammelled by unscrupulous European civilisation; all who hold, as we hold, that a further extension in China, of the infamies of Russian rule in Asia and in Europe, or, for that matter, of the infamies of British rule in India, would be most injurious to mankind, must necessarily wish well to Japan in the coming struggle.

. . . all Social Democrats must long to see the exhaustion of Russia in any event. Let the Muscovite despotism once be shaken in earnest, whether by defeat or costly victory, and a new era opens up before that great country and its European neighbours. Moreover I hope that the result of this war will be to awaken China in earnest too. I hope that the people of that great and ancient civilisation, encouraged and enlightened by Japanese example and Japanese leadership, will, ere long, make a clean sweep of the Russian, French, German, English and other marauders who wish to break down her Empire and dominate her peaceful and industrious population. That is what I hope. We have had in our day, it seems to me, enough of the loathsome hypocrisy of our ruinous and baleful capitalist proselytism. It is high time for us English Social–Democrats, therefore, in common with our fellows of other nationalities, to declare against the policy of buccaneering commercialism and blood-sucking Christianity in the Far East, and to claim for Asiatics, as for Europeans, the right to work out their own destinies in their own way.[8]

The position of European socialists on the Russo–Japanese conflict was an interesting, indeed paradoxical, one. To begin with, the pacifist programme of the European socialist movement proved a great stumbling-block so far as the attitude of its members towards Japan was concerned. It appeared difficult, therefore, at least in the first instance, to come out actively in favour of a belligerent. In fact many hesitated; some remained pacifist throughout. In Paris, for example, a meeting of socialists in early 1904 condemned both belligerents and then proceeded to set up a relief fund for wounded on both sides.

But to others the issues at stake were so high that they rallied round the Japanese cause. Even Jean Jaurès, one of the more outspoken pacifists, admitted that though he would not actively back Japan he wished for Japanese victory, now that war was under way. What European socialists ignored, or chose to ignore, however, was that the country they began to hail as a great crusader – the yellow hope – was, at the same time as waging war on Russia, carrying out a ruthless campaign against its own socialists. Japanese socialists, in particular Kōtoku Shūsui, were opposed to Japan's war against Russia. The Japanese socialist organ, *Heimin Shinbun*, appealed to socialists throughout the world to unite against the war. Eventually, for their pains, Kōtoku and a number of his comrades were to hear of the rest of the war from behind bars. As the war progressed, and in Japan's favour, the momentum among Western socialists supporting Japan increased and so did the Japanese government's determination to imprison its dissident pacifist socialists. The anti-war appeals lodged by the *Heimin Shinbun* appeared in Western newspapers, but for some reason they seem to have been ignored by many Western socialists. Henry Hyndman, in particular, remained a fervent supporter of Japan. The war leading to Japanese victory, according to his view, would have the most beneficial repercussions in Asia.

> The late Sir Louis Malet, for many years Permanent Under-Secretary of State for India, said to me in 1879: 'We shall have to see a revolution in England, Mr. Hyndman, before we get justice to India'. I used to think so myself. I am not so sure now. Even this splendid move of Japan will have some influence. There is not an educated Asiatic living who will not feel heartened and encouraged by what the Japanese are doing and have done. I hope their pluck and success will breathe new life and hope into the oppressed and starved millions upon millions of British India.

So far our study of the yellow hope and its influence has been restricted mainly to Asia, what Japan would do for the Asiatics. But for the oracles of the yellow hope Japan also had an important mission to accomplish in Europe: namely the destruction of absolutist and oppressive Russian Tsarism. As Hyndman exclaimed, 'One of the chief reasons why we are favourable to Japan is because we are friends to the Russian people and hate the Russian Government. The breakdown of existing Russian rule in Europe and in Asia will benefit mankind. Russian patriots wish well to Japan.'[9] For many anti-Tsarists, whether Russian or not, Japan herself was not so important; it was the result in Russia that mattered. British and French socialists, including Hyndman, Jaurès, Anatole France and Jules Guesde, welcomed the war since they felt it would herald the downfall of the Tsarist state. It is known that Russian revolutionaries cooperated with the Japanese and, among other things, were instrumental in letting the Japanese know the route of the Baltic fleet as it advanced towards its awaiting destiny in the Tsushima straits. Lenin and Trotsky were two who expressed satisfaction at the course events were taking.

There was another group of people, however, whose admiration for the Japanese went far beyond mere consideration of what Japan could or could not do to Russian Tsarism. Henry Dyer, for example, saw much greater universal implications in Japan's struggle:

> Since the outbreak of this war, as well as during the period of suspense that preceded it, the quiet self-possessed attitude of the Japanese people has been a theme of constant admiration and surprise to foreign onlookers, and has been described in eulogistic terms by foreign journalists. In truth, the country is just as it has always been. The Japanese people are not swayed by any frenzy of revenge or fired by any heat of territorial ambition. They are fighting for what they believe to be the minimum of their just right; for the cause of free institutions; the cause of security against the spread of military despotism; the cause of a commercial field untrammelled for all, and the cause of lasting peace: causes which they have fervently embraced and for which they are ready to make any sacrifice. Under such circumstances this war has not impaired in the slightest degree the friendly

feeling entertained by the Japanese nation for the peoples of Europe and America. On the contrary, it has greatly intensified that feeling, inasmuch as the crisis has elicited throughout nearly the whole of the Occident expressions of sympathy with Japan, which she welcomes with profound gratitude and satisfaction. She appreciates that the purpose for which she is shedding blood and treasure have the full endorsement of the enlightened nations of the West, and she sees that by lending her whole strength to the promotion of those purposes, she has drawn greatly closer the bonds of amity between herself and the Occident.[10]

Japan's historical transformation, according to Gulick, would herald in its wake a better world:

From being the most secluded and self-sufficient people of the earth, Japan has advanced to the forefront of progressive open-mindedness. The white peril so long feared has proved to be the very tonic and stimulus required to place her in the advance guard of progressive nations. She now takes her part in doing the world's work and seeks, in ways at once wise, humane, just and powerful, to restrain the greedy aggressor and to build up the weak and backward.[11]

The news of Japan's victory brought mixed feelings. To those who relished Japan's advance against Russia as sounding the death bell of the Tsarist regime the end was premature. Thus *Justice* declared:

We are not of those who receive the news of peace between Russia and Japan with unmixed and uncritical gratification. Certainly war is a frightful thing . . . Nevertheless a peace which is merely temporary would be worse than the continuance of the war. Should that prove to be the case with the Peace of Portsmouth, then it would have been far better never to have entered upon negotiations until Linievitch's army had been completely crushed by the overwhelming forces of Oyama. Such talk as we have heard lately from the Russian side has scarcely been encouraging, and those who are most eager to see the new Russia take her rightful place in the world must feel doubtful about any Treaty which even partially saves the old Muscovite reactionism from final defeat and humiliation. That has been our view from the very first. We see no reason to change it now. Convinced that Japan would worst the Great Russian Empire on land and on sea – though none could possibly have foreseen the unchecked career of victory on both elements by which the Japanese have astonished mankind – we welcomed the prospect, and the realisation of this overthrow even more for the effect it would have upon Europe than that which it must have upon Asia. If now, as many of our Russian comrades believe, the conclusion of peace or the continuance of war equally makes for a revolution in Russia proper then from this point of view peace is preferable. If, also, the Japanese, having gained, as they have gained, all for which they took up arms, are satisfied that, by arrangements with China and by an extended alliance with Great Britain, they have so secured the position in the Far East that further aggression by Russia, or further development of the White Peril in that region is impossible; . . . then, unquestionably, peace today with certainty of a long period for re-organisation and re-cuperation, is better than peace eighteen months hence, after still more expenditure and national exhaustion. Russia has been shaken, probably for a century, as an aggressive Power. Asia has been placed in quite a new light before the world. The future of Japan is assured. The integrity of China is practically beyond attack, after certain marauders have been removed. All this is a stupendous result for an 18 months war.

The article concluded in writing Russia's epitaph and cheering the murderer:

With all that the Russian debacle is complete. Her power in Asia is gone for ever, whilst her activity in Europe as a 'great' Power, is paralysed for a quarter of a century. We can only rejoice at that. No longer will Russia play the European gendarme, and no longer will William and his precious allies, the French chauvinists, find in her a source of strength. The 'yellow peril' has done that, and to the 'yellow peril' we offer three cheers. May it continue to grow and gather strength, and ultimately drive the whole of the 'white salvation' bag and baggage out of Asia! Long has it suffered from that 'salvation' unspeakable insults and horrible injury – we hope the day of reckoning is not far off.

Whether due to prescience or pure chance *Justice* saw the contradiction and frailty of the Anglo–Japanese alliance, renewed and extended in 1905 before the end of hostilities:

> One word of conclusion. Great Britain has an offensive and defensive alliance on a wider basis than ever with an Asiatic Power now of the first rank. This deliberate derogation from the prestige of the white man is supposed, in some inscrutable fashion, to strengthen our hold upon India and the East. For us who cry boldly, 'Asia for the Asiatics', and 'India for the Indians', such incredible fatuity is thoroughly welcome. The rise of Japan will, ere long, mean the end of our rule of mean despotism and infamous famine-manufacture in Hindostan.

Nor did *Justice* fail to see that, in spite of the apparent friendship which Japan presently enjoyed with Britain and the United States, it could not last:

> Japan has concluded peace, having renounced her claim for an indemnity. All the world is struck by her 'generosity', and encomiums, one louder than the other, are poured out on her hapless head. Japan has come to the end of her financial resources, and her English and American friends have left her in the lurch. The Moor, to quote Schiller, has done his duty, the Moor can go. It is not in the interest of England that Russia be so weakened as to yield the military dictatorship in Europe to Germany, nor is it in the interest of America that Japan should grow so strong as to gain the total supremacy on the Pacific. Hence the gentle pressure on Japan, and – the moral hysterics.[12]

But these protestations and forebodings for the future were a minority view in Britain. It would seem rather that the general atmosphere was one of admiration for the Japanese, not only for their valour but also for their magnanimity whether in war or peace. *The Times* expressed great praise for the Japanese on the way the war had been both fought and won:

> To-day the tremendous conflict which for more than eighteen months has engrossed the attention of the world is transferred from the category of the present to the category of the past. It is still too soon to pass upon it the final judgement of history. Many of its details are hidden from us, and its lessons cannot be fully grasped and appreciated until the requisite *data* are known. But we have seen enough to feel assured that, in many of its most vital features, this war transcends all other wars of modern times. We have seen an Oriental people, which has made its way into the comity of nations within the last three decades, meet one of the most formidable military Powers of the Old World with its own weapons, and inflict on it an unbroken series of crushing defeats. That, on the whole, is the first and most abiding impression left by the war – the absolutely uninterrupted course of victory which has rewarded the Japanese arms. One searches in vain through modern warfare to find a parallel to these extraordinary successes, lasting over so long a period and gained with equal decisiveness by land and sea. Oyama's record and Togo's would be sufficiently remarkable, if each stood by itself; taken together, they constitute an achievement unprecedented in its completeness. . . . These results have been attained by a people whose civilisation, measured by European standards, was still medieval at the date of the battle of Königgrätz [1866]. . . .
>
> So much Japan owes to the courage, endurance, and devotion of her people, and to the brilliant leadership which, whether on sea or land, has always led her troops to victory. She makes peace in the hour when she had every reason to expect further and still greater success. Never has a belligerent been placed in a position where he could better

163

afford to show magnanimity; never has a peace been more clearly the fruit of that virtue, and not of weakness or faint-heartedness.

Japan's war against Russia may well have been spectacular and decisive, but it was expensive both in human and financial terms. The statements above regarding Japan's magnanimity and generosity in peace refer to the victorious power's decision not to demand an indemnity at the peace conference – whereas extracting an indemnity from the vanquished was a normal custom. In fact there is a considerable amount of hypocrisy involved here. Initially the Japanese government had both wanted and expected an indemnity; as to the Japanese people, they were so certain that an important and much-needed indemnity would be obtained that when the provisions of the Treaty of Portsmouth were made known, and that these excluded an indemnity, severe rioting broke out in Tokyo and other urban centres. The Russians refused steadfastly to consider even the possibility of an indemnity, let alone haggle over the sum. The Japanese government wisely realised that it could not push hostilities any further as the expenditures of the war effort had practically emptied the coffers. But the role of the friendly powers, and particularly Japan's ally, was displeasing to the Japanese and to some a reminder of the ten-year-old Triple Intervention. It was felt that, although no protestations had been made when Japan demanded an indemnity from China, now even those so-called friendly powers could not countenance the victorious Oriental exacting an indemnity from the defeated White. *The Times* sought to justify the non-indemnity provision by heaping praise on the 'generosity' and 'magnanimity' of the Japanese:

Borne upon the flowing tide of victory and ready to strike with a heavier hand and a more assured prospect of success than ever, she has renounced her claim for an indemnity and taken the burden upon her own shoulders. Her old chivalrous spirit has led her to disdain the prosecution of war for merely monetary considerations. Her Sons have shed their blood freely for their country and for their Sovereign. By the

Samurai tradition their laurels would be tarnished were they now bidden to fight for gold.[13]

But perhaps the last word on the matter should be left to Lord Redesdale (A. B. Mitford), who, in a letter to *The Times*, wrote: 'Sir, The World stands amazed at the magnanimity of the Japanese. . . . Various epithets have been given to Kings and Conquerors. We have had Philip the Handsome, William the Conqueror, Ivan the Terrible. Perhaps the reign of the present Emperor of Japan will be known in history as the reign of Mutsuhito the Generous.'[14]

Western feelings about and reactions to the momentous events taking place in the Far East were mixed. While many rejoiced for whatever reason, many others expressed alarm. But in all instances one feeling that was shared was amazement over the speed and unpredictability of the course of history:

When in the month of February 1854 the American Commodore Perry, at the head of a small fleet, forced open the doors of Japan, hermetically sealed for more than two centuries, and Occidental nations began sending their ships, their consuls, their merchants, certainly no one could have predicted in what a strange way the fiftieth anniversary of this event would be celebrated. At that time the warriors with two swords, picturesque but impotent, had had to bow before the menace of three frigates and four sloops, and open, with rage in their hearts, the doors of their country to the 'barbarians' whose mores, customs and ideas they abhorred. Today, barely fifty years later, the sons of these same samurai, having imported all the techniques of production and destruction of the Occident, not satisfied merely with competing with European commerce in the markets of Asia and elsewhere, dare measure their strength against the vastest empire of the world, whose modern war fleet torpedoes their battleships and bombards their fortresses. One can understand why Europe is baffled by this extraordinary adventure and by the excellent students it had not expected to form. We must not be surprised if from now on we must take account of these Yellow people whom we have roused from slumber and forced out of isolation.[15]

To some the writing had been on the wall for a few years; they stressed vigilance on the part of Europe. One correspondent to *The Times* must surely have appeared prophetic a few years after his letter was published. He was commenting on certain problems raised by the allied expedition against the Boxers in China. At the time of his letter a commander-in-chief of the allied troops had yet to be named and as usual there was bickering among the different nationalities involved as to which of the nations the commander should hail from. As the Japanese were supplying the most numerous force, certain quarters felt the commander should be Japanese. In an impassioned letter, the correspondent rejected this view and raised more concerns:

Sir, – The attitude taken by the Japanese Government in the present crisis in China appears to me to be worthy of all praise; but there is a danger lest we should allow our admiration and sympathy for this fascinating and energetic people to lead us into playing their game to our own peril.

No student of the problems of the Far East can fail to see that sooner or later Manchuria and the extreme north of China must fall under the dominion of one of two powers, Russia or Japan. Let us hope that it be not under that of Japan. It must be remembered that barely a quarter of a century has lapsed since Japan was murdering foreigners with as wild a fanaticism and as unreasoning a cruelty as China. True, in that interval she has donned a veneer of Western civilisation. But how deep does it go? Can the leopard have changed his spots so quickly? The words Daimio, Samurai, Ronin have disappeared in to the limbo of the past. But the Yamato Damashi, the spirit of old Japan, by which the men who bore those titles were fired, has that died too? Is the volcano extinct or only slumbering? – a knotty question for the professor of political seismology to solve. The national character of Japan is restless, ambitious, and aggressive in the highest degree. Her statesmen were clever enough to see thirty years ago that it was only by adopting the science and civilisation of the West that she could hope to take her place among the nations, and so at one leap she bounded from the 13th into the 19th century, from the darkness of the feudal system into the light of a constitutional government. No sooner did she feel herself armed than she picked a quarrel with China about Korea that she might put her newly found strength to the test. We all know the result. She conquered; but her great ambition, the ambition to become military leader of a vast Manchu–Chinese–Japanese league, or even nation, was foiled by European diplomacy [the Triple Intervention of 1895]. At the present moment it would almost seem as if circumstances were bringing the coveted prize once more within her reach.

Japan is spoken of as the principal factor in the relief of Peking, and this on account of her proximity to the scene of disturbance. Is Japan really so important in this crisis as some people appear to think, and as she herself would have us believe? At any rate, there can be no justification for giving her a leading part. For the forces of the allied Powers to be placed under the orders of a Japanese commander-in-chief appears to me, as it must to all who know the East, a proposition which no responsible statesman could seriously entertain. If we want peace in the future, it is to Russia, and not to Japan, that we should look for the civilisation of the North of China. Since a change there must be, let Peking be a Russian city – never again a Chinese capital . . . To drive the hated white man out of Asia is the dream of every Asiatic ambition. To this end neither China by herself nor Japan by herself is formidable. But a combination of the two? Although it seemed hard at the time, the Powers were well advised to possess herself of the Leao-Tung peninsula. Once given Japan a foothold on the continent of Asia, place her in command of the countless hordes of Tartars and Chinese (the best of fighting material), drilled and licked into shape by her marvellous power of organisation and her military instinct, and you will have given shape and substance to that yellow terror which was the phantasm of the German Emperor's too prophetic nightmare. You will have conjured into existence a disturbing force that may alter the map of Asia, if not of the world.[16]

As it turned out the question of the nationality of the commander-in-chief was easily solved by a fortuitous event, namely the assassination by the Boxers of the German head of legation. Thus, with due deference for the death of one man, his compatriots were permitted to select the one who would take command over the annihilation of those responsible. Nevertheless, for the 'yellow perilists', this correspondent to *The Times* gave vent to many of the nightmares to which events five years later seemed to give credence.

No doubt one of the most terrifying aspects of this important turning point in history was the terrible fear of the unknown:

The extreme remoteness of the field of battle, the sheer dimensions of a war in which two great states, one of them European, meet in conflict; the seemingly endless railway at whose limit the drama is taking place; the country itself, with its barbaric names which our lips have difficulty even in pronouncing; the savage races, Manchus and Mongols, who in the past, with their *Inflexible Emperor* (Genghis Khan), were the conquerors of the world and who now suddenly reappear on the stage; even the landscape where the action takes place, where trains move over ice and towards which, on moonless nights, destroyers glide silently – everything the actors, the stakes and the setting – contributes to emphasise the gripping image this war has produced on all the peoples of Europe from its very first hour. A conflict in the Balkans, though much closer to us, would strike the imagination less; there, in the classical domain of diplomatic complications, everything is foreseen, calculated in advance. In the East, though, what we see is the preparation of some mysterious destiny whose menace worries and fascinates. The inscrutable enigma of the yellow soul adds to everything we hear of the Far East something of the shudder man feels in front of secrets he cannot penetrate: the Romans must have felt something analogous before the fathomless depths of Barbarity.[17]

What made present events all the more unpalatable to one German writer, Baron von Falkenegg, was that this terrifying yellow menace had arisen largely as a result of the stupidity of Europeans themselves:

Our attitude towards the Chinese and Japanese was so lacking in logic and understanding of the natural tendencies, the historical development and the dangerous aspirations of the Mongolians. . . . And the Japanese, 'the little Japs', were regarded from above as little schoolboys, quick to learn, who, we assumed, once returned to their idyllic Nippon, would obtain from the West, for domestic consumption, all those nice little European gadgets, from cannons to the bicycle, and who would always look up obediently and respectfully to their masters.

We revealed to them all the mysteries of our civilisation, showed them round all our factories and workshops and laboratories, let them look behind the scenes of the most sophisticated methods of manufacture, and were delighted when the cute, polite little people, who looked so harmless, left with a pleasant smile. We were deluded, so future historians will judge.

Are we to imagine that the Japanese would have revealed even the smallest part of the achievements of their civilisation to the foreigners, the 'foreign devils', if they had been in possession of fighting techniques superior to those of the West?

No, but a thousand times no!

But the Europeans, disregarding the consequences, have armed the hand which one day will fill them with terror.[18]

The spectrum of opinion on the yellow peril in 1904–5 ranged from a predatory view of yellow hordes descending on the West to more specific attacks on the Japanese. An Englishman, Crosland, alarmed by the apparent blindness of his compatriots, urged a more realistic view of the Japanese:

A stunted, lymphatic, yellow-faced heathen, with a mouthful of teeth three sizes too big for him, bulging slits where his eyes ought to be, blacking-brush hair, a foolish giggle, a cruel heart, and the conceit of the devil – this, O bemused reader, is the authentic dearly-beloved 'Little Jap' of commerce, the fire-eater out of the Far East, and the ally, if you please, of John Bull, Esquire, the omnipotent.

Since the beginning of the Russo–Japanese war what have you not heard about him? His 'pluck', his 'heroism', his 'amazing adaptability', his 'unparalleled zeal', and 'energy', his 'unquenchable patriotism', not to mention the general lovableness of his disposition, have been held up for your unreserved admiration by every newspaper in the kingdom. The ha'penny papers have vied with one another in the invention of endearing epithets for him – 'little Jappy Atkins', 'little Jap Tar' . . . And the people who call themselves caricaturists have done him up in the most favourable guises, and always with his pagan foot upon the neck of Russia.

. . . The English love of fair play prompts him to stand by and applaud. . . . 'Go it, my darling, little Jap! Remember always that you have the moral support of the greatest, honestest, and most Christian nation in the world! Let 'em have it hot! Give 'em hell, in fact! We never could have done it ourselves, and we never really believed that you could do it. But wonders refuse to cease. Give 'em hell!'

. . . It is a grave question whether Japan with her marvellous gifts of imitation, her extraordinary energy, her cunning rapidity, and her total want of conscience is in the least likely to become 'a world power' of the kind that Europe is likely to find useful or satisfactory. Indeed the only restraints that could be put upon her are the restraints of the Christian religion. Can she be brought to submit to them? Does she desire in her heart to submit to them? Will she ever be other than pagan and heathen and cruel and unconscionable under the surface? The answer is No.

. . . When Japan builds an arsenal, or invents a new smokeless powder, or a new projectile, we must remember that it is not as though the things had been done by a European power. An instinctive appreciation of the recognised rule of war and the spirit of Christian civilisation that should be behind it are in all probability not there. During the course of her campaign against Russia, Japan has sagaciously put on all the appearance of a civilised nation. That is to say, she has treated her foe in the manner approved by the European peoples. But she does not beat Russia in every encounter on her military superiority alone. She beats Russia because her ranks are packed with men who would rip themselves up rather than suffer defeat, and to whom life is not a matter worth a moment's consideration. They are men, in fact, who believe themselves to be without souls. That they are careful to respect the usage of civilised armies is because they hold it to be expedient so to do.

At the moment they are desperately in need of the moral support which has been extended to them by the English. But let them beat Russia, and be allowed to possess themselves of the legitimate spoils of war, let them proceed with their civilisation, assisted at both elbows by the indulgence and cupidity of Europe, let them become really recognised as a properly-established world-power, and if there be anything at all in the primal instincts, we are pretty sure to see sights.[19]

The theme of Christian versus heathen was bound to loom large in the writings of the 'yellow perilists'. In the Kaiser's drawing of the yellow peril, the peril was represented as Buddha, while the caption read: 'Nations of Europe! Join in the defence of your faith and your home.' By the beginning of May 1905, with the prospect of Russia's defeat almost certain, the Kaiser felt obliged to comment on the implications of recent events. He was reported in the *Evangelische Kirchenzeitung* as having

> attributed the Japanese victories to patriotism, family affection, and discipline, but he added that the fact that these victories had been won by a heathen over a Christian nation did not warrant the conclusion that Buddha was superior to Jesus Christ. If Russia had been defeated it was, in his opinion, due to the fact that Russian Christianity must be in a very sad condition, while the Japanese exhibited many

Christian virtues. A good Christian meant a good soldier, but unhappily, Christianity among the German people was also in a bad way, and he doubted whether in the event of a war 'we Germans had any longer the right to ask God for victory and to wrestle in prayer with Him for this favour like Jacob with the angel'. The Japanese were a 'scourge of God' like Attila . . . It was the business of the Germans to see to it that God should not one day have to chastise them with a scourge of that kind.[20]

What then was the nature of this scourge? Most 'perilists' did not isolate Japan as a single factor; the really terrifying – and to some inevitable– spectre was the alliance of Asian nations under Japan. Japan would first organise China and then move on to South and South-East Asia, until ultimately all of the East would confront the West:

In the last few weeks the development of public opinion in the different countries of the civilised world has shown, how under the influence of events in the Far East, the conscious-ness of people is reforming itself– a notion which, in Europe, had begun to weaken, even to disappear, the notion of an enemy outside threatening to destroy their civilisation and their lives. Little by little, as events develop, as the conflict grows and threatens to extend itself to China, the people, regardless of their preferences in the first instance, are be-coming alarmed at the future consequences of this stupen-dous upheaval in the yellow world. The oracles may well ask whether there is a 'yellow peril'; public opinion believes there is; it fears these Asiatic revolutions which in times past threw on to the Occident successive waves of barbaric invasions; it notes that each time Europe has come into con-tact with the Far East, the result has been bloody episodes and new advances of the 'yellows' in armaments and in their hatred of 'foreigners'. Whether one likes it or not, the 'yellow peril' has entered already into the imagination of the people, just as represented in the famous drawing of the Emperor William II: in a setting of conflagration and carn-age, Japanese and Chinese hordes spread out over all

Europe, crushing under their feet the ruins of our capital cities and destroying our civilisations, grown anaemic due to the enjoyment of luxuries and corrupted by vanity of spirit. Hence, little by little there emerges the idea that even if a day must come (and that day does not seem near) when the European peoples will cease to be their own enemies and even economic rivals, there will still be a struggle ahead to face and there will rise a new peril, the yellow man. The civilised world has always organised itself before and against a common adversary: for the Roman world, it was the Barbarian; for the Christian world, it was Islam; for the world of tomorrow, it may well be the 'yellow man'. And so we have the reappearance of this necessary concept, without which peoples do not know themselves, just as the 'Me' only takes conscience of itself in opposition to the 'non-Me': the enemy.[21]

And, they stressed, this enemy was not an unknown quantity. This time it was the Japanese, but in reality the Oriental soul was always the same; the danger confronting the West from the East in the beginning of the twentieth century was not significantly different from that which had faced Europe in centuries past. The history of the West was fraught with bloody encounters with the East. Again and again Europe had had to repel Asian invasions to safeguard its civilisation. So, argued the 'perilists', Europe once again was facing aggression from the East. The West should have been much quicker in realising the danger that it would have to confront, argued Baron von Falkenegg, one of the more alarmed 'perilists'.

The European powers should have realised in good time, that the cunning, skilled and valiant Japanese people would soon be uttering the slogan 'Asia for the Asians'.

And we were still further deluded. Even today there are thousands of Europeans, supposedly educated in historical matters, who are rejoicing wildly over the victory of Japan over Russia. But they are not well educated historically, and do not see that in Manchuria, not Russia, but Europe was beaten.

173

But those whom the Gods wish to destroy, they make blind.

The idea of world power is not confined to the Caucasian race alone; the Mongoloids can also refer in their history to the fact that they several times succeeded in shaking the Western world in its foundations, and that three times they came near to establishing a powerful world empire – under Attila, Genghis Khan and Tamerlane.

As soon as the Mongoloids were set in a belligerent direction, they always showed the fighting characteristics for which we use the French expression *élan* – they knew no retreat, even when the bodies piled as high as hills. Exactly like the Japanese. Here, as there, we find that uncanny, wild bravery, incomprehensible to the European mind, which sets the value of the individual at naught.

The clever Japanese, with the knowledgeable Mikado at their head, have enough understanding of historical matters to interpret Mongoloid history, and from this understanding to draw the conclusion that as soon as the mighty will of an energetic ruler set in motion the elementary nationalist fervour of the Mongoloid people, they were irresistible.

With the increasing success of the Japanese, might not the idea have taken root in the mind of Emperor Mutsuhito that he was destined by Providence to lead Japan to a high position of world power, far superior to that of the West?

To the Japanese, victory over Russia means victory over Europe.

From Seoul, the Capital of the Land of the Morning Calm, to Bangkok, the capital of Siam, word is spreading fast of the invincibility of Japan, the most important power in Asia, the leader of all Asia. 'Asia for the Asians' has become the slogan in Japan, and is directed at all those Europeans who want to take political and commercial advantage in Asia.

But for the Japanese, 'Asia for the Asians' has the obvious implication, 'Japan dominates Asia, and Asia dominates Europe'.

Japan is beginning to think of herself as the centre of the world, as the Land of the Chosen People. A new nation is awakening in world history, and like a *Mene Tekel Upharsin* we can read into these fantastic thoughts of the Japanese the words, 'Thou art weighted in the balances, and art found wanting; we are taking your place; dismiss!' For what is nearer now than the thought that Japan after such pleasing success in Russia, no longer has any respect for any European power? For indeed, to these European states the Russian 'Colossus with Feet of Clay' appeared to be the *non plus ultra* of military strength and prowess. As far as Japanese conviction of her military supremacy is concerned, and as regards her self esteem, which has been engendered and supported by the logic of the facts, even Germany is no exception. Unfortunately, so I say as a German, but that does not help, to close one's eyes to the force of events would be stupidity. The Japanese must, by reason of their success and their skills (for their successes were no accidental victories!) consider themselves to be the first military power in the world.

Their teachings of an ethical nature, such as their *Bushido*, and their secret art of the development of physical strength, *Ju-jitsu*, give us a rough idea of what might go on in the minds of the Japanese when they compare themselves with Europeans.

To express it in a word, the Japanese consider themselves to be a thoroughly masculine people, whereas most Western nations, especially those above all, on whom, in any conflict with the Mongoloid races, everything will depend, have, without exception, become 'feminine'; that is, the Japanese have absolutely manly aspirations, and allow themselves to be influenced only by strong, masculine thoughts; the people of Europe are mostly dependent on feminine and womanly influences; they are imitators and degenerates.

The Japanese is manly and strong in matters which affect the fatherland and national feeling – where decisions are made, Mars is in the ascendancy, Venus and her erotic companions must be silent. Japanese policy, supported by the power of success, can only have one aim in sight; Asia for the Asians, or, more so, Asia for the East-Asians, at whose head stand the Japanese, who only need to re-organise vast, densely-populated China, to become ruler of the world. The 55 million Japanese at the head of the 400 million Chinese, whom the former will arm and fill with enthusiasm for war – now feel called to the forefront of the world powers, and to dictate the law to Asia, and perhaps also to Europe. *Videant consules!*[22]

The alarmists could not fathom another course than that which must, by the nature of things, join all Asians together in a common crusade against the West under the leadership of Japan. To some, even after Japan had defeated Russia at Port Arthur, Japan alone was not the danger. The real yellow peril consisted of a much more formidable spectacle, as explained by one of the 'perilists':

In China, news of the triumph of Oyama and Togo, announced in the newspapers, with comments from Japanese agents operating in the very depths of provinces still closed to foreigners, has created an incredible stir the consequences of which only the future will show. In Annam and in the whole French empire of Indo–China . . . the government has had to forbid the entry of Chinese newspapers, often edited by Japanese, which were commenting on the fall of Port Arthur and the defeat of Europeans with too much satisfaction and excited the natives to revolt. In Siam, the ruling aristocracy, threatened in its privileges and in its peaceful exploitation of power through foreign influences, turns its glance towards Japan as if towards a natural protector. In the Philippines, the Tagal population sees in the soldiers of the Mikado eventual auxiliaries against the Americans and hopes that, if the conquerors of the Spaniards delay in giving the natives the promised independence, a liberating help could, one day, come from the north. In Java, in the entire Malayan empire, where several thousand Dutch govern millions of natives, the automatist tendencies, even more developed, have been encouraged and stimulated by the events of the war. The same phenomenon is taking place in the English Empire of India; the party, not yet to be feared, despite its intelligence and activity, which dreams of gaining the government of India for Indians, will now seek its watchword from that Empire of the Rising Sun whose symbol appears as the portent of the great destinies reserved for the Asiatic races. The English were afraid they would one day see the Muscovite monster descend on India from the heights of the Afghan mountains; in order to divert this menace, albeit distant, Lord Curzon and his friends pushed for a Japanese alliance and paved the way for the present war; it may well be that one day they will live to regret having helped Japan to success . . . as Japan may become too powerful a neighbour for her allies, and, for the aspirations of native nationalism, too encouraging an example. As far away as the populations of the island of Madagascar, as far away as the English Empire of the Cape, where, thanks to the fighting between English and Boers, the black races are developing with such disconcerting speed, the victory of Japan has had profound repercussions among the natives. Hence, everywhere where European domination or influence extend, the fall of Port Arthur has awakened hopes which will translate themselves in a not too distant future into threatening facts for the world hegemony of Old Europe. . . .

Hence the fall of Port Arthur will have been the point of departure of a new era where our arms and our machines will be used by new civilisations. The period when the nations of Europe set forth to the conquest of new territories has come to an end.[23]

This was one of the repercussions on which those who saw Japan as yellow hope and those who saw Japan as the yellow peril agreed: it was the beginning of the end of European imperialism and domination of the world. But the perilists were not concerned only with the political or military implications of these momentous events; for people who believed that imperialism was a 'bread and butter issue', the economic ramifications were also most alarming. Ten years before the awful events, Valentine Chirol had warned: 'More formidable even than the political dangers which threaten us from the Far East, and I have no wish to underrate them, appears to be the economic danger. The time is not far distant when not only ourselves, but industrial Europe altogether will rue the day when we introduced to the labour markets of the world the enterprising genius of Japan and the countless hosts of Chinese labour.'[24] Japan's military defeat of Russia made the yellow economic peril all the more real.

The competition of yellow labour, perhaps not the imminent peril sometimes depicted, is still very far from being an imaginary peril. Japanese industry in the last few years is no longer progressing and production has almost ceased to grow, for if labour is cheap, it is nevertheless very mediocre in quality and of feeble return; Nippon labour does not seem to be the cause of the depreciation of salaries in occidental Europe; but would it be the same if Japan, victorious over Russia and master of the Celestial Empire, organised Chinese labour and acclimatised China to industrial civilisation and the regime of wage-earning? It is undoubted that the markets of the Far East would be closed to European manufacture and that the exports of the yellow countries would invade all the regions which presently are the clients of Occidental manufactures; it would be surprising indeed if the result were not the lowering of salaries, which could be remedied only by raising ultra-protectionist barriers. This peril is so far from being imaginary that for a long time the United States and Australia have taken severe measures to protect white labour against the competition of yellow labour; even recently, the European workers of the Cape Colony have energetically protested against the importation of Chinese coolies in the Rand mines. The victory of Japan over Russia will be the point of departure of a new era in which the yellow race, under the control of the Nippons, will adopt all the processes and tools of our civilisation; the result for Europe will be economic perturbations which will notably delay any solution to the grave social problems.[25]

Thus one sees the various implications – social, political, economic, military – of the yellow peril. Above all, perhaps, it was a terrible psychological shock; the white race had been

178

challenged and lost. The Russian débâcle 'must cause grave anxiety to all those who believe in the great commercial and civilising mission of the white race throughout the world. For one moment all frontiers and all differences of nationality are abolished, and from the wreck of the Russian Armada there arises the gigantic conception of the unifying belief in our own race and the common sorrow over its defeat.'[26]

Among the perilists some were not content to express sorrow and alarm, but urged their governments to action: 'the new world power notion should be knocked out of her [Japan] forthwith. There cannot be a world power which is other than white. Any deviation from this principle is the sure way to Armageddon.'[27] One author, after stating that 'it is not just Russia which is involved, it is our entire race and our entire civilisation', developed a programme for action divided into three parts:

1. Use all our influence in Peking to prevent the Japanese from penetrating Southern China; do the same in Bangkok in regard to Siam; persuade all Europeans that it is a common peril; persuade Britain that, even if Russia is her enemy, Japan is just as dangerous for her intrigues in the Yangtse valley, in Siam and even in India. In a word unite all European powers in the Far East against Japan;
2. By every possible means, especially financial ones, prevent Japan from increasing her fleet; consequently never lend money to Japan.
3. Prepare for war.[28]

Japan never had a chance. As the military-surgeon-novelist-poet, Mori Ogai, wrote in a poem during the war:

> Win the war,
> And Japan will be denounced as yellow peril.
> Lose it,
> And she will be branded a barbaric land.

He was of course right. The yellow hope dream quickly vanished; within little more than a decade the European left had a new hope in the new Russia. Within less than two decades Great Britain abandoned her ally under pressure from those countries passing anti-Japanese immigration legislation – Australia, Canada and the United States. At the Conference of Versailles the Western powers vetoed the harmless Japanese-sponsored racial equality clause they wished to include in the Covenant of the League of Nations. The hope was ephemeral, the stigma of the peril remained. Japan in the beginning of the century was neither the yellow hope nor the yellow peril; she was an imperialist nation, slightly different from the others, of course, but no better or worse than the others, and no more dangerous than the others.

Among all the spectators of the carnage in the East, there was one solitary voice crying in the desert – Tolstoy's. On the question of the Japanese as the yellow peril, he said: 'They are what they are, nothing more, with their qualities and their defects, many of which must be common to all men.' He refused to participate in this war; the ordinary Russian men and women and the ordinary Japanese men and women were not each other's enemies; the enemy was those who deceived them and those who took advantage of them. He asked:

But when will all this come to an end? When, at last, will deceived men take matters in their own hands and declare, 'You, kings, mikado, ministers, metropolitans, priests, generals, journalists, businessmen, whatever name you give yourselves, you, who are without pity, go face the bullets and the shells, but we, we will not go! Leave us alone, leave us to till our soil and sow our seeds.' Yes, the great struggle of our times is not that which is taking place now between Russians and Japanese, nor that which could explode between the white and yellow races, it is the spiritual struggle which never ceases and is taking place now, the struggle between the enlightened conscience of humanity, ready to manifest itself, and the darkness of oppression, which surrounds it and overwhelms it.[29]

APPENDIX

I have relied more on the following writers than on others.

Sir Rutherford Alcock, a diplomat, was Britain's first permanent representative and head of legation in Edo. He took up his post in 1858 and left in 1865; Alcock's period of residence was a particularly difficult one as the officials of the shōgunal government were far from helpful and open. Alcock was responsible for the gunboat diplomacy carried out in Kagoshima in 1863 and in Shimonoseki (the British fleet being joined by the French, Dutch and American) the following year. Alcock feared that proper relations with Japan could only be established following some sort of military action, probably even war. Alcock's successor, Sir Harry Parkes, was able to involve himself to a far greater extent in Japanese politics (initially thanks to his very active secretary, Ernest Satow) and remained as head of legation in Japan for eighteen years. Alcock wrote a two volume work on Japan, entitled *Capital of the Tycoon*, which is encyclopedic in breadth.

Sir Edwin Arnold was a very widely travelled author and journalist. He knew Asia well and received numerous decorations from a variety of Asian courts, including Officer of the White Elephant of Siam, Commander of Lion and Sun of Persia, and the Order of the Rising Sun of Japan. Twice widowed, he married as his third wife a Japanese women, Tama Kurokawa, from Sendai. His numerous publications include *Light of Asia*, *Light of the World* and *The Voyage of Ithobal*.

William George Aston, the great expert of Japanese literature, came to Japan in 1864, four years before the Imperial Restoration, as a student interpreter attached to the British legation. He remained in Japan and published numerous books on the country's language, literature and religion. These include *A Grammar of the Japanese Spoken Language*, *A Grammar of the Japanese Written Language*, his *History of Japanese Literature* and a work entitled *Shintô: The Way of the Gods*. He also translated the *Nihongi*, the chronicles of old Japan completed in the eighth century.

John R. Black, an Australian, arrived in Japan before the Restoration. He was the editor of Japan's first English language newspaper, the *Japan Herald*, later edited the *Japan Gazette* and a monthly, the *Far East*. Black also owned and edited a Japanese language newspaper, the *Nisshin Shinjishi*.

Georges Bousquet was for four years, from 1872 to 1876, adviser to the Japanese government on the compilation of a civil and criminal code. He contributed frequently to the Yokohama French language newspaper, *L'Écho du Japon*, and was one of those who advised prudent and slow progress, rather than too rapid change.

Basil Hall Chamberlain was undoubtedly the Westerner who was most knowledgeable about Japanese civilisation. He was Professor of Japanese and Philology at the University of Tokyo and also published numerous books, among them *Classical Poetry of the Japanese, Handbook of Colloquial Japanese, Practical Introduction to the Study of Japanese Writing* and his famous small encyclopedia on Japan, entitled *Things Japanese*. He left Japan at the time of the First World War and spent the remaining twenty years of his life living at the Hotel Richmond in Geneva, where he wrote books on French literature.

Sir Valentine Chirol travelled very extensively throughout Asia, including Japan and China. In 1899 he became director of the Foreign Department of *The Times* and wrote numerous works dealing with political and economic problems of Eastern countries.

T. W. H. Crosland was a journalist, writing for the popular press, and a prolific writer; his works include such titles as *The Unspeakable Scot* (1902) and *The Wild Irishman* (1905).

George Nathaniel Curzon, journalist, writer and politician, certainly needs no introduction, except perhaps to remind readers that he was Viceroy of India from 1899 to 1905. He had wide experience of most of Asia, travelling a great deal, contributing articles to *The Times* and influencing the editorial policy of that newspaper.

Dr J. E. de Becker, a British doctor residing in Japan, married a Japanese woman and became a naturalised Japanese citizen himself, taking the name Kobayashi Beika.

Arthur Diósy was born in London of a Hungarian father. He was a writer and a lecturer, a strong advocate of the Anglo–Japanese

Alliance and founder in 1891 of the Japan Society as well as being a member of the Société Franco–Japonaise. He was made a knight commander of the Order of the Rising Sun.

William Gray Dixon, a Scot, was Professor of English at the Imperial College of Engineering of Tokyo from 1876 to 1880. He was a minister of the Church of Scotland and after leaving Japan served in numerous Presbyterian churches in Australia and New Zealand.

Henry Dyer, another Scot, Order of the Sacred Treasure (2nd class), Order of the Rising Sun (3rd class) and Emeritus Professor of Tokyo Imperial University, was an engineer by training and was appointed the first principal of the Imperial College of Engineering, Tokyo, and Professor of Civil and Mechanical Engineering in 1873. He resided in Japan until 1883. He published numerous works on education, science and technology and a most interesting book on Japan, *Dai Nippon, The Britain of the East.*

Baron von Falkenegg was a German publicist and writer and strong advocate of German expansionism.

Mrs Hugh Fraser, novelist and writer of travelogues, was the wife of a British diplomat who was minister in Japan towards the end of the century. With her husband she lived in various countries of Europe and South America and accompanied him on his postings to China and then to Japan. Her many books include a novel based on old Japan, entitled *The Stolen Emperor: A Tale of Old Japan* (1904).

William Griffis, an American missionary, arrived in Japan in 1870 and taught in various parts of the country, though especially the south, for many years.

Sidney L. Gulick, another American missionary, seems to have followed his vocation and a desire to enlighten the West on Japan with equal zeal. His first book, *The Growth of the Kingdom of God* (1895), was followed by the two works we have used here, *Evolution of the Japanese* and *The White Peril in the Far East: An Interpretation of the Russo–Japanese War.* He continued to write books and indeed in 1935 as the clouds of war were beginning to appear over the Pacific he wrote *Towards Understanding Japan: Constructive Proposals for Removing the Menace of War.*

Lafcadio Hearn was born in 1850 in the Ionian islands of Irish and Greek parentage. He went to the United States in 1869 and worked as a journalist, then to Martinique where he lived for three years, 1887-9, and arrived in Japan in 1890. He married a Japanese woman and became naturalised, taking the name Koizumi Yakumo. From 1896 to 1903 he lectured on English literature at Tokyo Imperial University; his successor was the novelist Natsume Sôseki. Lafcadio Hearn wrote numerous books on Japan, which are listed in the bibliography; more than anyone else Hearn was responsible for creating the more romantic image of Japan in the West. He died in Japan in September 1904.

Henry Mayers Hyndman was a joint founder in 1881 of the London Democratic Federation, which in 1884 became the Social Democratic Federation. He edited *Justice*, wrote numerous books – including one entitled *The Awakening of Asia* (1912) – pamphlets and tracts and was a frequent public speaker. He was, however, not on speaking terms with Engels. Hyndman's life and thought can be studied in the work by Chushichi Tsuzuki, *H. M. Hyndman and British Socialism* (Oxford University Press, 1961).

Paul Leroy-Beaulieu was a writer and lecturer and travelled widely. He was a staunch advocate of French imperialism in the course of the Third Republic. His *De la Colonisation Chez les Peuples Modernes* is perhaps the most important work in terms of understanding the motivations behind the French empire.

Pierre Loti (born Viaud) was a naval officer who sailed extensively both in the Middle and Far East, thus providing himself with an exotic décor for his numerous novels.

Sir Henry Norman was on the editorial staff of the *Pall Mall Gazette* and held other positions in journalism. He travelled extensively throughout North America and Asia and produced numerous publications.

Laurence Oliphant was a novelist, war correspondent, mystic, and Member of Parliament. He accompanied Lord Elgin when the latter was sent as chief plenipotentiary for the signing of Britain's first treaty with Japan and then returned to Japan as secretary to the legation in 1861. He was the victim of a night raid by xenophobic terrorists on the legation and almost lost his life. He returned to Britain and though he continued to lead a very active life –

travelling widely and writing profusely – it is said that he never completely recovered from the incident.

Lord Redesdale (A. B. Mitford) joined the Foreign Office in 1858. He was posted to St Petersburgh in 1863, Peking in 1865 and in 1866 to Edo, where he stayed until the year of the Restoration. He returned to Japan almost four decades later in order to accompany the mission there of Prince Arthur of Connaught.

Sir Edward Reed was Liberal M.P. for Pembroke from 1874 to 1906. He visited Japan in 1879 and as a result wrote a two-volumed work, *Japan*; he took a very pro-Japan stance and advocated revision of the unequal treaties. Apart from his interest in Japan, he wrote on ships, including *Our Iron-clad Ships* (1869), and also published some poems.

So far as *The Times* is concerned, as pointed out in note 12 of Chapter 1, details can be obtained from the *History of the Times* (London, 1947). The story behind *The Times*'s East Asian policy need not concern us unduly as this was not something which the general reading public would necessarily have been aware of. However, a very brief summary may be in order. Initially *The Times*'s correspondents in Japan were people residing in the country and involved in some occupation or other. By the mid-1880s, however, the then manager of *The Times*, Donald Mac-Kenzie Wallace, became convinced of the importance of East Asia and of the need to expand British interests there. Although special *Times* correspondents had occasionally gone to Japan (as part of an Asian tour), in 1885 the first full-time correspondent was appointed in the person of Colonel Palmer. Palmer was followed in 1894 by Captain Brinkley. So from the 1880s onwards *The Times*'s coverage of East Asian affairs was fairly extensive. Another reason for this, and perhaps the most important, was the presence of the very able, if somewhat controversial, correspondent in Peking, G. E. Morrison.

In 1894 *The Times* was critical of Japan for going to war with China. However, with Japan's rapid victory *The Times* became fully conscious of the importance of this victory, the change in the balance of power that resulted from it, and the undisputed fact that Japan was becoming a world power with which Britain had to deal intelligently.

Also, it was during these two years that Valentine Chirol travelled to China and Japan. Chirol was impressed by what he saw in Japan and had no doubt that the country must henceforth be taken very seriously indeed. It should be made clear that *The Times*'s policy towards Japan was not so much a sentimental one as a sensible one, worthy of the great newspaper it was at the time. By and large Chirol dominated *Times* policy on the East for the ensuing decades, writing many of the articles which have been cited. Japan, as we have seen in Chapter 6, got a very good press from *The Times* during the Russo–Japanese war, thanks mainly to Chirol and to Morrison. In the course of the peace negotiations at Portsmouth, New Hampshire under the chairmanship of Theodore Roosevelt, Japan got a bad press from *The Times*. This is not dealt with in this book. Suffice it to say that this apparent change of policy resulted from the anti-Japanese and pro-Russian stance of *The Times*'s chief U.S. correspondent, George Smalley.

NOTES

INTRODUCTION

1 Akira Iriye, *Mutual Images; Essays in American–Japanese Relations* (Harvard University Press, 1975) and *Pacific Estrangement: Japanese And American Expansion, 1897–1911* (Harvard University Press, 1972).
2 George Alexander Lensen, *Japanese Diplomatic and Consular Officials in Russia. A Handbook of Japanese Representatives in Russia from 1874 to 1968* (University of Florida Press, 1968), *Report From Hokkaido; the Remains of Russian Culture in Northern Japan* (Hakodate, 1954), *Russian Diplomatic and Consular Officials in East Asia* (University of Florida Press, 1968), *The Russian Push Toward Japan; Russo–Japanese Relations, 1697–1875* (Princeton University Press, 1959), *Russia's Japan Expedition of 1852–1855* (Gainsville, 1955).
3 For very interesting accounts of Westerners in early modern Japan see Pat Barr, *The Coming of the Barbarians* (Macmillan, 1967), *The Deer Cry Pavilion* (Macmillan, 1968), and Harold S. Williams, *Foreigners in Mikadoland* (Tokyo, 1963), *Shades of the Past Or Indiscreet Tales of Japan* (Tokyo, 1959) and *Tales of the Foreign Settlements in Japan* (Tokyo, 1958).

CHAPTER 1

1 *Edinburgh Review*, January–April 1863, vol. 117, p. 517.
2 Douglas Sladen, *Queer Things About Japan* (London, 1904), p. vii.
3 See Richard Storry, *A History of Modern Japan* (Penguin, Harmondsworth, Middlesex, 1967). Introduction.
4 Rudyard Kipling, *From Sea to Sea* (London, 1900), vol. 1, p. 335.
5 William Gray Dixon, *The Land of the Morning* (Edinburgh, 1882), p. 125.
6 *The Times*, 17 September 1887.
7 Basil Hall Chamberlain, *Japanese Things* (Charles E. Tuttle reprint, Rutland, Vermont and Tokyo, 1971), p. 496.
8 Dixon, op. cit., pp. 125–6.
9 *The Times*, 21 October 1879.
10 *The Times*, 4 June 1881.
11 *The Times*, 6 June 1881.
12 The policy of *The Times* on Japan obviously depended to a fairly great extent on the views of the individual *Times* correspondents in Tokyo: see vols. II and III of *History of The Times* (London, 1947).
13 *The Times*, 19 May 1887.
14 *The Times*, 19 April 1889.
15 *The Times*, 28 December 1889.
16 *The Times*, 17 September 1899.
17 Chamberlain, op. cit., p. 496.
18 *Edinburgh Review*, August–October 1872, vol. CXXXVI, p. 252.
19 *MacMillan's Magazine*, May–October 1872, vol. XXVI, p. 496.
20 Georges Bousquet, *Le Japon de Nos Jours* (Paris, 1877), vol. II, pp. 351–2.
21 'Le Japon depuis l'abolition du Taïcounat, les réformes et les progrès des Européens', *Revue des Deux Mondes*, 15 March 1873, vol. 104, pp. 480–1.
22 *MacMillan's Magazine*, May–October 1872, vol. XXVI, p. 497.

23 René Pinon, 'Après la Chute de Port Arthur', *Revue des Deux Mondes*, 1 June 1905, vol. 27, p. 558.
24 *Edinburgh Review*, August–October 1872, vol. CXXXVI, p. 256.
25 Lafcadio Hearn, *Glimpses of Unfamiliar Japan* (AMS Press reprint, New York, 1969), vol. I, p. 239.
26 Kipling, op. cit., vol. I, p. 410, 451 and 360.
27 *The Times*, 18 September 1876.
28 André Bellesort, 'Voyage au Japon – I – Premières Impressions', *Revue des Deux Mondes*, 15 December 1899, vol. 156, pp. 771–2.
29 Louis Couperus, *Nippon*, translated from the Dutch by John de La Valette (London, 1926), p. 129.
30 Dixon, op. cit., p. 124.
31 George N. Curzon, *The Problems of the Far East* (London, 1896), pp. 52–3.
32 Pierre Leroy-Beaulieu, *The Awakening of the East*, translated by Richard Davey (London, 1900), p. 171–4.
33 J. Morris, *Advance Japan: A Nation Thoroughly in Earnest* (London, 1896), p. xvi.
34 *Le Petit Journal*, Supplément Illustré, 2 April 1905.
35 Henry Dyer, *Dai Nippon: The Britain of the East* (London, 1904), pp. 48–9.
36 *The Times*, 30 May 1876.
37 Dyer, op. cit., p. 50.
38 *The Times*, 28 November 1889.
39 Lafcadio Hearn, *Kokoro: Hints and Echoes of Japanese Inner Life* (London, 1906), p. 11.
40 John R. Black, *Young Japan: Yokohama and Yedo 1858–1879* (Oxford University Press reprint, Tokyo, 1968), vol. I, p. 151.
41 Leroy-Beaulieu, op. cit., pp. 177 and 182.
42 Chamberlain, op. cit., pp. 7–8.

CHAPTER 2

1 C.H.F., 'A Japanese Inferno', *Chambers' Journal*, 1 March 1895, Part 134, p. 118.
2 Sir Rutherford Alcock, *Capital of the Tycoon* (London, 1863), vol. I, p. 414.
3 Lafcadio Hearn, *Glimpses of Unfamiliar Japan* (AMS Press reprint, New York, 1969), vol. I, p. 7.
4 Rudyard Kipling, *From Sea to Sea* (London, 1900), vol. I, p. 455.
5 John LaFarge, *An Artist's Letters from Japan* (New York, 1897), pp. 126–7.
6 *The Times*, 18 August 1876.
7 Kipling, op. cit., vol. I, p. 332.
8 *Edinburgh Review*, October 1852, vol. XCVI, p. 351–2.
9 Charles Baudelaire, *Journaux Intimes*, 'Mon Cœur mis à nu' (José Corti, Paris, 1949), p. 75.
10 John Ruskin, *Time and Tide*, Letter VI (George Allen, Orpington, Kent 1882), p. 33.
11 M. C. de Varigny, 'L'Asie à l'Exposition Universelle, *Revue des Deux Mondes*, 1 October 1889, vol. 95, p. 612.
12 Kipling, op. cit., vol. I, p. 316.
13 'A Cruise in Japanese Waters', Part II, *Blackwood's Magazine*, January 1859, vol. 85, p. 54.
14 Arthur Diósy, *The New Far East* (London, 1904), p. 195–6.
15 Henry Norman, *The Real Japan* (London, 1908), p. 210.

16 Georges Bousquet, *Le Japon de Nos Jours* (Paris, 1877), vol. I, p. 331.
17 Sir Edward J. Reed, *Japan* (London 1880), vol. II, p. 50–51.
18 *The Times*, 4 December 1885.
19 *The Times*, 15 December 1885.
20 For an account of the impact of Japan on European and American art and literature see Earl Miner, *The Japanese Tradition in British and American Literature* (Princeton University Press, Princeton, New Jersey, 1966) and William L. Schwartz, *The Imaginative Interpretation of the Far East in Modern French Literature* (Edinburgh and Paris, 1926).
21 Norman, op. cit., p. 137.
22 LaFarge, op. cit., p. 160.
23 Hearn, op. cit., vol. I, pp. 166 and 168.
24 M. T. de Wyzewa, 'La Peinture Japonaise', *Revue des Deux Mondes*, 1 July 1890, vol. 100, p. 115.
25 Bousquet, op. cit., vol. II, pp. 197–8.
26 Mortimer Mempes, *Japan: A Record in Colour* (London, 1905), pp. 31–2.
27 Henry Houssaye, 'Voyage Autour du Monde à l'Exposition Universelle', *Revue des Deux Mondes*, 15 July 1878, vol. 28, p. 373.
28 T. W. H. Crosland, *The Truth About Japan* (London, 1904), pp. 46–8.
29 Maurice Paléologue, 'Trois Palais d'Asie', *Revue des Deux Mondes*, 15 November 1886, vol. 78, p. 421.
30 For the influence of Japanese poetry on Ezra Pound see Lawrence W. Chisolm, *Fenollosa: The Far East and American Culture* (Yale University Press, New Haven, Connecticut, 1963), Miner, op. cit., especially Chapter V, and Noel Stock, *The Life of Ezra Pound* (Penguin, Harmondsworth, Middlesex, 1970).
31 Douglas Sladen, *Queer Things about Japan* (London 1904), p. 140.
32 F. Marnas, *La Religion de Jésus Ressuscitée au Japon dans la Seconde Moitié du XIX Siècle* (Paris, 1896), p. 98.
33 J. B. Chaillet, *Monseigneur Petitjean (1829–1884) et la Ressurection Catholique au Japon au XIX Siècle*, Montceau, 1919, p. 85.
34 Basil Hall Chamberlain, *Japanese Things* (Charles E. Tuttle reprint, Rutland, Vermont and Tokyo, 1971), p. 409.
35 Henry Dyer, *Dai Nippon: The Britain of the East* (London, 1904), p. 36.
36 Rudolpe Lindau, *Un Voyage Autour du Japon* (Paris, 1864), p. 37.
37 Hearn, op. cit., vol. I, pp. 34–5.
38 William George Aston, *A History of Japanese Literature* (Charles E. Tuttle reprint, Rutland, Vermont and Tokyo, 1972), pp. 398–9.
39 Hearn, op. cit., vol. I, pp. ix–x.
40 Percival Lowell, *Occult Japan: The Way of the Gods* (Boston, 1895), p. 42.
41 Lindau, op. cit., p. 41.
42 Chamberlain, op. cit., p. 411.

CHAPTER 3

1 Sidney L. Gulick, *Evolution of the Japanese* (London, 1905), p. 102.
2 H. Norman, *The Real Japan* (London, 1908), p. 177.
3 William E. Griffis, *The Mikado's Empire* (New York, 1883), pp. 551 and 554.
4 Gulick, op. cit., p. ix.
5 James A. Scherer, *Japan To-Day* (London, 1904), p. 102.
6 ibid., pp. 110–11.
7 Gulick, op. cit., p. 259.

8 Basil Hall Chamberlain, *Japanese Things* (Charles E. Tuttle reprint, Rutland, Vermont and Tokyo, 1971), pp. 416 and 502.
9 Griffis, op. cit., p. 559.
10 Georges Bousquet, *Le Japon de Nos Jours* (Paris, 1877), vol. I, p. 87.
11 F. de Fontpertuis, *Le Japon Civilisé* (Paris, 1883), p. 195.
12 Scherer, op. cit., pp. 113–14.
13 Griffis, op. cit., p. 555.
14 J. E. de Becker, *The Nightless City or the History of the Yoshiwara Yûkwaku* (Charles E. Tuttle reprint, Rutland, Vermont and Tokyo, 1971), p. 324.
15 See Fernando Henriques, *Prostitution and Society, A Survey*, vol. I, *Primitive, Classical and Oriental* (Macgibbon & Kee, London, 1962), especially chapter II.
16 de Becker, op. cit., pages 84, 85, 201, 121 and 163.
17 William Gray Dixon, *The Land of the Morning* (Edinburgh, 1882), p. 472.
18 G. Layrle, 'Le Japon en 1867 – I', *Revue des Deux Mondes*, 1 February 1868, vol. 73, p. 640.
19 Griffis, op. cit., p. 556 fn.
20 Norman, op. cit., p. 305.
21 Alice Mabel Bacon, *Japanese Girls and Women* (Boston, 1902), p. 291.
22 de Becker, op. cit., p. xviii.
23 Douglas Sladen, *Queer Things about Japan* (London, 1904), p. 6.
24 Bacon, op. cit., p. 291–2.
25 Arthur Diósy, *The New Far East* (London, 1904), p. 259.
26 Mrs Hugh Fraser, *A Diplomatist's Wife in Japan* (London 1904), p. 522–5.
27 Gulick, op. cit., p. 354.
28 Dixon, op. cit., p. 489.
29 Diósy, op. cit., pp. 262–3.
30 ibid., p. 263.
31 Chamberlain, op. cit., pp. 310–11.
32 Lafcadio Hearn, *Out of the East: Reveries and Studies in New Japan* (Charles E. Tuttle reprint, Rutland, Vermont and Tokyo 1972), pp. 95–9.
33 Inazo Nitobe, *Bushido The Soul of Japan* (Charles E. Tuttle reprint, Rutland, Vermont and Tokyo, 1969), pp. 153–4.
34 Sir Edwin Arnold, *Japonica* (New York, 1892), pp. 104–5.
35 Chamberlain, op. cit., p. 312.
36 Diósy, op. cit., pp. 255–6.
37 Arnold, op. cit., p. 104.
38 Norman, op. cit., p. 183.
39 Gulick, op. cit., p. 278–9.
40 Bousquet, op. cit., vol. I, p. 88.
41 Diósy, op. cit., p. 272.
42 Mrs Fraser, op. cit., pp. 533–4.
43 Arnold, op. cit., p. 97.
44 Bousquet, op. cit., vol. I, pp. 348–9.
45 Chamberlain, op. cit., p. 501.
46 Taken from Earl Miner, *The Japanese Tradition in British and American Literature* (Princeton University Press, Princeton, New Jersey, 1966), p. 40.
47 Arnold, op. cit., pp. 68–9.
48 Lafcadio Hearn, *Japan An Attempt At Interpretation* (New York, 1907), p. 393.
49 Norman, op. cit., pp. 177–8.
50 *The Times*, 27 September 1860.
51 Arnold, op. cit., p. 4.

52 Hearn, op. cit., p. 394.
53 Le comte de Beauvoir, *Pékin, Yeddo, San Francisco, Voyage Autour du Monde* (Paris, 1872), p. 160.
54 John LaFarge, *An Artist's Letters from Japan* (New York, 1897), pp. 179–80.
55 Rudyard Kipling, *From Sea to Sea* (London, 1900), vol. I, pp. 353–4.
56 Bacon, op. cit., p. 79.
57 See Earl Miner, op. cit., p. 48.
58 William L. Schwartz, *The Imaginative Interpretation of the Far East in Modern French Literature* (Edinburgh and Paris, 1926), p. 131.
59 Mrs Fraser, op. cit., p. 595.
60 Chamberlain, op. cit., p. 220.
61 Sidney McCall, *The Breath of the Gods: A Japanese Romance of To-Day* (London, 1906), pp. 50 and 431.
62 Diósy, op. cit., pp. 257–8.
63 H. G. Ponting, *In Lotus-Land Japan* (London, 1922), p. 10.

CHAPTER 4

1 Lawrence Oliphant, *Narrative of the Earl of Elgin's Mission to China and Japan* (London, 1859), vol. II, p. 244.
2 Rudyard Kipling, *From Sea to Sea* (London, 1900), vol. I, p. 315.
3 *Blackwood's Magazine*, April 1862, vol. XCI, p. 431.
4 *The Times*, 2 November 1858.
5 *Edinburgh Review*, October 1852, vol. XCVI, p. 381.
6 *The Times*, 4 November 1863.
7 *Edinburgh Review*, October 1852, vol. XVCI, pp. 364–5.
8 Oliphant, op. cit., vol. II, p. 143.
9 *Blackwood's Magazine*, April 1862, vol. XCI, p. 433.
10 Le Marquis de Moges, *Souvenirs d'Une Ambassade en Chine et au Japon* (Paris, 1860), p. 326.
11 Karl Marx, *Capital* (Lawrence & Wishart, London, 1974), vol. I, p. 672.
12 Sir Rutherford Alcock, *The Capital of the Tycoon* (London, 1863), vol. II, pp. 237 and 348.
13 John R. Black, *Young Japan: Yokohama and Yedo 1858–1879* (Oxford University Press reprint, Tokyo, 1968), vol. II, p. 32.
14 David Murray, *Japan* (London, 1906), pp. 381–2.
15 William E. Griffis, *The Mikado's Empire* (New York, 1883), pp. 323–4.
16 Murray, op. cit., pp. 386–7.
17 ibid., p. 389.
18 Augustus Mounsey, *The Satsuma Rebellion* (London 1879), pages 110–12 and 214–15.
19 Black, op. cit., vol. II, p. 498.
20 A. Laurié, *Autour d'un Lycée Japonais* (Paris, 1886), p. 192.
21 Murray, op. cit., pp. 393–4.
22 Griffis, op. cit., p. 589.
23 Sir Edward Reed, *Japan* (London, 1880), vol. I, pp. 353–4.
24 Ernest W. Clement, *A Handbook of Modern Japan* (Chicago, 1904), p. 145.
25 *The Times*, 5 April 1888.
26 Henry Norman, *The Real Japan* (London 1908), p. 345–346.
27 *The Times*, 21 February 1889.
28 *The Times*, 22 March 1889.

29 Murray, op. cit., p. 392.
30 *The Times*, 22 October 1889.
31 Chamberlain, op. cit., p. 135.
32 *The Times*, 22 October 1889.
33 An article which first appeared in the *Japan Weekly Mail* and was reproduced in *The Times* of 28 December 1889.
34 Murray, op. cit., p. 396.
35 Chamberlain, op. cit., p. 135.
36 Dyer, *Dai Nippon: The Britain of the East* (London, 1904), pp. 276–7.
37 George N. Curzon, *The Problems of the Far East* (London, 1896), pp. 18–21 and 24.
38 *The Times*, 23 January 1905.
39 Curzon, op. cit., pp. 37–8.
40 Pierre Leroy-Beaulieu, *The Awakening of the East*, translated by Richard Davey (London, 1900), p. 161.
41 *Justice*, 26 June 1897; I am indebted to my colleague Dr James Young for bringing this passage to my attention.
42 See *Petite République* of 25 November 1903.
43 Curzon, op. cit., pp. 362–3.
44 Clement, op. cit., pp. 128, 129 and 132.
45 Henry Norman, *The Peoples and Politics of the Far East* (London, 1900), p. 390.

CHAPTER 5

1 Rudyard Kipling, *From Sea to Sea* (London, 1900), vol. I, pp. 315 and 366.
2 *The Times*, 23 April 1888.
3 Arthur Diósy, *The New Far East* (London, 1904), p. 337–8.
4 George Wm. Knox, *Imperial Japan* (London, 1905), p. 215.
5 Pierre Leroy-Beaulieu, 'Le Japon. L'Eveil d'un Peuple Oriental à la Civilisation Européenne', *Revue des Deux Mondes*, 1 April 1890, vol. 98, pp. 683–4.
6 James A. B. Scherer, *Japan To-Day* (London, 1904), p. 246.
7 F. de Fontpertuis, *La Chine et le Japon et l'Exposition de 1878* (Paris 1878).
8 Kipling, op. cit., vol. I, p. 383.
9 Scherer, op. cit., p. 249.
10 *The Times*, 23 April 1888.
11 ibid.
12 *Le Moniteur des Soies*, 4 September 1880.
13 Henry Dyer, *Dai Nippon: The Britain of the East* (London, 1904), p. 152.
14 *The Times*, 27 March 1894.
15 Dyer, op. cit., pp. 189–90.
16 David Murray, *Japan* (London, 1906), pp. 419–21.
17 Diósy, op. cit., pp. 293–4, 155 and 288–9.
18 T. W. H. Crosland, *The Truth About Japan* (London, 1904), pp. 63–5.
19 Henry Norman, *The Real Japan* (London, 1908), pp. 356–7.
20 William Gray Dixon, *The Land of the Morning* (Edinburgh, 1882), p. 119.
21 Valentine Chirol, *The Far Eastern Question* (London, 1896), pp. 131 and 133.
22 Pierre Leroy-Beaulieu, *The Awakening of the East*, translated by Richard Davey (London, 1900), p. 140.
23 Chirol, op. cit., pp. 128 and 132.
24 Leroy-Beaulieu, 'Le Japon. L'Éveil d'un Peuple Oriental . . .', p. 655.
25 Norman, op. cit., p. 357.

26 Knox, op. cit., p. 217.
27 Basil Hall Chamberlain, *Japanese Things* (Charles E. Tuttle reprint, Rutland, Vermont and Tokyo, 1971), pp. 95 and 261.
28 Dyer, op. cit., p. 153.
29 Lafcadio Hearn, *Japan An Attempt At Interpretation* (New York, 1907), pp. 488 and 493–4.
30 Murray, op. cit., pp. 422–3.
31 Dyer, op. cit., pp. 202–3.
32 Henry Norman, *The Peoples and Politics of the Far East* (London, 1900), pp. 389–90.

CHAPTER 6

1 Karl Kautsky, *Ethics and the Materialist Conception of History* (Chicago, 1918), p. 11. I am indebted to my colleague Dr Robin Law for bringing this passage to my attention.
2 Lord Redesdale, *The Garter Mission to Japan* (London, 1906), p. 50.
3 *The Times*, 6 February 1904.
4 ibid.
5 *The Times*, 11 February 1904.
6 Sidney L. Gulick, *The White Peril in the Far East: An Interpretation of the Russo–Japanese War* (New York, 1905), pp. 164–80.
7 Anatole France, *Sur La Pierre Blanche* (Paris, 1904), pp. 211–23.
8 *Justice*, 13 February 1904.
9 *Justice*, 27 February 1904.
10 Henry Dyer, *Dai Nippon: The Britain of the East* (London, 1904), pp. 419–20.
11 Gulick, op. cit., p. 115–116.
12 *Justice*, 2 September and 9 September 1905.
13 *The Times*, 30 August 1905.
14 *The Times*, 31 August 1905.
15 Pierre Leroy-Beaulieu, 'Le Japon et ses Ressources dans la Guerre Actuelle', *Revue des Deux Mondes*, 15 March 1904, vol. 20, pp. 389 and 419.
16 *The Times*, 12 July 1900.
17 René Pinon, 'La Guerre Russo–Japonaise et l'Opinion Européenne', *Revue des Deux Mondes*, 1 May 1904, vol. 21, p. 188.
18 Baron von Falkenegg, *Japan Die Neue Weltmacht* (Berlin, 1905), pp. 11–16.
19 T. W. H. Crosland, *The Truth About Japan* (London, 1904), pp. 1, 2, 5, 41, 42 and 43.
20 Extract from an article in the *Evangelische Kirchenzeitung*, which appeared in *The Times* of 9 May 1905.
21 Pinon, op. cit., pp. 218–19.
22 Falkenegg, op. cit., pp. 16–52.
23 René Pinon, 'Après la Chute de Port Arthur', *Revue des Deux Mondes*, 1 June 1905, vol. 27, pp. 562–3.
24 From *History of the Times* (London, 1947), vol. III, p. 196.
25 Pinon, 'La Guerre Russo–Japonaise . . .', pp. 194–5.
26 *National Zeitung*, 31 May 1905.
27 Crosland, op. cit., p. 71.
28 Charles Petit, *Pays de Mousmés! Pays de Guerre!* (Paris, 1905), pp. 240–1.
29 Leo Tolstoy, *Dernières Paroles* (Paris, 1904), pp. 79 and 87.

BIBLIOGRAPHICAL NOTE

Many more books and articles about Japan were written in the period covered in these pages than have been listed in the notes. A far higher percentage of those Westerners either living in or simply visiting Japan wrote about the country than is the case today. Going to Japan in the Victorian period was obviously a very different proposition from what it is now. It took weeks and weeks to get there. There were numerous ports of call on the way and though the seas by then were free from pirates excitement was not lacking. The whole approach to Japan was necessarily different. *En route* one would have time to read and get to know one's fellow travellers; inevitably one would meet the 'old Japan hand', the 'I can remember . . .' sort, full of exciting tales about the country towards which one was slowly advancing. Today one has hardly the time to digest the in-flight John Wayne film before the aircraft has touched down at Tokyo airport.

Another important point, of course, is that although some complained that Osaka was becoming the Manchester, Chicago, Lille or Hamburg of Japan, the country even in the early twentieth century was very different from Western countries. There was a whole new world to discover.

Many aspects of Japan described by Westerners do not appear in the pages of this book. For example, many of the books contained at least a chapter on the *Aino* – the original inhabitants of the Japanese isles, then (as now) to be found only in the northern island of Hokkaidō. These Victorian works on Japan were encyclopedic. In the same binding would appear chapters dealing with Japanese history, geography, the customs of family life, the treatment of women, descriptions of the major cities and of rural villages, religions, political developments, major imports and exports, flora and fauna, and narratives of personal experiences. Very few of the books were dry, though a number of authors could not resist the opportunity to pontificate; many, however, were very amusing.

One thing this book could not do was to reproduce the excitement of individual experiences and discoveries as they occurred day after day in the peregrinations of some of the more intrepid travellers. For this one has to turn to the original works, many of which can be found accumulating dust in second-hand bookshops (too often, alas, at exorbitant prices – which may explain the dust) and, of course, in well stocked libraries.

Some of the more entertaining and interesting books relating the experiences and impressions of Western residents in or visitors to Japan are the following:

Alcock, Sir Rutherford, *The Capital of the Tycoon: A Narrative of Three Years Residence in Japan*, 2 vols (London, 1863). Alcock was Britain's first head of legation in Edo. His two-volume work is a good example of the encyclopedic nature mentioned above. It also conveys the atmosphere of loneliness and insecurity of the West's first residents in a far from hospitable Japan.

Bird, Isabella, *Unbeaten Tracks in Japan*, 2 vols (London, 1880). A Yorkshire spinster, this admirable woman began globe-trotting at the age of 47. Apart from her book on Japan, she left an impressive record of her travels around the world, including *Six Months in the Sandwich Islands* and *A Lady's Life in the Rocky Mountains*. (See Pat Barr, *A Curious Life for a Lady: the story of Isabella Bird* (Macmillan, London, 1970).)

Black, John R., *Young Japan: Yokohama and Yedo 1858–1879*, 2 vols (Oxford University Press, reprint, Tokyo, 1968). Black was a pioneer of journalism in Japan.

Eliot, Sir Charles, *Letters from the Far East* (London, 1907).

Faulds, Henry, *Nine Years in Nippon* (London, 1887).

Finck, Henry T., *Lotos-Time in Japan* (London, 1895).

Harris, Townsend, *The Complete Journal of Townsend Harris*, introduced by M. E. Conenza, 2nd ed. (Tokyo, 1959). Harris was the first U.S. diplomatic representative in Japan, preceding by two years his French and British colleagues.

Hartshorne, Anna C., *Japan And Her People*, 2 vols (London, 1904).

Holtham, Edward G., *Eight Years in Japan, 1873–1881* (London, 1883).

Jephson, R. Mounteney and Elmhirst Edward Pennell, *Our Life in Japan* (London, 1869).

Knox, George William, *Imperial Japan* (London, 1905).

Lensen, George Alexander, ed., *Trading Under Sail Off Japan 1860 to 1889, The Recollections of Captain John Baxter Will, Sailing-Master and Pilot* University of Florida Press, Tallahassee, 1968).

Lensen, George Alexander, ed., *The d'Anethan Dispatches From Japan, 1894–1910*, (Sophia University Press, Tokyo, 1967).

Morse, Edward Sylvester, *Japan Day By Day, 1877, 1878–79, 1882–83* (The Morse Society, Tokyo, 1936). Morse was a pioneer in the field of geology and seismology in Japan.

Oliphant, Lawrence, *A Narrative of the Earl of Elgin's Mission to China and Japan in the Years 1857–1859*, 2 vols (Edinburgh, 1860).

Redesdale, Lord (A. B. Mitford)
The Garter Mission to Japan (London, 1906). Redesdale accompanied Prince Arthur of Connaught to Japan in 1906 in order to carry the Order of the Garter to Emperor Mutsuhito and a bundle of other decorations to sundry Japanese officials. Redesdale had been a secretary to the British legation in Japan before and during the Restoration. As he admits, this return voyage almost forty years later was very much of a Rip van Winkle experience. *Memories*, 2 vols (London, 1915).

Rittner, George H., *Impressions of Japan* (London, 1904).

Satow, Sir Ernest, *A Diplomat in Japan*, introduced by Gordon Daniels (Oxford University Press reprint, Tokyo, 1968). Satow was also attached to the legation in the middle and late 1860s, during which time he established close links with the Satsuma people whom he strongly favoured against the shōgunate. He returned as minister at the end of the century.

Sladen, Douglas
  The Japs at Home (London and Glasgow, 1906).
  Queer Things About Japan (London, 1904).

Thomas, J. H., *Journeys Among the Gentle Japs in the Summer of 1895* (London, 1897).

Tristam, H. B. (canon of Durham), *Rambles in Japan: The Land of the Rising Sun* (London, 1895).

Watson, Gilbert, *Three Rolling Stones in Japan* (London, 1903).

Also worthy of attention is Japan's first guidebook for Western tourists, *Murray's Handbook for Travellers in Japan* (London, 1899).

On religion the books by Percival Lowell, *Occult Japan: or the Way of the Gods* (Boston, 1895) and *The Soul of the Far East* (Boston, 1893), are of great interest.

Alice Mabel Bacon's *Japanese Girls and Women* (Boston, 1891) remains to this day the best account in English of Japanese women's status, life and customs in the nineteenth century. J. E. de Becker's *The Nightless City or the History of the Yoshiwara Yukwaku*, fortunately reprinted by Charles E. Tuttle (Rutland, Vermont and Tokyo) in 1971, is absolutely fascinating.

Basil Hall Chamberlain's *Things Japanese*, also reprinted by Charles E. Tuttle in 1971 (though why did they alter the title to *Japanese Things?*), is a mine of information and perception.

Western observations on Japan's developing army and navy receive little attention in this volume, apart from the chapter dealing with the Russo–Japanese war. The following books specifically dealt with this problem:

Grierson, J. M., *The Armed Strength of Japan* (compiled by the Intelligence Branch of the War Office, London, 1886).

Jane, F. T., *The Imperial Japanese Navy* (London, 1904).

Norman, F. J., *The Fighting Man of Japan* (London, 1905); mainly a study of Japanese martial arts (*budō*).

Petillot, L., *L'Organisation Militaire du Japon: Armée et Marine* (Paris, 1904).

Rein, J. J., *Japan: Travel and Researches Undertaken at the Cost of the Prussian Government*, translated from the German, 2nd ed. (London, 1888).

Smith, G., *Supremacy in the Far East: The Navies of Japan and Russia* (London, 1905).

Similarly very little is said in this book about Western reaction to the Sino–Japanese war of 1894–5. This was Japan's first major foreign war and radically altered the *status quo* in the Far East. For Western attitudes to these events, see:

Allan, J., *Under the Dragon Flag: My Experiences in the Chino–Japanese War*, (London, 1898).
Aveta, F., *La Guerra Cino–Giapponese 1894–1895* (Turin, 1895).
Eastlake, F. W. and Y. Yamada, *Heroic Japan: History of the War Between China and Japan* (London, 1897).
Villenoisy, F. de, *La Guerre Sino–Japonaise, Ses Conséquences Pour l'Europe* (Paris, 1895).
War Office, *An Epitome of the Chino–Japanese War, 1894–1895*, compiled by N. W. H. Du Boulay (London, 1896).

On the Russo–Japanese War in general and the yellow hope–yellow peril phenomenon in particular, apart from the works listed in the notes for Chapter 6, the following should be of interest:

Barry, R., *Port Arthur: A Monster Heroism* (New York, 1905).
Burleigh, B., *Empire of the East; Or Japan and Russia at War, 1904–1905* (London, 1905).
Chasseur, A., *A Study of the Russo–Japanese War* (Edinburgh, 1905).
Halot, A., *L'Extrême Orient; Etudes d'Hier, Evénements d'Aujourd'hui* (Brussels, 1905).
James, D. H., *The Siege of Port Arthur: Records of an Eye-Witness* (London, 1905).
Kann, R., *Journal d'un Correspondent de Guerre en Extrême-Orient* (Paris, 1905).
Mackenzie, F. A., *From Tokyo to Tiflis: Uncensored Letters From the War* (London, 1905).
'O', *The Yellow War. By 'O'* (Edinburgh, 1905).
Richardson, T. E., *In Japanese Hospitals During War-Time* (Edinburgh, 1905).
Russo–Japanese War. *Press Cuttings Relating to the Russo–Japanese War* (London, 1904).
Russo–Japanese War. *The War in the Far East*, by the military correspondent of *The Times* (London, 1905).
Russo–Japanese War. *A Collection of Russian Cartoons on the Russo–Japanese War*, (Moscow and St Petersburgh, 1904).
Théry, E., *Le Péril Jaune. La Transformation du Japon* (Paris, 1901).
Tolstoy, L. N.,*En Ecoutant Tolstoi: Entretiens sur la Guerre* (Paris, 1904).
Tolstoy, L. N., *La Guerre Russo–Japonaise*, translated by E. Halpérine-Kaminsky (Paris, 1905).
Wilson, H. W., *Japan's Fight for Freedom. The Story of the War Between Russia and Japan* (London, 1904).

Finally, one should not miss reading the novel by Pierre Maël, *Blanche Contre Jaunes: Grand Roman d'Aventures sur la Guerre Russo–Japonaise* (Paris, 1905). It is a masterpiece of its genre, containing all possible and imaginable racial stereotypes of the late nineteenth and early twentieth centuries. One will find, for example, an illustration depicting a group of Japanese attacking the white heroine, Sonia; although the action takes place at Port Arthur in February, the Japanese are practically naked, dressed only in loincloths, headbands and sandals! There are many more gems in this novel.

Needless to say, Kipling's observations on Japan are excellent reading; to my knowledge, apart from the articles contained in *From Sea to Sea* (London, 1900), Kipling did not write anything else about Japan. In any case Kipling's works hardly need recommending. The same is probably true of Pierre Loti. By far the best known work of Loti's on Japan is *Madame Chrysanthème* (Paris, 1887), which is available in Livre de Poche and also in English translation. Loti wrote another novel set in Japan, *La Troisième Jeunesse de Madame Prune* (Paris, 1895). His *Japoneries d'Automne* (Paris, 1893) is not a novel, but well worth reading. So are some of his articles on Japan, notably 'Escales au Japon', which appeared in the *Revue des Deux Mondes* (on 15 December 1904, 1 and 15 January and 15 February 1905). Also recommended are 'Kiôto, La Ville Sainte' in *La Nouvelle Revue*, 1 March 1887; 'Un Bal à Yeddo', *La Nouvelle Revue*, 15 December 1887 and 17 January 1888; and 'La Sainte Montagne de Nikko', *La Nouvelle Revue*, 15 September, 1 and 15 October 1888. There are also a number of his experiences in and impressions of Japan in his correspondence to Juliette Adam, *Lettres de Pierre Loti à Madame Juliette Adam, 1880–1922* (Paris, 1924).

Undoubtedly, however, the most enchanting and fascinating accounts of Japan are to be found in the works of Lafcadio Hearn: *Exotics and Retrospectives*, (Boston, 1898); *Gleanings in Buddha Fields* (New York, 1897); *Glimpses of Unfamiliar Japan*, 2 vols, (New York, 1894); *In Ghostly Japan* (Boston, 1899); *Japan: An Attempt at Interpretation* (New York, 1904); *A Japanese Miscellany* (Boston, 1901); *Kokoro* (New York, 1896); *Kotto* (New York, 1902); *Kwaidan* (Boston, 1904); *Out of the East* (Boston, 1895); *Shadowings* (Boston, 1900). For a more intimate acquaintance of Hearn and his life in Japan there are two works by Elisabeth Bisland: *The Life and Letters of Lafcadio Hearn*, 2 vols (London, 1911) and *The Japanese Letters of Lafcadio Hearn* (London, 1911). Two further interesting studies of Lafcadio Hearn are: George M. Gould, *Concerning Lafcadio Hearn* (Philadelphia, 1908) and Albert Mordell, *Discoveries: Essays on Lafcadio Hearn* (Orient/West, Tokyo, 1964).

INDEX

Acollas, É. 112
Adam, J. 198
administrative areas, terms to denote 97
agitators, juvenile 111–12, 115
Aino 194
Alcock, Sir R. 43, 102–3, 181, 195
Allan, J. 197
American influence 34
Anglo-Japanese Alliance 20, 147, 161, 162, 182–3
anticolonialism 156–7
anti-Tsarism 159, 160–1
architecture: brothels 74–5; domestic 45
Arinori, M. 66, 116
armed forces 196; conscription 23, 24, 106, 144; European expertise and arms 128–9, 144; modern army formed 54, 129, 144; navy 151, 154; privileges of *samurai* 54, 104, 144; Red Star Army 123
Arnold, Sir E. 82, 86, 87, 181, 190nn
arsenals 126, 170
art, Chinese 57, 58
art, Japanese 53, 54–9: comparisons with classical Greece 56–7; criticisms of 55–8; exhibitions 58; museum 58; native preferences 59; nature and 54–5, 56; part of daily life of all classes 56; Western reaction to 54–5, 56, 57–9
art; Western impact of Japan on 54, 58, 189n
artisans 124
assassinations 66, 101, 114–15, 116, 117, 168; *see also* terrorism
assemblies, deliberative 104, 109
Aston, W. G. 17, 19, 59, 63, 65, 181
Attila 172, 174
Aveta, F. 197

Bacon, A. M. 77, 91, 190n, 196
balance of power 146, 148
banking 125
Barr, P. 187n, 195
Barry, R. 197

baskets 131
bathing, mixed 44, 90–1
Baudelaire, C. P. 48
beauty of Japan 42, 45, 49, 54–5, 91
Beauvoir, L. de, *Comte* 90
Beika, K. 182
Bellesort, A. 188n
Bingham, J. A. (judge) 50
Bird, I. 195
Bisland, E. 198
Black, J. R. 39–40, 103, 181–2, 191n, 195
Blackwood's Magazine 18, 98, 101
Blanche Contre Jaunes 197
Boer War 156, 177
Bousquet, G. 51, 182, 187n, 189n, 190nn
Boxer rising 148, 155n; commander-in-chief of allied troops 166–8
Breath of the Gods 94–5
Brinkley, F., Captain 185
Britain, Japanese friendship with 20, 147, 161, 162, 170, 171, 177, 180, 182–3
British diplomacy 28–30; German rivalry 29; gunboat diplomacy 61, 98–9, 181
British Social Democratic Federation 156, 184
bronze 131
brothels, *see* prostitution
Buddhism 62, 63, 64, 66, 171; concept of women 71
budō 143
Burleigh, B. 197
Bushidō 143, 175
Buxton C. 99

Cabinet: Whig Cabinet analogy 119
capitalism: social prerequisites of 126–7; struggle against feudalism 125
Chaillet, J. B. 189n
Chamberlain, B. H. 17, 19, 40, 66, 71, 82, 86, 115, 117, 137, 182, 187n, 189n, 190n, 191n, 196
Charter Oath 23, 24, 103, 104, 105, 109

Chasseur, A. 197
Chateaubriand, F. R. 100
cheapness of Japanese products 131, 134
children 46, 49; employment of 127–8, 142
China: cultural influence of 21, 52, 53; customs compared with Japanese 46–7; exploitation by West 126; feet-binding of girls 68; government corruption 126; ideographic script 52–3; industrialisation 125–6; Japanese future influence surmised 156; Jesuit missionaries 62; Manchu Ch'ing dynasty overthrown 147; Opium War 23, 46, 60, 152; scramble for concessions by West 148; war indemnity 129, 147, 164; war with Japan (Sino-Japanese War) 94, 121, 129, 145, 146–7, 148, 164, 185, 196–7
Chinoiseries 58
Chirol, Sir V. 18, 134, 136, 177, 182, 185–6
Chisolm, L. W. 189n
Chōshū 61, 107, 109
Christianity 14, 15; banned in Japan 60–1; clandestine Christians 61; espousal by Japanese 34, 36, 65; marriage and 79, 82; 'military and commercial' 154; missionaries 34, 60–2 *passim*, 65 68, 72, 76, 79, 83–5 *passim*, 105, 122, 155, 183; non-acceptance by Japanese 64–5, 66; treaties and 27, 60–1; versus heathen 170, 171–2
cleanliness as Japanese trait 46
Clement, E. W. 191n, 192n
clocks 130, 131
clothing: adoption of Western 24, 34–5, 36, 75; native Japanese 44
colonialism, opposition to 156–7
commerce, *see* trade
Commercial High School, Tokyo 132–3
Communist Manifesto 121
Concert of Powers system 148
concubinage 83–5
Conference of Versailles 180
Confucianism: component of Japanese religion 63; concept of women

70–1; Jesuit interest in 62; moral standards 64; pupil-teacher relationship 54
Connaught, A. W. P. A., *duke of* 185, 195
Constitution 97, 109, 116, 118, 129; abolition of 114; deification of Emperor 113; German model 112; Western reception of 112–14
consular jurisdiction, abolition of 30
'coolies' 43
co-operatives 129
corruption: Chinese 126; Japanese 122
cotton yarn 129, 131, 132, 136
Couchoud, P. L. 59
Couperus, L. 35, 39
crockery, foreign 75
Crosland, T. W. H. 133, 169, 182, 189n, 193n
cultural invasions 21, 24, 33–9 *passim*, 142
curios 43, 58
Curzon, G. N. 18, 36, 117, 118, 119, 121, 122, 177, 182
customs (behaviour): Chinese and Japanese compared 46–7; European and Japanese compared 43–4, 77
customs (tariffs) 26, 124

daimyō 22, 95, 97, 102, 104
De Becker, J. E. 73, 74, 76, 77, 182, 196
death: Japanese concept of 44; marriage and 80
debating clubs 110
decorations: Asian 181, 183; British 195
Dejima, Dutch traders at 21
deliberative assemblies 104, 109
dental care 44
'desertion, novel of' 91–95
diet (food), adoption of Western 24
Diet (parliament), *see* parliament
Dillon, F. 52, 54
Diósy, A. 85, 123, 182–3, 188n, 190nn, 191n, 192n
diplomacy: British 28–30, 61, 98–9, 181; Japanese 31, 32, 61
diplomats: American 195; British 28–9, 43, 59, 78, 101, 102–3, 143, 144,

diplomats—*contd.*
165, 181, 185, 195, 196; French
58, 102, 189n
divorce 70–1
Dixon, W. G. 183, 187n, 188n, 190nn,
192n
dockyards and harbours 126, 130
dogs 46
drama, military 144
Du Boulay, N. W. H. 197
Dyer, H. 38, 129, 130, 138, 139, 141,
159, 183, 188n, 189n, 192n
dynamite 39

Eastlake, F. W. 197
Écho du Japon 182
economy, Japanese: agrarian 124;
competitor to West 131, 134, 141;
ignored by West 123–4; problems
22; Westernisation 24; *see also* industrialisation
economy, Western 124
Edinburgh Review 18, 32, 46, 99
Edo 73–4, 181, 185
education 16; Christian missionary
influence 61; commercial and industrial 129, 132–3; compulsory universal 23, 24; Ministry of 116, 131;
national learning 22; system and
syllabus revised 54; Western
teachers 33, 61, 132
Eiichi, S. 125
elections 114, 117, 129
Elgin, J. B., *earl of* 101, 184
Eliot, G. 134
Eliot, Sir C. 195
Elmhirst, E. P. 195
embassies in Western countries 23
emperors: deification of 113;
Mutsuhito (Meiji Tenno) 104, 110,
112, 113, 116, 165, 174, 195; *see
also* mikados; shōguns
Engels, F. 184
English spoken by Japanese and
Chinese 50
entrepreneurs 125
epithets, royal 165
Evangelische Kirchenzeitung 171
exhibitions: art 58; industrial 130, 136
experts, foreign 17, 28
exports 131–2
extraterritoriality 26, 27, 128, 155

Falkenegg, F., Baron von 169, 173,
183
famines 22
Far East 182
Faulds, H. 195
fauna and flora 45
fear of the West 98
feet-binding 68
female infanticide 68
Fenollosa, E. and M. 59
feudalism 21, 102, 103; abolition 23,
105, 106; attitude to women 71;
idealisation of 138–41 *passim*; Japan
compared with medieval Europe
102; struggle against capitalism
125
fiefs 61, 97, 102, 109; abolition 106
Finck, H. T. 195
First World War 148–9
flora and fauna 45
flower arrangements 55
Fontanesi, A. 17
Fontpertuis, F. de 190n, 192n
foreign experts 17, 28
foreign policy 26
Formosa expedition 145
France, A. 154, 155, 159
Fraser, Mrs H. 78–9, 85, 183, 191n
free thought 33
freedom and popular rights movement 109, 112
Freeman-Mitford, A. B., *see* Mitford,
A. B.
frugality as Japanese trait 127
Fukoku-kyōhei programme 124, 129,
141, 143
functions terms to denote 97

gardens 45, 46
Garter, Order of the 195
Genghis Khan 168, 174
geographic position 20; presumed
effect on racial characteristics 48
geology 195
Gneist, R. von 112
Gould, G. M. 198
government 22–4, 32, 60, 97–9 *passim*,
101, 102, 104–22 *passim* 181; Western support for 117–18
Greek art compared with Japanese
56–7
Grierson, J. M. 196

Griffis, W. E. 68, 76, 105, 183, 190nn, 191n
Guesde, J. 159
Guimet, E. 58
Gulick, S. L. 69, 79, 83–5 *passim*, 152, 153, 160, 183, 189n
gunboat diplomacy 61, 98–9, 181

haboutaye 135
haiku 59
Halot, A. 197
han 61, 97, 102, 109: abolition of 106
handkerchiefs, silk 135
hara-kiri 44, 104; *see also* suicide
harbours and dockyards 126, 130
Harris, T. 195
Hartshorne, A. C. 195
hats 35
Hearn, L. 17, 19, 34, 39, 44, 55, 59, 63, 64, 81, 82, 88, 89, 139, 141, 184, 198
heavy industries 125
Heimin Shinbun 158
Henriques, F. 190n
Heredia, J.-M. de 59
Hideyoshi, T. 144
Hirobumi, I. 112
Hiroshige, A. 54
Hokkaidō 194
Hokusai, K. 54
Holtham, E. G. 195
horses, stabling and harnessing 44
hospital for VD treatment 76
hotels 127–8
houses and gardens 45, 46
Houssaye, H. 189n
human resources 127
Hyndman, H. M. 18, 156, 158, 159, 184

ideals, contradictory 33
ideographic script, Chinese 52–3
ideology, lack of 120
Ii Kamon-no-kami 116
Ii Naosuke 115
immigration laws, anti-Japanese 180
Imperial College of Engineering 129, 183
imperialism 33, 145, 146, 177, 180, 184
impressionist painting 54, 58
India 176–7, 182

industrialisation 13, 15, 24, 38, 42, 123–42 *passim*; artistic originality in design 136; Chinese 125–6; effect on quality of life 136, 138–9, 140–1, 142; foreign loans 128–9, 133; impact on love suicides 80; Japanese compared with Chinese 126; obstacles to 124–7 *passim*, 133; social relationships 139; Western criticisms of 133, 135, 136–7, 138–42 *passim*; *see also* modernisation, Westernisation
industriousness as Japanese trait 127
infanticide, female 68
inns: Chinese 46; Japanese 128
institutions, adoption of European 34, 37
institutions, political: terminology 97
insurance 125
international relations 26–7
invincibility, military 20, 46
Iriye, A. 13
isolationism 21, 22, 98
Itagaki Taisuke 112
Ito, Count 119
Itō Hirobumi 112
Iwakura mission 32, 61

James, D. H. 197
Jane, F. T. 196
Japan: as economic competitor to West 131, 134, 141; customs compared with European and Chinese 43–4, 46–7, 77; friendship with Britain 20, 147, 161, 162, 170, 171, 177, 180, 182–3; future influence on China surmised 156; market for Western products 131
Japan Gazette 182
Japan Herald 182
Japan Society 85, 183
Japan Weekly Mail 192n
Japanese language: development of 54; language reform societies 52; use of Chinese roots 54; Western attempts to speak 50–1
Japoneries 54, 58, 91
Japonisme 54
Jaurès, J. 158, 159
Java 176
Jephson, R. M. 195
Jesuits 21, 60, 62

jinrikisha 43
Jiuroda, H. 108
jiyūminkenundō 109, 112
ju-jitsu 175
judō 143
jurisprudence, *see* law
Justice 18, 120, 121, 156, 160, 162, 184

Kaempfer, E. 64
Kagoshima, bombardment of 99, 181
Kaiser Wilhelm II 149, 150, 171, 172
Kamikaze (typhoon) 20
Kamon-no-kami, I. 116
Kann, R. 197
karate 143
Kautsky, K. 143
kendō 143
Kipling, R. 17, 18, 19, 25, 34–5, 45,
    46, 49, 90, 97, 123, 127, 198
kite-flying 44
Knackfuss, H. 149
Knox, G. W. 192n, 193n, 195
Kobayashi Beika 182
Kobe, VD hospital at 76
kōgisho 104
Koizumi Yakumo 17, 184
Königgrätz, battle of 163
Korea 105, 145, 146, 147, 167
Kōtoku Shūsui 121, 158
Kublai Khan 20, 144
Kurokawa, T. 181
Kyoto Industrial Exhibition 136

lacquer 130, 131
LaFarge, J. 17, 54, 90, 188n
land tax 124
language, Japanese, *see* Japanese
    language
language reform societies 52
Laurié, A. 191n
law 16; civil and criminal codes 23,
    27–8, 182; constitutional 112;
    foreign criticism of 30; Meiji re-
    forms 23, 27–8; Peace Preservation
    Law 111–12; press laws 115–16
Law, R. 193n
Layrle, G. 190n
League of Nations 180
lectures 110
legislation, *see* law
Lenin, V. I. 159
Lensen, G. A. 13, 195

Leroy-Beaulieu, P. 37, 40, 120, 126,
    127, 135, 136, 184, 188n, 193n
Liaotung Peninsula 146, 147, 167
light industries 125
Lindau, R. 189n
literature 59–60, 77: Japanese girl in
    87–8, 91–3, 94–5; novels 91–3, 94–5;
    plays 92; poetry 59–60, 87–8, 92
loans, foreign 128–9, 133
locks 44
London Democratic Federation 156,
    184
Loti, P. 17, 18, 91, 92, 93, 94, 184, 198
Louis XVIII 100
love suicides 79–80
Lowell, P. 65, 196

McCall, S. 94
machinery 130, 131; effect of intro-
    duction 127
Mackenzie, F. A. 197
MacMillan's Magazine 18, 32
Madagascar 177
Madame Chrysanthème 91–2, 93, 94, 198
Maël, P. 197
Malayan empire 176
male dominance 70, 72, 82, 84, 86
Malet, Sir L. 158
Manchu Ch'ing dynasty overthrown
    147
Manchuria 147, 154, 166, 173
Manet, E. 58
manual workers 43
manufactures 129–31 *passim*, 134–5:
    imitations of Western products 134,
    135
Marnas, F. 189n
marriage: adultery 85; attitudes to
    love and marriage 78–9, 81–2;
    Christianity and 79, 82; concub-
    inage and 83–5; courtship absent
    from 78; death and 80; husband-
    wife relationship 79, 81–2, 83, 84,
    85–6; Japanese and Western cus-
    toms 78, 79, 81, 82, 83, 85; love
    suicides 79–80; mothers-in-law 82–
    3; polygamy 68, 83; private nature
    of 81; wedding ceremony 80;
    Western attitudes 78–9, 81–2, 84
martial values and arts 143–4
Marx, K. 102
matches 135

Meiji Restoration 23, 103, 104, 105, 106; opposition from *samurai* 105–9; opposition from progressive pressure groups 109, 110; reforms 23, 103, 105–6, 111, 144
Mempes, M. 189n
merchants: Europeans 58, 126, 129, 137–8; Japanese 22, 124–5, 136–8
middle class Westernisation 24
mikados 67, 97, 100–1; apprehension over victory by 101–2; Komei 22, 23; Mutsuhito (Meiji Tenno) 104, 110, 112, 113, 116, 165, 174, 195; relationship to shōguns 99–100
militarism 121, 122, 167
military aristocracy 143
military service, *see* armed forces
military strength 20, 46, 93, 142
Miner, E. 189n, 190n, 191n
mineral resources 124, 133
mining 125
Mishima, Y. 123
missionaries 34, 60–2 *passim*, 65, 68, 72, 76, 83–5 *passim*, 105, 122, 155, 183
Mitford, A. B. 59, 143, 144, 165, 185, 195
Mitsubishi 125
Mitsui 125
modernisation 13–14, 16, 24–5, 32–41 *passim*; concubinage and 83–4; foreign reservations 30–6 *passim*; motivation for 37–8; religion and 63–7; slogan 124, 129, 141, 143; Western errors of judgment 93; *see also* industrialisation; Westernisation
Moges, A. de, *marquis* 102
monarchy 109: *see also* emperors; mikados; shoguns
Mongols 174
Moniteur des Soies 128
morality; commercial 136–8; Confucian 64; judgments on prostitution 76, 77; sexual 72, 73, 76, 77, 91, 92, 93
Mordell, A. 198
Mori Arinori 66, 116
Mori Ogai 179
Morris, J. 188n
Morrison, G. E. 185, 186
Morse, E. S. 195

'most favoured nation' clause 25, 26
Mounsey, A. 107, 191n
Murray, D. 116, 131, 140, 141, 191nns, 192n
Musée Guimet 58
museum, art 58
music, Japanese girl in 91
'Musmée, The' (quoted) 88
mythology 69–70

Nagasaki: children in 49; VD hospital at 76
Naosuke, I. 115
Napoleon I 33, 100, 143
national identity and character 35–6, 38, 39, 41, 142, 166
National Zeitung 193n
nationalist movements 149, 176–7
nationalist spirit 126, 175
Natsume Sôseki 184
natural resources 124, 133
nature and art 54–5, 56
neatness as Japanese trait 46
Newton, G. (naval doctor) 76
Nicholas II 17, 93–4, 149
Nisshin Shinjishi 182
Nitobe, I. 81
nobility 97–8, 99, 142, 143; *see also* daimyō; samurai
Norman, F. J. 196
Norman, Sir H. 192nns, 193n
novels 91–5
Noyes, A. 87
nudity 44, 90–1

'O' 197
objets d'art 54, 58, 130, 131
Ogai, M. 179
Oji 142
Ōkubo Toshimichi 115, 116
Ōkuma Shigenobu 39, 112, 116
Oliphant, L. 97, 101, 184–5, 195
operas and operettas 87, 91
opium trade 126, 152
Opium War 23, 46, 60, 152
order as Japanese trait 46
Osaka 130, 132, 194
Oyama, I., Marshal 155, 160, 163, 176

pacifism, socialist 33, 157–8
painting 54, 58
Paléologue, M. 58, 189n

Pall Mall Gazette 184
Palmer, M., Colonel 185
Paris World Expositions 57, 58
Parkes, Sir M. 28–9, 181
parliament: Cabinet responsibility 114, 117; establishment of 110
patriotism 38, 67, 108, 121, 151–2, 170, 171, 175; female 93–4, 95, 96
Peace Preservation Law 111–12
peasants: minimal Westernisation of 24; ranking in soical hierarchy 124
pégrine (silk-worm blight) 127n
people: attitude of Japanese to West 160, 175; British admiration for Japanese 163–5; characteristics of Japanese 43–4, 45–50, 123, 127–8, 175; ideas of good breeding 81–2; Japanese self-comparison with Europeans 175; religion 63, 64–6, 170, 171–2; Western attitude to Japanese 13, 14–15, 45–50, 92, 93, 123, 127–8, 151, 159–60, 163–5, 168–71, 174, 175, 180; Western contact with Japanese 43, 187n, 194
Perry, Commodore M. C. 22, 144, 165
Petillot, L. 196
Petit, C. 193n
Petit Journal 38
Petite République 121
Petitjean, B. (missionary) 61
Philippines 176
Pinon, R. 187n, 193nn
plane, carpenter's 44
politics: European analogies 119–20; parties 118–20; 'personal elements' 117; political clubs 118; 'professional politicians' 118; public meetings 118; religion and 66; Western influence 109, 118; Western interest in 110–22 *passim*
pollution 132, 138
polygamy 68, 83
Ponting, H. G. 191n
porcelain 130, 131
Port Arthur 143, 147, 153, 155, 176, 177, 197
Portsmouth, treaty of 160, 164, 186
Portugal: Jesuit influence on Japan 21, 60
positivism 33
Pound, E. 59
prefectures, institution of 106

press 110, 115–16
products 129–31 *passim*, 134–5: imitations of Western goods 134, 135
progressive pressure groups 109, 110
prostitution: brothel architecture 74–5; foreign clothing and crockery 75; moral judgments on 76, 77; motives for choice of 73; photograph albums for selection 75; public exposure of prostitutes 75; suburban location 76; venereal disease 73, 76; virtual slavery of prostitutes 77; Western influences 74–6; Yoshiwara system 73–7
Protestantism 33
Puccini, G. 91

quality of Japanese products 134–5

race 16; presumed effect of geographic position on characteristics 48; racial equality clause vetoed (League of Nations covenant) 180; racial significance of Russo-Japanese War 149; Western attitudes to Japanese 13, 14–15, 45–50; white peril concept 152–3, 154–5, 156, 160, 161; yellow peril concept 124, 149–50, 153–4, 155, 166–80 *passim*, 197
railways 129; used for love suicides 80
Rangakusha 21
Red Star Army 123
Redesdale, A. B. Freeman-Mitford, *baron* 59, 143, 144, 165, 185, 195
Reed, Sir E. 28–9, 110 185, 188n
reforms 23, 103, 105–6, 111, 144
Rein, J. J. 196
religion 14, 16; Confucianism as component 63; espousal of Western 34, 36, 65; indigenous Japanese beliefs promoting modernisation 66–7; modernisation and 63–7; multiple religious adherence of Japanese 62–3; politics and 66; popular attitude to 63, 64–6; toleration accepted 23; 62; Western interest in Japanese 62
revolution 102, 103, 105
Revue des Deux Mondes 18
Richardson, C. L. 99
Richardson, T. E. 197
rickshaws 43

Rittner, G. H. 195
roads 46, 130
Roesler, H. 112
Romajikai 52
Roman Catholicism 33; missionaries 60–2
Roosevelt, T. 186
Rousseau, J.-J. 33, 109
Ruskin, J. 48
Russian Revolution 148–9
Russo–Japanese War 66, 96, 129, 133, 170, 197; consequences predicted 145–6; cost of 164; effects of victory 143, 148–9; European response to 150, 160–6 *passim*, 178–80, 186, 196, 197; indemnity question 162, 164; 'magnaminity' of Japanese 162–5 *passim*; origins 145, 147; peace treaty 160, 164, 186; racial significance of 149; revenge as motive for 153, 159; universal implications 159–60

Saigō Takamori 107–8, 109, 145
samurai 22, 54, 71, 81, 94, 99, 115, 142, 165; new careers for 106; oligarchy of 109; opposition to Meiji government 105–9; ranking in social hierarchy 124; social values 124–5, 136, 137, 144; stipends commuted 106–7
Satow, E. 181, 196
Satsuma 61, 99, 109, 115, 196
Satsuma Rebellion 107–8, 109, 115, 116, 145
Scherer, J. 127, 128, 189n, 190n
Schwartz, W. L. 189n, 191n
secret society 148
seismology 195
Sekigahara, battle of 21
Sengoju kidai 21
seppuku, see suicide
'Seven Reasons for Divorce' 70–1
sex 16–17, 72, 73, 76, 77, 91, 92, 93
Shibusawa Eiichi 125
Shigenobu, Ō. 39, 112, 116
Shimonoseki, gunboat diplomacy at 146, 181
Shintoism 62, 63, 64, 66; concept of women 71
shipbuilding 130
shipping 125

Shiroyama 108
shizoku 142
shoes 130
shōguns 22, 23, 32, 60, 97, 100, 101, 102; relationship to mikados 99–100; Tokugawa Yoshinobu 103–4
Shūsui, K. 121, 158
Siam 176
silk 127n: products 135
Sino–Japanese War 94, 121, 129, 145, 185, 196–7; consequences of 146–8; peace settlement 146; war indemnity 129, 147, 164
Sladen, D. 187n, 189n, 190n, 196
Smalley, G. 186
smallness of Japanese life 44–5, 49
Smiles, S. 25
Smith, G. 196
Social Democratic Federation 156, 184
social values: Tokugawa period 124–5, 136, 137, 144; transformation needed 127
socialism 111, 112, 120–1; anti-colonialism 156–7; attitudes to Russo–Japanese War 157–9; literature 18, 120, 121; pacifism 33, 157–8
Société Franco-Japonaise 183
Sôseki, N. 184
sōshi 111–12, 115
Soulie, F. 100
South Africa 156, 177
Spain: Franciscan missionaries 60
steamers 129–30
Stein, L. von 112
stitching by tailors 44
Storry, R. 187n
suicide 44, 104, 108, 123; love suicides 79–80
Sumitomo 125
suttee 68
suzerainty proposal 25
Swift, J. 20n
sword-wearing 104

Taiping Rebellion 126
Tairō (Ii Naosuke) 114–15
Taisuke, I. 112
Takamori, S. 107–8, 109, 145
Tama Kurokawa 181
Tamerlane 174
tariffs 26, 124

taxation, land 124
tea houses 46
terrorism 17, 101, 115, 116, 117; *see also* assassinations
textiles 24, 55, 125, 126, 129, 131, 132, 136
Théry, E. 197
Thomas, J. H. 196
timber shortage 133
Times, The 18, 134, 182; accredited correspondents 185, 186, 187n; articles in 27, 29–30, 38, 89, 98, 111–15 *passim*, 118, 119, 123, 128, 129, 145, 149, 150–1, 163, 164; East Asian policy 185–6; letters to 28, 30, 35, 39, 46, 52–3, 99, 165, 166–8
Togo, H. Admiral 151, 155, 163, 176
Tokugawa dynasty 22, 60; idealisation of 138–41 *passim*; social values 124, 136, 137; Yoshinobu 103–4
Tokyo 73–4, 129, 181, 183, 185: University 182, 183, 184
Tolstoy, L. N. 13, 180,197
Tomomi Iwakura 32, 161
torture 28
Tosa 109
Toshimichi, Ō. 115, 116
Toyotomi Hideyoshi 144
trade: disdained by *samurai* 124–5, 137; Dutch 21; Japanese-Western relations 136–8
trade unions 121
Trafalgar, battle of 143
Trans-Siberian Railway 146
travel restrictions, foreigners' 26, 42–3
treaties 22–3, 25–7, 29, 30–1, 42, 101, 128; Christianity and 27, 60–1; revision 27, 29, 31, 39, 61, 65, 124, 129, 146; 'unequal treaties' 25–7, 31, 61, 124, 146; Yeddo 101, 184
Treaty Ports 25–6, 42, 43, 61, 148, 153
Triple Intervention 147, 148, 164, 167
Tristam, H. B. 196
Trotsky, L. D. 159
Tsarism, opposition to 159, 160–1
Tsuzuki, C. 184
T'ung-chih restoration 126
Tycoons, *see* shoguns
typhoon 20

'unequal treaties' 25–7, 31, 61, 124, 146

urban landscape, changes in 132
Utamaro 54

Varigny, M. C. de 188n
Victoria, Queen 101
Villenoisy, F. de 197
violence 122
visits to Japan 17, 42–3, 187n, 194–6, 198

Wallace, D. M. 185
war indemnities 129, 147, 162, 164
War Office 197
Watson, G. 196
Western fear of the unknown 168
Western prejudices 14–15
Westernisation 13, 14, 23–5, 31; brothel architecture 74–5; indigenous Japanese religion promoting 66–7; influence evaluated 34–5, 39–40; selective assimilation 36–7, 38, 39, 53–4; *see also* industrialisation; modernisation
white peril 152–3, 154–5, 156, 160, 161
Wilhelm II (Kaiser) 149, 150, 171, 172
Williams, H. S. 187n
Wilson, H. W. 197
Wirgman, C. 17
women 16–17, 48, 68–96; as chattels 72–3; beauty 88–9, 90, 91, 92, 93; chastity 72; comparative status 68–9; Confucian concept of 70–1; costume 91; courage 93–6 *passim*; European attitude in feudal times 71; flirtation 77–8; *geisha* 87, 96; Greek and Japanese compared 89; idealised by West 86–90, 91–3; kissing 77; *musmée* 87–9, 93; obedience and disobedience 70–3 *passim*, 82; patriotism 93–6 *passim*; reasons for inferiority 69–73; role in contemporary society 71; Shinto concept of 71; smallness of 91; status 68–71, 86; suicide 93, 94, 95
woodblock prints 54, 58
world power, Japan as 145, 148, 149, 156, 162, 163, 167, 170, 171, 174, 175, 179, 185
writing 14, 44, 51–3
Wyzewa, M. T. de 189n

xenophobia 23, 101, 115, 148, 155, 172, 184

Yakumo, K. 17, 184
Yamada, Y. 197
Yamato Damashi 166
Yami's hotel 127
yashiki 142
Yasuda 125
Yeddo, treaty of 101, 184
yellow hope, Japan as 150, 156, 158–62, 177, 179, 180, 197
yellow peril 149–50, 153–4, 155, 166–80 *passim*, 197; action programme

to oppose 179; Christian versus heathen 170, 171–2; drawing of 149–50, 172; economic 124, 150, 178; European stupidity as cause of 169; Japan as example to nationalist movements 176–7; psychological shock 178–9; spectre of Asian alliance under Japan 172–6
Yokohama 42, 50; VD hospital at 76
Young, J. 192n

zaibatsu 125
Zen Buddhism 143
Zola, E. 33, 58